95

Rancho Palos Verdes, Calif.

The Effective
Church Board

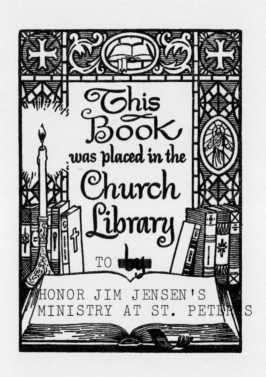

This
Book
was placed in the
Church
Library
TO by

HONOR JIM JENSEN'S
MINISTRY AT ST. PETER'S

The Effective Church Board

A Handbook for Mentoring and Training Servant Leaders

Michael J. Anthony

Saint Peters By The Sea

Church Library

Rancho Palos Verdes, Calif.

254
Ant

Baker Books
A Division of Baker Book House Co.
Grand Rapids, Michigan 49516

© 1993 by Michael J. Anthony

Published by Baker Books
a division of Baker Book House Company
P.O. Box 6287, Grand Rapids, Michigan 49516-6287

Library of Congress Cataloging-in-Publication Data

Anthony, Michael J.
    The effective church board : a handbook for mentoring and training
servant leaders / Michael J. Anthony.
       p.   cm.
    Includes bibliographical references.
    ISBN 0-8010-0230-3
    1. Church management. 2. Lay ministry—Recruiting. 3. Church
committees. I. Title.
    BV652.A74   1993
    254—dc20   93-13092

Printed in the United States of America

Scripture quotations not otherwise identified are from the New International Version.
Copyright © 1973, 1978, 1984 International Bible Society. Used by permission of
Zondervan Bible Publishers.

All names used in case studies have been changed to protect the identity of people
involved.

2293

This book is dedicated to

Ron Van Groningen

His friendship has been a tremendous source
of encouragement to me and my ministry. In
addition, his eleven years of service as a
deacon at First Baptist Church of San Jose,
California, most of those years as chairman of
the board, have provided me with insights
regarding the valuable work of a church board
member. His spiritual gifts of wisdom and
giving helped make this book possible. A son
couldn't want a better father-in-law than you!

Contents

Appendixes

Foreword

n a speech delivered at Dartmouth College in 1986, William H. Spoor recalled the words of Winston Churchill. Apparently the British Prime Minister remarked, while reflecting on his own leadership during World War II, "There is a special moment when a person is figuratively tapped on the shoulder and offered the chance to do a very special thing, unique to him and fitted to his talent; what a tragedy if that moment finds him unprepared or unqualified for the work which would have been his finest hour." I have not attempted to verify the quote, but the spirit of this sentence is very Churchillian. It also lends support to the premise of this book which deals with preparing and qualifying church leaders for what may very well be, by eternity standards, their finest hour.

Across the continent today churches struggle over congregational control and authority. In some churches (usually with a more congregational polity), imperial pastors tend to abuse lay leaders until the church splits or the congregation rises up and fires the pastor. In elder-governed churches, power struggles between seminary trained pastors and lay elders often result in gridlock or some form of abuse by one side or the other. Michael Anthony has written this book to correct that problem and numerous others which corrupt the functioning of servant leaders in the vineyard of the Lord. Even the section headings—"Laying the Groundwork for Service" and "Mastering the Art of Serving Others" indicate the teamwork model to which Anthony calls his readers, a model intensely biblical and extremely practical.

At first glance one may assume Anthony addresses only pastors, urging them to develop board members in their churches. But that would betray his teamwork commitment. I am reminded of an illustration which appeared in *Leadership* a few years ago.

> A sea captain and his chief engineer were arguing over who was the most important to the ship. To prove their point to each other, they decided to swap places. The chief engineer ascended to the bridge, and the captain went to the engine room. Several hours later, covered with oil and dirt, the captain suddenly appeared on the deck. "Chief!" he yelled, waving aloft a monkey wrench. "You have to get down there; I can't make her go!" "Of course you can't," replied the chief. "She's aground!" On a team we don't excel each other; we depend on each other (Fall 1991, Vol. XII, No. 4, p. 44).

Anthony does not assume the basics but offers foundational information for fledgling pastors and newly elected board members. He treats pastors, elders, and deacons separately so each can find his or her particular place and respond in the multiple leadership context of a modern congregation. Finally, he doesn't sidestep the tough issues but devotes his entire third section to "Leading During Crisis Periods of Ministry." How desperately we need to hear about "Moral and Ethical Dilemmas" and "Healing a Divided Church."

This is not a book about power but about service. Leadership is a sacred trust in which the well-being of other church leaders depends on the spirituality and competence of an effective church board. A certain amount of authority may rest with the title, but the right to lead and the influence to make decisions which affect other people's lives must be given leaders by followers. This book will greatly assist men and women in reaching the potential to which God has called them and for which he has gifted them. I commend it to pastors, church staffs, church boards, and students of Christian leadership everywhere.

Kenneth O. Gangel
Dallas, Texas

Preface

*E*ffective ministry in a local New Testament church is not a mystical concept. Rather, it is built on a foundation of biblical teachings and instructions. The methods used require teamwork between paid professional clergy and volunteer lay leaders, both of whom are essential for the effective functioning of the body of Christ. Together they form a bond designed to withstand the pressures mounted against the church by the eroding social, legal, and moral standards of our secular culture. Because Christian ministry is at the forefront of all spiritual battles, those who serve in positions of leadership in the church should not be surprised when conflict or disaster strikes. That's what war is all about. Our enemy has a well-equipped arsenal, but the joy of the corporate body is in knowing that our resources are stronger and readily accessible. The danger lies in trying to solve our ministry problems with our own devices.

This book was written with the express intent of helping church board members and senior pastors work together effectively. Regardless of doctrinal positions, denominational distinctives, or theological orthodoxy, the church of Christ must be united in its leadership. Jesus put it best when he warned that "every city or household divided against itself will not stand" (Matt. 12:25). Spiritual battles must be fought with spiritual weapons, and one of our strongest weapons is our unity in Christ as Christian leaders.

Training leaders for church ministry has been a constant challenge since the days of the early church. Who is responsible for providing the training? What materials will be used? What is the best format or agenda to be followed? These and many other questions have been the basis for countless conferences and training seminars across the country. It is my contention that the best person to train and equip church board members is the senior pastor of the congregation. As the shepherd of the flock, he is responsible for preparing the leaders who will serve with him.

Source Material

This book was put together from a variety of sources. Because Scripture is the best source of authoritative guidance regarding training for spiritual leadership in a church ministry, each chapter begins by addressing the scriptural teachings that serve as a foundation for how we should conduct our leadership. I have also gathered information from some of the latest journals and books available today. Many of these materials were written by pastors and board members who have drawn on their wealth of practical experience. Their successes and failures stand as guideposts for others to follow or avoid. The third component of my materials comes from a national survey that I conducted among senior pastors and church board members. The responses from one hundred pastors and almost an equal number of board members were tabulated and analyzed. This is by no means a comparative sample of the church in North America, but it does present evidence of what is being done in some local churches today.

Finally, I also conducted numerous personal and telephone interviews of pastors and board members, to follow up on what I found in my surveys and elicit additional information. For example, chapter 18, "Healing a Divided Church," and chapter 19, "Issues Involved in a Church Day-Care Center" were based almost exclusively on interviews, since so little has been written on these subjects. The experiences of pastors who have tasted the joys and defeats of these ministry issues can provide us with rich insights and wisdom.

The Survey

To help you put your own ministry experience in context with those involved in my sampling, summaries of the survey's demographics and general findings are provided below.

Senior Pastors

The length of time the senior pastors had been in ministry ranged from a few months to forty years, with twelve years being the average. Denominations represented in the sample included Baptist, Bible Church, Christian & Missionary Alliance, Church of Christ, Covenant, Episcopalian, Evangelical Free Church, Fellowship of Grace Brethren, Independent, Lutheran, Methodist, Nazarene, and Presbyterian. Some pastors simply checked "other" but provided no specific details.

Attendance (as opposed to membership) in these churches ranged from 14 to 1,800. An average of 282 people attended on Sunday morning. Regarding church administration and lay leadership in this sampling, 45 churches had a board of trustees, with an average of 3 trustees per board; 58 churches had an elder board, with an average of 3 or 4 elders per board; 65 churches had a deacon board, with an average of 4 deacons per board; and 49 churches had a deaconess board, with an average of 7 deaconesses per board.

In terms of undergraduate education, 72% of the senior pastors had graduated from either a Bible institute or a Christian college or university; 82% had graduated from a seminary. The churches ranged across the country according to the following geographic distribution: NE = 2; PNW = 18; CN = 51; SO = 9; PSW = 20.

Roughly 88% of the senior pastors said that their church had a written mission statement. Only 44% said that they had written goals for the ministry of the church. When asked how often they faced interpersonal conflicts in their church, the pastors responded as follows: weekly = 14%; monthly = 25%; quarterly = 28%; annually = 33%. Half of the pastors said they involved their church board members in the resolution of these conflicts.

When asked to describe their style of leadership in the church, 7% of the senior pastors said they were "autocratic"; 60% said "democratic"; 7% said "laissez-faire"; and 25% said "other"—such as "servant leader," "paternal leader," "benevolent dictator," and a host of miscellaneous descriptions. Only 12% of these pastors had ever experienced a split in their church.

The pastors were also asked to rank-order how they spend their time (1 = time most spent; 8 = time least spent). The average rankings were: 1, sermon preparation; 2, administration of the church; 3, Bible study; 4, pastoral care; 5, prayer; 6, counseling; 7, conflict resolution; 8, other. In characterizing their relationship to their church board, the vast majority described it as either "excellent" or "good." A few said it was "weak," and only one said it was "a battle zone."

For describing a church's growth or decline, I used the criteria established in much of the current literature. About 38% of the churches were experiencing an attendance plateau (1 to 5% growth or decline); 45% of the churches were experiencing moderate (6 to 15%) growth or decline; and 17% were experiencing a significant degree (16% or more) of growth or decline.

A little more than half (55%) of the churches had written job descriptions for their church board members.

Church Board Members

The length of time the members had served ranged from a few months to thirty-three years, with nine years being the average. Congregations that were represented in the sample were the same as those for the senior pastors, since it was the pastors who gave me the board members' names and addresses.

Of the church board members represented in this sampling, 8% of those who responded were trustees; 50% were elders; 35% were deacons; and 5% were deaconesses.

In terms of their undergraduate education, 21% of the board members had graduated from a college or university, and 8% had either attended or graduated from a seminary. The churches represented by the board members varied according to geographic location as follows: NE = 3; PNW = 14; CN = 47; SO = 4; PSW = 24.

The occupational experience of the church board members was extensive and varied. About 40% were professionals; 23% were in business-related jobs; 3% were in sales; 5% in skilled labor; 2% in service industries; 5% were homemakers; and 19% were in "other" situations, including para-church ministries, retirement, and so on.

About 95% of the board members said that their church had a written mission statement (compared to 88% of the pastors); 55% said that their church also had written goals (compared to 47% of the pastors).

When asked to describe their style of leadership in the church, 7% of the board members said they were "autocratic"; 91% said "democratic"; 2% were "laissez-faire." A significant number (37%) of the board members had experienced a split in their church (compared to 12% of the pastors).

In describing their relationship with the senior pastor, 60% said it was "excellent"; 31% said it was "good"; 6% said "weak"; and 2% described it as "a battle zone."

Regarding their church's growth or decline (using the same criteria as with the pastors), 47% of the board members said they were plateaued (compared to 38% of the pastors); 36% reported moderate growth or decline (compared to 45% of the pastors); and 16% said they were experiencing significant growth or decline (compared to 17% of the pastors).

I also examined the current issue of whether someone who was divorced should be allowed to serve on a church board. In my sample, 60% said they would accept a divorced person on the board. Of those churches, 37 said they had at least one divorced adult currently serving in that capacity.

It is interesting to note that there were both similarities and differences between the responses of the pastors and those of their church board members. Some of these issues will be discussed in more detail in the text. Generally speaking, the input provided by both groups through the survey and follow-up interviews added a great deal to the development of this manuscript.

Using This Book

I hope that *The Effective Church Board* will serve as a basis for discussion between senior pastors and members of their church boards. Many of the board members expressed a genuine desire to be mentored and discipled by their pastor, since they had a tremendous respect for the pastor and desired a closer relationship with him.

An excellent way to use the contents of this book would be to set aside a weekend retreat at a local lodge or hotel during which a pastor and church board could discuss the portions of the book that apply to their own church. If that is not possible, assigning a chapter per month for board discussion might be just as useful. Having board members come to the meeting with a specific chapter read and marked for discussion would be an excellent way to cover the essential items of concern. Such a dialogue will usually contribute to the mutual respect and cooperation between a senior pastor and the church board.

One final note: The majority of churches in America have male leadership in both senior pastor and board positions, but some churches have female pastors and board members serving in their ministries. For this reason, I have tried to use inclusive language (where possible) to recognize the contribution of both men and women. However, in order to avoid a cumbersome use of English pronouns (him/her, he/she, his/hers), I have generally used male descriptors. Until we create more reader-friendly terms that are gender neutral, such distinctions will need to be made and clarified.

Acknowledgments

A book of this nature could not have been accomplished without the significant contribution of many people. The majority of this manuscript was prepared while I was serving as visiting professor of Christian education at Moffat College of the Bible in Kenya, East Africa. I want to express my appreciation to Dr. Sherwood Lingenfelter, provost and senior vice president at Biola University, and Dr. H. Bingham Hunter, former dean at Talbot School of Theology, for granting me a sabbatical leave to teach overseas and complete this manuscript. I also want to thank Phillip Bustrum, the academic dean at Moffat College of the Bible, who was very cooperative in arranging my teaching schedule so I would have large sections of time to write.

In addition, several people at Baker Book House have been very encouraging and helpful to me throughout the process of preparing this manuscript. It is a pleasure to work with them.

I especially want to thank the senior pastors and church board members (trustees, elders, deacons, and deaconesses) who responded to my survey and allowed me the opportunity to interview them. These materials were priceless to me in my desire to gain practical wisdom and advice from a multi-denominational perspective. Although I received over two hundred completed surveys from these individuals, some wished to remain anonymous in their contribution. Those who participated in this study and who have allowed me to mention their names are listed below.

To each of them I say a very big "thank you." I really couldn't have done it without you!

Senior pastors: C. Robert Allred, Dan Amerson, Anthony F. Andres, John J. Aranda, Kerry Ascher, John W. Auxier, Gary Basshow, Paul R. Bawden, Jim Beard, David Beckwith, Kenton Beshore, John B. Bryan, Charles Bloyer, Patrick Bonnie, James Borror, James Bull, Ron Bystrom, Harris Campbell, Mark Campbell, Dan Carlson, Erwin L. Carlson, Robert Carter, Harvey Clark, James R. Cook, Richard Cryder, J. Larry Dean, Ray Dimino, Keith Essex, Jerry D. Ester, David Ewert, J. W. Fischer, Jim Gilbreth, Wayne Gropp, Robert E. Hilderman, D. Ray Hoke, Lynn Holm, Dale R. Hutchcraft, Lee K. Iseley, Bufe Karrakor, Charles Kelley, D. Wayne King, John Kitchen, Ian R. Hoover, Richard Kraft, Ridley Latimer, Donald Leach, Dorington G. Little, Thomas P. Lynn, Russell L. Lyon, Wayne Matejka, Dan McAtee, Roy McAtee, Clyde N. McCammack, Rick McRostie, Kenneth Nesselroade, Thomas A. Nite, Walter R. Peterson, Herman R. Pieper Jr., David Presher, Scott Roen, William R. Ross, Jerry L. Rouse, Raymond Schmautz, Gary R. Schroeder, Paul R. Shackelford, Chuck Simonson, John E. Skanse, James R. Snyder, John E. Stensether, Gary Templeton, B. Dale Thomas, Robert Tibbs, John Tornfelt, Roger Trautmann, Larry L. Spader, Jim Spicklemier, Paul G. Thyren, L. James Tieszen, Bradley Utterback, Jon M. Van Dine, John Vawter, Daniel J. Waite, Mike Weber, Sam Williams, Kevin Wilson, Duke Winser, Duane T. Wuggazer.

Board members: Sue Adkins, Bert Aunan Jr., Forrest Beatty Jr., Michael A. Bell, John R. Brunt, Joe Bush, Don Culp, Doris De Witt, Kenneth Dobson, W. Duane Eckert, Lee Ettenger, James Feldman, Paul Fields, Craig Hofer, Tom Hagen, James W. Hamer, Lawrence Harpe, Paul Harris, Keith Has-Ellinson, Bill Hatch, Steve Henning, Jim Johnson, Brian J. Jones, James P. Keenan, Michael Kellogg, Robert Kiner, David Kuhlers, Herbert R. Langthorp, Robert A. Leafblad, John Lester, Jerry McKinney, Elwood B. Meadows, Tony Mennenga, Thomas P. Moser, John Nelson, Curt Oberholtzer, Dennis O'Keefe, Annette M. M. Oppedahl, David Pressuall, William L. Reese, Richard K. Roth, Charles A. Rudd, Jerry Sanhey, David Shaver, Gary Smith, William J. Stricker, Steve Sturdiuant, Lee Tate, Bill Travis, Ron Van Groningen, Stanley R. Van Keuren, Randy Van Peursem, Del Velenchenko, Roger Waldron, Rick Walton, Jim Willard, Carol Williams.

I also want to express my appreciation to my wife, Michelle, who has been a team player with me in many years of church and para-church ministry. Her insights have been very helpful to me when making important decisions. I value her contribution and thank God for the gift of such a wonderful helpmate.

Part One

Laying the Groundwork for Service

The Mythical Senior Pastor

erhaps as you reflect on your childhood upbringing, you have fond memories of your pastor as a mild-mannered man who always seemed kind and concerned about the events of your life. He spoke with a soft yet commanding voice and knew everyone by name. Because he was highly admired in the community, he attended the city council meetings to begin their sessions with prayer and was always the person who threw out the baseball at the beginning of the Little League season. This flattering image of a local pastor is not uncommon among people across North America.

However, not everyone has positive qualities in mind as they reflect on their own experiences in a local church. For some people, their ideas about a senior pastor are based on memories of a dictatorial leader who condemned everything that was fun to do in the community. He seemed cold and self-righteous, as if he enjoyed making everyone else feel miserable and guilty. Even if he did not actually abuse his parishioners through emotional manipulation, he rarely acted as if he cared about their welfare.

Exaggerated as either portrait may be, most people have some preconceived notions of how a member of the clergy should behave, and they judge their own pastor according to those standards. After years of research, someone has put together this "job description" of an ideal senior pastor:

> He preaches for exactly twenty minutes, then sits down. He condemns sin, but never hurts anyone's feelings. He works from 8:00 A.M. to 5:00 P.M. in every type of work from preaching to custodial services.
>
> He makes $100 a week and wears good clothes. He buys good books regularly, has a nice family, drives a good car, and gives $50 a week to the church. He also stands ready to contribute to every good work that comes along.
>
> He is twenty-six years old and has been preaching for thirty years. He is tall and short, thin and heavyset. He has one blue eye and one brown eye. His hair is parted in the middle. The left side is blonde and straight; the right side is brown and curly.
>
> He has a burning desire to work with teenagers and spends all his time with older folks. He spends most of his time with a straight face because he has a gregarious sense of humor that keeps him dedicated to his work.
>
> He makes fifteen calls a day on church members, spends all his time evangelizing the unchurched, and is never out of the office.

Such an image is humorous, to be sure. However, it also underscores the fact that the wide and conflicting variety of qualities demanded of a local pastor sets up unrealistic expectations that are impossible for *any* pastor to attain.

As previously explained, in the process of preparing this book I surveyed one hundred senior pastors from across the country and almost as many church board members. Pastors were asked: "In your opinion, what is the greatest misconception church board members have about the senior pastor?" Board members were asked: "In your opinion, what is the greatest misconception a senior pastor has about being a board member?" These first two chapters reflect some of the most frequent responses I received.

Common Misconceptions About Senior Pastors

Misconception #1. A seminary degree prepares the pastor for leading a church. This myth is based on the educational level of most pastors in America today. Preparation for the ministry usually includes four years of college, a graduate degree (two to four years postgraduate work), and in some cases in-service training in the form of special seminars and workshops (denominational conferences, time-management seminars, video programs, etc.). A senior pastor may also have earned a doctorate degree in theology or ministry.

Such an extensive academic background leads many church members to believe that their pastor must know everything there is to know about the specifics of managing a local church. After all, what else could better prepare a pastor than four to ten years of classroom study? The sad reality is that a college and seminary education does not guarantee adequate training for leading a congregation.

First of all, the majority of church members don't understand the content of most seminary programs. In many seminaries the Master of Divinity (M.Div.) degree is packed full of required courses, such as Systematic Theology, Church History, Hermeneutics, Apologetics, Philosophy of Religion, Sermon Preparation, Cults, Religions of the World, and multiple years of studying the Hebrew and Greek languages. These courses, and many more like them, are designed to provide the would-be pastor with a broad range of studies related to his career development.

Few seminaries require courses in premarital or marital counseling, leadership and administration, training and developing volunteers, understanding human development, principles of educational learning, financial accounting, interpersonal communication, managing multiple church staffs, or conflict resolution. Yet these areas consume most of the working hours in a pastor's week. Preparing a sermon may involve eight to fifteen hours for an average pastor, but that is a small percentage of the sixty to seventy-two hours he will work in most weeks.

It is true that a seminary degree *should* provide pastors with a set of tools that can be applied in a ministry context. However, as with many professions, there are no guarantees that young pastors will be able to use those skills with confidence and expertise once they become members of the clergy.

It is not uncommon for young men or women entering the ministry to remember their seminary training with disappointment. Within a few years they have lost their ability to read or translate Hebrew or Greek. The names and dates they learned in church history become foggy, and the lists of facts they memorized for theology exams provide little help in the midst of personal crisis or corporate confusion. Neither ministry nor life itself is nearly as simple as their seminary professors taught them it would be.

Misconception #2. Pastors have all the answers to today's complex social problems. This false conclusion is drawn from much earlier periods of American history, when the local pastor always seemed able to solve his town's problems just in time to prevent catastrophe. This makes for a good movie plot, but it is seldom based on reality, given the nature of our society today.

The increased complexity of ethical decisions facing the medical and legal professions has inevitably created a dilemma for pastors who try to confront such issues with an open mind. Decreasing educational scores among our nation's children, juvenile delinquency, chemical and substance abuse, the fractured nature of the American family, and a host of other concerns present the clergy with difficult choices as they seek to interpret and apply God's Word to these disturbing problems. Is it any wonder that some parishioners become disillusioned when their pastor does not go along with their view on such issues? It simply isn't possible to provide a Bible verse as a remedy for every social ailment.

Misconception #3. Pastors have model families. It is true that most pastors try hard to have a family life that can serve as a model for the rest of the congregation to follow. Paul's instruction to Timothy states that a church leader "must manage his own family well and see that his children obey him with proper respect. (If anyone does not know how to manage his own family, how can he take care of God's church?)" (1 Tim. 3:4–5). This biblical requirement is a very high standard to maintain.

Many pastors, feeling the pressure to attain perfection at home, become overly legalistic and restrictive on their family members. This often causes their children to rebel and adopt lifestyles that bring public embarrassment to the pastor. Even nationally renowned ministers and evangelists have had children who were rebellious and undisciplined. Some came back to Christ as adults, but throughout their years of adolescent development they created turmoil and emotional pain for the entire household.

No pastor's family is perfect. By the time children reach their teen years, they develop a natural desire to test their own limits of ethical and moral decision making. In essence, they need to try their wings and see if they can fly on their own. Sometimes these "test flights" are successful, and the children grow to become responsible adults. But sometimes they fail, and the young people turn away from their spiritual upbringing. Pastors must not be held accountable for all the shortcomings of their children. It is a great challenge to raise a family in our social context today. Because the declining moral and ethical fabric of modern society takes its toll on a pastor's family, just as it does everyone else's, a pastor's home life is not exempt from failure and pain. Family harmony should be seen as a reasonable goal, but not necessarily a final product. Church members who demand perfection on the part of their pastor's family are unrealistic and contribute to the tension that causes some pastoral family members to break under this unfair expectation.

Misconception #4. The pastor's only "real" day of work is Sunday. Here we see the lack of understanding that many parishioners have of their pastor's daily life. The average church member sees his or her pastor for only one hour on Sunday morning, although some members see him on Sunday evening for another hour. An even smaller number may also see him on Wednesday evening for a third hour in the week. During a pastor's work week of sixty to seventy hours, most members will see him only at worship services or official church functions, leaving them to assume that the pastor is not working very hard the rest of the time. After all, how hard can it be to sit and read the Bible and pray for the remaining hours in a week?

The reality of a pastor's life is far different. Depending on the size of the church, his average day begins before dawn with disciplined prayer and Bible study. After breakfast he may arrive at the church to answer correspondence and attend to business matters for several hours. He may then lead a church staff meeting, providing direction and supervision for several staff personnel and volunteer workers. After lunch with a board member or perhaps a businessman from the congregation, he will probably proceed to the hospital (or several of them) for a few hours of visitation. An hour or two of visiting shut-ins in their homes will follow that. By late afternoon, the pastor will be back at his office for several hours of counseling and conflict resolution among his church members or staff. After dinner at home, he will usually depart for the church for three or more hours, to attend meetings of any of a dozen committees or boards. By 10:00 P.M., he has had a full schedule of activities and is tired and exhausted from the demands of the day. This routine is repeated throughout the year and is punctuated by denominational meetings, training conferences, and crises, which arrive on a regular basis.

It is no wonder the pastor may appear weary and worn by the time Sunday morning comes around. Yet Sunday is the heaviest day of the week—what with teaching Sunday school or preaching multiple services, meeting with church members between services, being a "one-minute counselor" at the door as people shake hands to leave, an afternoon committee meeting, evening service, and pie and coffee with someone after that service.

It is not surprising that many pastors "resign on Monday" a dozen times in their mind during a grueling Sunday. Such a wearing routine prompted one pastor to write a book entitled "Never Resign on a Monday." The lifestyle of a senior pastor may seem to be one of ease and comfort unless you have followed in his footsteps for a day.

Misconception #5: The pastor is the only one called (and paid) to do the work of the ministry. It may be true that the pastor receives an annual salary to accomplish a list of ministerial duties. However, it is clearly not biblical to say that it is the pastor's responsibility to do all the work of the ministry in the local church.

Paul's writings in Ephesians 4:11–16 and 1 Corinthians 12 set forth clear teaching regarding who is to be involved in the ministry of a local church. We are told that God gave spiritual gifts to all believers (1 Cor. 12:7; 1 Peter 4:10), so that they could build up and equip the members of the body of Christ. When each member uses his or her area of giftedness (administration, pastoral care, healing, teaching, evangelism, etc.), the church functions as a spiritually healthy body. If any one gift is missing, the whole body suffers (1 Cor. 12:21–26). No one person has all the gifts, not even the senior pastor! He probably has the spiritual gift of "shepherding" or discipleship. He may even have an additional gift or two, such as evangelism or administration, since such a gift cluster is not uncommon among those who are employed full-time in the ministry. However, we must not succumb to the misconception that only a member of the clergy is gifted to carry out ministry in the local church. Each believer is gifted in some way and has a responsibility to use that gift to strengthen the local church. One of the major responsibilities of the senior pastor is to help church members discover their gifts and provide training to use those gifts in the context of the local church. Churches that rely completely on the senior pastor to perform the entire work of the ministry will find themselves with discouraged pastoral leadership and ultimately have a high turnover rate of pastors.

Misconception #6. Pastors never struggle with their personal spiritual development. This is one of the few myths that is perpetuated more by the pastor than by his parishioners. Most pastors do not feel secure enough to admit before other church members that they, too, sometimes struggle with spiritual concerns. Everybody knows that the average church member is constantly striving toward spiritual maturity, but everybody also assumes that the pastor always has his spiritual life under control. Nothing could be further from the truth. James implies that nobody enters into the kingdom of God without "trials of many kinds" (James 1:2). It is a clear teaching from Scripture that those who are church leaders will face tough spiritual battles and testings. After all, if Satan can cause a pastor to fall he might be able to bring down many members of the pastor's church at the same time. Certainly this was seen with the recent backsliding of several television evangelists. A considerable number of their followers were disillusioned in the faith and said to themselves, "If he can't live the Christian life, how can I be expected to do so?"

As a conference speaker, I have had the opportunity to visit many churches and camps throughout the world. In my travels I have met a number of pastors whose lives were on the brink of spiritual ruin. Because they were spiritually dry, they were guilty of doing the work of the ministry in the power of the flesh. I must confess that there have been times in my own ministry when I have exhausted my spiritual reserves through overwork and fatigue.

It has been said that if Satan can't cause you to fall into sin, he will keep you so busy that you will dry up spiritually. I have seen the truth of that, especially in the lives of young pastors who are so busy doing the work of God that they forget about being *people* of God. Their inner, spiritual journey has been pushed aside by the demands of a heavy schedule of meetings, decisions, messages, ceremonies, and other ministerial duties. Although many, if not most, of these activities are beneficial for the body of Christ, the strain to maintain the pace has taken them away from their first love: following their Savior.

Jesus reminded his disciples that no servant is greater than his master (John 13:16). If Jesus felt compelled to retreat periodically from his busy schedule of ministering to ever-present needs and spend time alone with his heavenly Father (Mark 1:35), is it not even more important that a senior pastor get away to renew his personal walk with his Creator? One of the greatest assets a minister can have is an accountability group, consisting of several trusted members of the congregation who will meet with the pastor on a regular basis to help him maintain this essential component of ministry.

Misconception #7. Pastors need not be concerned about their personal finances. During the early period of American history, a pastor was provided with a home, commonly called a manse or parsonage. He did not have to pay directly for his housing, although it was included in his pay package. He also received discounts for goods purchased at retail stores, usually around 10 to 20 percent of the price of an article, which helped lower the cost of living for members of the clergy. In many agricultural areas, church members loaded the pastor's pantry with a storehouse of meat, vegetables, and dairy supplies. It was the local community's way of helping to offset the low pay that a minister received from his congregation.

Consider the modern pastor's income. A 1991 study from the National Council of Churches reports that the average parishioner's contribution to the church is only 2.64 percent of his or her annual income, or $399.63. The highest level of giving—an average of $1,192 per member—was reported by the Presbyterian Church in America. The average annual figure for Southern Baptists was $308. United Methodists gave an average of $300 each, and Episcopalians averaged $764 per year. Those amounts are very modest when you consider that the average church in America has under one hundred members.

Now consider the pastor's expenses. Few pastors today could afford to live in the manse adjacent to the church parking lot, and his housing arrangement does not allow for building up personal equity in a home for retirement living. The average cost of a house on either the East or West Coast is approximately $225,000. Many lending institutions require a 20-percent down payment ($45,000) to qualify for a mortgage loan. Furthermore, since many pastors do not contribute to a Social Security account, they find themselves scrambling to make ends meet financially when it is time to retire.

When one considers the staggering high costs for medical coverage and for educating children throughout their academic career, in addition to expenses for food, clothing, life insurance, taxes, transportation, and so on, it is no wonder that many pastors feel the need to moonlight to bring in additional income for the family (most commonly as real estate agents, salespersons, or substitute teachers). The other alternative is for the spouse to enter the work force and help meet the family's financial needs.

Pastors have never been exceptionally high on society's pay scale, and perhaps it is commendable that they are not overpaid. However, economic realities have changed greatly since a parson was paid with a chicken. Church members must realize that just as their own expenses have risen dramatically over the past decade, so have the expenses of their pastor. It is a misconception to believe that a pastor is not concerned with providing for his family's security and financial stability. Not to do so, according to Paul, would make him "worse than an unbeliever" (1 Tim. 5:8).

Implications

Those seven misconceptions about the local clergy are but a few of the ideas that can circulate through a congregation. Church members, perhaps more than any other segment of society, are difficult to change in this regard. Their minds have been so thoroughly influenced by many years of tradition and stereotyping that their expectations of a pastor are difficult to correct. Church board members must educate themselves and others about the realities of life as a senior pastor if they are going to provide him with the support and encouragement that he so desperately needs and deserves. When board members hold to any of these common misconceptions, or others like them, they are guilty of being out of touch with the true needs of the senior pastor and greatly contribute to the feelings of being unappreciated, used, or unwanted that frustrate so many pastors.

The church board member is the first person in a congregation who should have a proper understanding of the realities of pastoral service. In principle, board members and the pastor form a team that provides the basis for biblical ministry. But no team can function properly if its players do not have a proper understanding of each other's roles. Misconceptions, such as those presented here and in the chapter to follow, can create disharmony. Once the pastor and every church board member have an accurate perception of each other's needs and responsibilities, they are able to interrelate with a greater degree of openness and trust. These qualities create a far more firm foundation for ministerial partnership than unrealistic expectations.

For Further Reading

Clark, George. "When the Minister Gets Angry." *Church Administration* 32, no. 6 (March 1990): 24–25.

Drucker, Peter. *Managing the Non-Profit Organization.* San Francisco: Harper/Collins, 1990.

Halverson, Richard. "The Pastor and the Board: Maintaining Healthy Relationships." *Leadership* 1, no. 1 (Winter 1980): 133–36.

Hubbell, Macklyn. "Calling Clark Kent." *Church Administration* 32, no. 6 (Mar. 1990): 8–10.

Osborne, Larry. "What's Your Role with the Board?" *Leadership* 10, no. 3 (Summer 1989): 56–60.

Rediger, Lloyd. "When Formulas Don't Come Out Right." *The Clergy Journal* 66, no. 2 (Nov.–Dec. 1989): 39–41.

Stedman, Ray. "Should the Pastor Play Pope?" *Moody Monthly* 77, no. 11 (July–Aug. 1976): 41–44.

Stubblefield, Jerry. "The Minister of Education as Educator." *Church Administration* 32, no. 12 (Sept. 1990): 23–25.

Swindoll, Charles. "Toward Better Board Relationships." *Leadership* 7, no. 4 (Fall 1986): 90–93.

Thornburg, Stan. "Administration through a Servant's Eyes." *The Christian Ministry* 18, no. 2 (Mar. 1987): 10–12.

The Mythical Church Board Member

henever several pastors get together to discuss how things are going in their ministries, you can be sure that one of the first topics of conversation will be their relationship with the church board. If there is one thing that all pastors have in common, regardless of denominational affiliation, it is a church board, whether it be a board of elders, a board of trustees, a board of deacons or—less frequently—of deaconesses. Due to the size of their congregation or their denomination, some pastors work with several boards in the church. Pastors in smaller churches often have just one.

As a result of serving on the pastoral staff at five churches, I have worked with each of the four different types of boards. Most of my experiences have been positive. A few were not. In seminary I was not prepared very well for working with these boards. It was as if the professors assumed that fledgling pastors would automatically know how to relate to them, train them, and negotiate ministry together. Nothing could have been further from the truth. In looking back, I now realize that my professors held a great many mistaken ideas about church board members and passed on many of those beliefs to the seminarians who would later become pastors.

The purpose of this chapter is to examine some of those myths and help both board members and pastors deal with the incongruencies that these stereotypes represent. When I conducted my survey of church board members, I asked them to identify one or more misconceptions they felt their senior pastor had about board members. Some responses were quite amusing (e.g., "That we are able to leap tall buildings with a single bound," or "That while he was on vacation we were meeting to overthrow him"). Others represented the heartfelt pains of deep misunderstanding.

Common Misconceptions About Board Members

Misconception #1. Board members know exactly what to do once they are elected to the board. Quite a number of church board members expressed frustration over what their pastor expected of them. It was as if the day they were elected to the board, the senior pastor assumed that a mantle of wisdom and discernment came magically on them from on high. It is far more productive to assume that a church board member's chief qualification is his or her willingness to serve. This is not to say that professional skill or knowledge is not useful, nor that informed decision making will not be required. However, making a policy decision at work—whether as a businessman, lawyer, or farmer—is not always the same as in a church setting.

Whenever I approach a new group of individuals to train or equip for ministry, I always like to start at the lowest point of common ground. That way, those who have little or no knowledge are not embarrassed to ask questions, and those with more expertise get a review. By the time we have had a few sessions, we are all at the same point and can begin moving ahead together. By not taking too much for granted, I avoid the risk of training beyond anyone's level of understanding. It is unrealistic to assume that everyone who has agreed to serve as a church board member understands what the Bible has to say about such important matters as interpersonal conflict resolution, church discipline, stewardship, servant leadership, and so on. These subjects take time to explain and discuss.

Many pastors, after discovering the need for board-member training, experience some frustration about how and when to conduct this training. The agenda of the monthly board meeting is usually filled with important business items and does not leave much time for anything else. At best, the pastor may lead a brief devotional, but sometimes the pressing decisions at hand make even that difficult.

Speaking of this need for training beyond what the regular business meetings allow, Pastor Larry Osborne writes, "Frustrated with our inability to find time to deal with these vital issues, I hit on an idea. Why not schedule an extra monthly meeting to deal with them exclusively? I wasn't sure if the board would go for it, but they agreed to try the meetings for the rest of the year. So I put together a series of 'shepherding meetings' to zero in on three areas: (1) team building, (2) training, and (3) prayer."[1]

Other churches I have served have also chosen to add a monthly meeting just for the purpose of leadership development. We made it a policy not to conduct business at these meetings. Instead, we set aside time each month to discuss one issue that would be helpful for the board members to focus on. We usually met at a member's home and began with breakfast, followed by a few hours of discussion and dialogue. Sometimes we would mail out an article or chapter from a book and ask that it be read before coming to the meeting. Such an assignment served several purposes. It reminded the members of the upcoming meeting, set the agenda for our discussion (to prevent chasing needless rabbits), and provided the participants with a file of support materials to which they could refer if the need warranted.

This kind of program is referred to as "in-service training." It is common in most corporate settings and is well accepted as a legitimate form of human-resource development. It is particularly beneficial if your church does not conduct an annual board-member training retreat, which might consist of a weekend at a camp, cabin, or hotel conference center.

Misconception #2. *Board members are not spiritually qualified to make important decisions.* Here we must take into consideration the perspective of a pastor who might hold this view. It is easy to throw stones at pastors for jumping to such a conclusion unless you understand their educational background (as discussed in chapter 1). If a pastor feels that volunteer leaders are not "spiritually qualified," what he really means is "academically trained." In comparison to his own formal preparation, that may be very true. However, it is important for every pastor to understand that a degree on the wall does not necessarily qualify one for ministry. Although graduate theological education is designed to provide the necessary tools for an effective ministry, a seminary degree does not guarantee that a person will know how to apply these tools properly. Board members may not have a great many years of formal theological training (although one-fifth of those in the survey had attended or graduated from a seminary), but they do provide a pastor with something that cannot be taught in seminary—common sense and perspective.

The church where I was ordained had a deacon board that consisted primarily of farmers and blue-collar workers. Because they were not highly educated by academic standards, the senior pastor had to give them the questions to ask at my ordination council. Although they could not explain the difference between "dichotomy" and "trichotomy," they could cut to the heart of an issue with amazing accuracy. These men knew the Word of God as a result of many years of sermons, Sunday school, and home Bible studies. They might not have been able to quote specific references for everything they said, but they did know what was right and wrong when applied to their church setting. They possessed a keen knowledge of the essence of what Scripture taught, and they knew the needs of the people in their church far better than I did. As I came to admire their insight and understanding of spiritual matters, I realized that I had once been guilty of basing my standard of spiritual maturity on academic know-how.

Most of the board members with whom I have served were elected by the congregation. They were chosen because they were seen as spiritual men and women of God. In a few cases I think the decision was more political than spiritual, but they were certainly the exceptions. Board members can assist the teachable pastor by clarifying issues, explaining the real needs of the membership, and providing the pastor with a sounding board for decision making. If some members of the board do not seem to possess the spiritual maturity to make important decisions, the pastor should address this need as part of his responsibility. The New Testament has much to say about how the pastor is to train and equip the members of his congregation. According to Ephesians 4:11–16, providing the board with a higher level of spiritual discernment fulfills his "job description."

So much of this comes down to the attitude of the pastor. He can see this apparent lack of spiritual preparation and depth as either a reason to be discouraged or as an opportunity for development, growth, and team training.

Misconception #3. Board members have a great deal of free time. This is certainly not true, especially in urban settings. In many parts of our country, it is no longer the norm for a wife to remain at home to care for the children. Due to the high costs of housing, medical care, insurance, and so on, many couples are finding it impossible to survive on one income alone. These two-income families are stretched to the limit, finding it very hard to shop for clothes and groceries, shuttle the children to a variety of school and civic events, attend to their own professional responsibilities, and still meet their weekly obligations at the church. It is no wonder why it is getting increasingly difficult to find leaders who are willing, or even able, to give extra hours of their week to serve on a church board.

In several of the churches where I have served, we instigated a policy that board members could not serve in any other capacity in the church. Those with leadership capabilities had found themselves being asked to teach a Sunday school class, sing in the choir, direct a youth group, or take on any number of other jobs. The result was inevitably an exhausted and overcommitted worker. We thought it wise to limit board members to the one area in which they could best focus their energies and provide a high level of contribution.

Speaking of a board member's lack of availability for numerous meetings at the church, Pastor Wayne Jacobsen writes, "It's tough to get people together. But when I look at ministry as touching people instead of attending meetings, I realize what makes them unavailable for my schedule makes them readily accessible to others. I can be at only one place at a time, dealing with a limited number of people, but my parishioners are spread out all over the city. And whereas I may need to schedule an appointment weeks in advance, some lay person will be free to go over tonight and spend hours helping someone. One farmer and his wife found fifteen hours in a single week to help a person through a major crisis."[2] A church board member who is not able to fit every business or committee meeting into his or her schedule may find it far easier to perform the relational aspects of ministry than the pastor.

Misconception #4. Decisions made by the board should always be in complete agreement with the pastor. I would love to believe that most pastors are secure enough to allow differences of opinion to be shared openly in board meetings. However, I have taught young pastors too long and served in enough churches to know that this simply is not true. Like most people, pastors are not immune from feelings of insecurity.

This misconception is known as the "rubber stamp" syndrome. It is based on the mistaken belief that pastors always know what is best for their congregations and that therefore the board would do best to go along with the pastor and not challenge or disagree with his agenda.

The average tenure of a senior pastor is less than five years, whereas it is logical to assume that most board members have been attending the church for a good many years longer than the pastor. Therefore, the board may know the needs and conditions of the church's membership far better than the pastor. It is inevitable that there will be disagreements regarding programs, priorities, or policies, but some controversy can be quite healthy.

The Book of Proverbs has several verses that help us understand the benefit of receiving input from others during any decision-making process:

> For lack of guidance a nation falls, but many advisers make victory sure (11:14).
> He who walks with the wise grows wise, but a companion of fools suffers harm (13:20).

Plans fail for lack of counsel, but with many advisers they succeed (15:22).

Make plans by seeking advice; if you wage war, obtain guidance (20:18).

For waging war you need guidance, and for victory many advisers (24:6).

As iron sharpens iron, so one man sharpens another (27:17).

It is not realistic to expect the board to agree with the pastor on all matters, and it is not biblical. When Paul and Barnabas were beginning their second missionary journey, they disagreed about whether or not John Mark should accompany them. John Mark had left them soon into their first missionary journey, and Paul did not feel that it was wise to take him along again. Because Paul and Barnabas then selected different partners and went their separate ways, the result was that they multiplied their ministry (Acts 15:36–41). Acts 6:1–6 tells of a disagreement that resulted in the formation of the first deacon board. Also in the Book of Acts is found a sharp division between the believers in Jerusalem (primarily of Jewish origin) and the believers who were from Gentile regions (of non-Jewish origin). Yet this disagreement resulted in a healthy dialogue between the church leaders (Acts 15:1–35).

Controversy can be very beneficial if it allows us to sort through the real issues and examine the motives behind the final decision. Mature individuals should be able to discuss their disagreements without this resulting in arguments, hurt feelings, or power struggles. It helps to remember the words of Peter: "To sum up, let all be harmonious, sympathetic, brotherly kindhearted, and humble in spirit; not returning evil for evil, or insult for insult, but giving a blessing instead . . ." (1 Peter 3:8–9 NASB).

This is an important matter and will be dealt with in more detail in chapter 9: "Team Ministry: The Biblical Ideal."

Misconception #5. The board should provide the vision and direction for the church. Many new pastors assume that since the board had been in place before their arrival, it has a clear understanding of the church's vision and purpose. This is not necessarily the case, however. It is true that an experienced board might have a sharper view of the church's goals than an incoming pastor. This does not mean that they know how the church should get there. In most of the churches where I have served, although the senior pastor was seen as the person who would provide the basic direction and vision for the church, the board of elders or deacons helped the pastor formulate the vision. Both bodies are needed. The pastor may supply most of the broad strokes of the picture, but it will be up to the board to "buy into" the vision and lend their support. This usually means that they have participated in the initial planning stages. Ministry should be viewed as a team process in which both the pastor and board make significant contributions.

Misconception #6. The board wants to direct and control the activities of the church. This may not be a prevailing view in all churches, but for churches that have a long history of tradition, change comes very slowly. In a few cases it does not come at all. In older, well-established churches, the board may choose to "stay on course" and maintain the status quo. Most pastors who accept a call from such a church know the board will be difficult to convince that change is needed.

Although a few churches are definitely board-controlled, most church boards are more than willing to share the responsibilities and burdens of the ministry with the pastor. In fact, a board in a new church may have a difficult time accepting its share of the leadership, especially if it was the pastor's vision and leadership that started the church.

Another important consideration in this regard is how long the church was without a pastor during a pastoral transition period. If the church lacked a senior pastor for an extended period of time (over two years), the board probably had to become decisive and somewhat controlling. Once the new pastor arrives, they must learn to relinquish much of its previously assumed authority. This shifting of power may be difficult to achieve, but it is an essential dynamic if the new pastor is going to be confident in his ability to lead the congregation.

Misconception #7. Discipling or mentoring of board members is not the senior pastor's responsibility. Board members who mentioned this as a view held by the clergy apparently felt that their own spiritual training had been set aside by their pastor for work he considered more important. In fact, there was a genuine disappointment among some about their level of personal involvement with the pastor. Many felt that agreeing to serve on the church board would give them ample opportunity to meet with the pastor "behind the scenes" and establish an intimate friendship with him. Then, shortly after arriving on the board, they became disillusioned by how little time they actually spent with the pastor.

It is certainly true that a pastor may feel too busy with other responsibilities to disciple the lay leaders of his congregation, especially in churches with more than one board. However, if board members are to serve as spiritual leaders in the church, it is critical that the senior pastor enjoy a close and honest relationship with them. This will take time to develop, but the process of interpersonal give-and-take will allow the pastor to mentor the board members and nurture their spiritual growth. Pastors who have set discipling of lay leaders as a high priority usually enjoy a better working relationship with their board. Disagreements and differences in philosophy of ministry may still occur, but when they do they are less likely to be in an explosive context. If "discussions" can sometimes take place in relaxed settings (such as on a golf course, while fishing together, or on a hunting trip), tension may ease as closeness is developed through mutual transparency.

Not all pastors, especially those in mega-churches, can adequately disciple their board members. Pastors in large churches have a difficult time just keeping up with their staff! They attend countless meetings every day and are exhausted when they get home at night; most also have at least a few evening meetings each week. Individual meetings with as many as twenty board members are simply not possible. It would be best for any board that interviews prospective pastors to discuss this matter before making a hiring decision. The potential for disappointment is greatly reduced if the board and new pastor have already agreed on the priority assigned to discipling of lay leaders.

Implications

These are a few common misconceptions about being a board member. Some are not entirely untrue, but are based on reality:

the denominational affiliation, size of congregation, history of the church, and experience of the pastor. Nevertheless, many of these misunderstandings can be eliminated through healthy dialogue if the pastor and each of the church board members are able to put these matters on the table and have an open discussion about them. Just reading about them and sharing personal feelings about these misconceptions could be the first step. It might also be a good idea for board members to write down in the space below a few additional "misconceptions" that seem worthy of discussion:

1.

2.

3.

4.

5.

For Further Reading

"An Interview with Howard Clark and R. Hudson Carlberg." *Leadership* 10, no. 4 (Fall 1989): 130–37.

Banks, Robert. "Introduction." *Theology, News and Notes,* June 1990: 3.

Larson, Bruce. "The Risky Business of Lay Ministry." *Leadership* 10, no. 4 (Fall 1989): 28–32.

The Biblical Basis for Pastors, Elders, Deacons, and Trustees

For members of the clergy, dealing with volunteer leaders may be the hardest part of ministering to a congregation. As one Southern California pastor put it, "You can't work with them, and you can't work without them." Nevertheless, it was in God's divine plan for laypersons to be involved in the day-to-day functioning of the body of Christ. The church with many dedicated volunteer leaders is blessed indeed. Those people can make things happen! It is the senior pastor's obligation, however, to be sure that each potential leader is placed in the proper position and trained for specific responsibilities. To do anything less is to waste the incredible resources that God has given to his church.

A search for an organizational chart in the pages of the New Testament will only lead to frustration. One must remember that principles of administrative management, which may be common in many of our twentieth-century churches, were not always evident in earlier times. Because geographical and cultural context, as well as the needs of the community, dictates a church's programs, worship structure, and patterns of leadership, rarely do we find one church duplicating the means and methods of another church in the Bible.

For this reason, coming to any definitive conclusions regarding the appropriate roles and responsibilities of church officers is not possible. Churches have different ways of handling issues such as how to format the worship service, design more contemporary ministry programs, and administer church governance. Their decisions take into account the variety of models found in church history, denominational distinctions, and congregational preferences.

The purpose of this chapter is to offer church leaders from a broad range of doctrinal and denominational backgrounds a basic pattern for delineating their roles. What one church may call an elder may be what another church calls a pastor. What one church refers to as the responsibilities of an elder may be assigned to a deacon at another church. It is not my intent to solve the age-old controversy of three-office versus two-office church leadership. Rather, I prefer to share the evidence I find in Scripture for each position's qualifications and responsibilities, and then allow each local church to make its own decision regarding the use of these roles. Although I will present the material from a three-office perspective, those who prefer to view the pastor and elder as synonymous church leaders (and therefore hold to a two-office view) should regard the first two sections of this chapter as referring to the same individual.

Pastor

The name *pastor* comes from the Latin term for "shepherd" and refers to the person who has general responsibility for a congregation. Although the word picture of a pastor as someone who watches over a congregation has been around since the early days of the Christian church, the use of the term as a position designation or formal title did not come about until quite recently. Its elevation to the preferred image and title first occurred among eighteenth-century Lutheran pietists, who were seeking to narrow the traditional gap between the professional minister and the average Christian leader.[1]

The Greek term for pastor, *poimen,* refers to one who guards, tends, feeds, and cares for the flock. This word came from the rural community and represents the character of a faithful shepherd who is providing for his sheep.

Qualifications

Clearly the primary qualification for a pastor is to be a born-again believer who is spiritually gifted for that role. The New Testament teaches that those with a specific gift—such as evangelists, counselors, teachers—must be placed in positions where they can exercise their gifts "for the common good" (1 Cor. 12:7; cf. 1 Peter 4:10). We must not assume that a person gifted in counseling is also gifted to be a pastor. Each gift is different, although one person may possess several gifts (e.g., pastor-teacher or pastor-evangelist). Care should be taken to be sure that an individual chosen as "pastor" is truly gifted in this area. Each spiritual gift listed in Scripture represents a ministry to be performed in the body of Christ. Since there is a distinct gift for pastoring, which is different from the other spiritual gifts mentioned in the New Testament, it is logical to assume that those who are going to perform such a ministry in the local church must be gifted "to be pastors" (see Eph. 4:11).

Responsibilities

Beyond having the appropriate gift, the biblical qualifications for pastors were identical to those for the elders in the church. Since the primary difference was one of giftedness, each assumed a slightly different set of responsibilities. The major difference between a pastor and an elder was that the former was held responsible for communicating the Word of God.

Elder

Despite a preponderance of materials devoted to the definition and description of the church elder, there is no clear-cut biblical answer to the question of who or what an elder is. Looking through

Scripture with an eye toward a historical overview reveals that "elder" meant different things in different settings. A brief look at how the term was used in both the Old and the New Testaments will serve as a foundation for understanding how the office came to exist in the early church.

Old Testament. The term *elder* comes from the Greek *presbuteros,* which indicates spiritual maturity in leadership. The term had been used in the Jewish culture, but it was also common among the Greeks. In reviewing the Old Testament teachings about the role of elder, several important trends emerge.

1. *The office of the elder was largely one of representation.* Since there is no Old Testament teaching regarding the qualifications and responsibilities of elders, the office must have gradually emerged after the period of the patriarchs. It was probably fully in place by the end of Israel's forty-year pilgrimage through the wilderness.

On several occasions, "elders" accompanied or were assembled by Moses (Exod. 3:16, 18; 4:29; 17:5–6; 19:7; 24:1, 10), and they also spoke and acted on behalf of the people (Lev. 4:13–15; Deut. 21:1–9; 1 Sam. 8:4; 2 Sam. 5:3; 1 Kings 20:7–8). At times the elders of the community were strong enough to rise to a position of prominence (as in the wilderness wandering, and during the periods of the judges, and the exile). However, while the monarchy was in place, and in the interval between the Old and New Testaments, elders had a seemingly lesser degree of influence and authority.

2. *The function of the elder was one of rule and governance.* Elders were assigned the responsibility of judging the civil arguments in the community (Deut. 19:12; 22:13–19; 25:1, 7–9; Josh. 20:4, 6). In addition they served as administrators of the civil code (Num. 11:16–17; Ruth 4:1–12) and, as a senate, provided counsel and leadership for matters of state (1 Sam. 4:3; 8:4; 2 Sam. 3:17–18; 5:3; 1 Kings 20:7–8; Ezra 5:9).

3. *There is no clear evidence that the ability to teach the Word of God was ever a condition of selection for eldership.* On the contrary, there was a separate and distinct office beyond that of the elder for communicating the Word. This office was that of levitical priest (Deut. 33:8–10). Although the elders of Israel shared with the

priests the responsibility for judging matters of national importance, teaching and communicating the Word of God was something that was not included in the role of elder. The Old Testament indicates clear lines of demarcation between the offices of priest and elder in the spiritual community of Israel. Some argue that these same distinctions exist today, while others believe they do not.

New Testament. The first Christians continued to observe many of the customs and teachings established in the Old Testament. Such practices as daily observance of temple prayers, keeping the Sabbath, maintaining the Jewish dietary laws, and reading from the sacred Hebrew Scriptures are examples of customs carried over into the early church. The responsibilities of its leaders may have changed, due to the doctrine of the priesthood of all believers, but the basic offices remained—for we find that sometime prior to the period mentioned in Acts 11:27–30, a body of elders had been formed in the Jerusalem church.

Examining the New Testament usages for the term *elder* reveals additional insights into their roles and responsibilities.

1. *The term "elder" includes those who also had the office of apostle* (1 Peter 5:1; 2 John 1:1; 3 John 1:1). It is thought by some that while an apostle was automatically considered an elder by virtue of his position of authority, an elder was not necessarily an apostle.

2. *Paul seems to draw a line of distinction between the gifts of pastoral teaching (pastor-teacher) and church governance (administrative leadership).* His teachings on the spiritual gifts (Rom. 12:4–8; 1 Cor. 12:1–31) imply a differentiation between the gifts of teaching and the gifts related to ruling. In many churches throughout the United States and Canada, "elder" probably comes closest to describing the status of most ordained pastors today.[2]

Qualifications

The New Testament indicates that those who were selected as elders were required to meet a host of carefully screened criteria. Because each of those elements related to character quality, it was clearly of primary importance to the early church that elders demonstrate lives of integrity. In essence, character was more important than any other component of an elder's résumé. The scriptural passages that most clearly portray the qualifications for the office of elder are 1 Timothy 3:1–7 and Titus 1:5–9. According to these passages, the qualities that an elder must possess—beyond being "above reproach," or "blameless as an example"—include:

Personal Qualities
- Temperate (calm and clear in thinking)
- Sensible or prudent (wise)
- Self-controlled (not given to impulsive behavior)
- Respectable (a well-ordered life)
- Not self-willed (able to allow others to share in governance)
- Devout (consistent in devotion to God)
- Free from the love of money
- Loves what is good
- Avoids drunkenness
- Not fond of sordid gain (can't be improperly influenced)

Family Life
- Husband of one wife (pure marriage relationship)
- Children who are believers and not rebellious
- Able to manage one's family (consistent testimony at home)

Relationships with Others
- Gentle (patient, kind)
- Uncontentious (not argumentative)
- Just (fair in decision making)
- Not pugnacious (doesn't attack others)
- Hospitable (ministry in the home)
- Not quick-tempered (controlled emotions)
- Good reputation with those outside the church

Spiritual Maturity
- Not a new convert
- Holds fast to the Word of God (practices spiritual discipline)

- Able to teach and exhort in sound doctrine (can apply the truth)
- Refutes false teachings (able to present a defense for the faith)

Responsibilities

Churches with elders in office may define their functions somewhat differently, but it is apparent that elders in the early church were involved in feeding and leading the membership. In general, they gave the congregation guidance and direction during important periods of decision making and also in the day-to-day operation of the church. Their responsibilities could be summarized as follows:

1. *Teaching the Word of God.* Elders in the early church were admonished to feed the congregation with spiritual food, which means they were in a position to teach biblical truth. Today, elders fulfill this responsibility by teaching home Bible studies or Sunday school classes and speaking at fellowship meetings, support groups, retreats, and so on.

2. *Decision making.* This responsibility was a continuation of the role played by elders in Old Testament times. In this capacity, for example, they were to receive and distribute financial aid to members of the congregation (Acts 11:30), presumably in accordance with individual need. Acts 21:18–25 provides us with a glimpse into the involvement of the Jerusalem elders in the decision-making process of the early church. After Paul's missionary journeys, he told the elders about the many Gentile converts the Lord had added to the universal church. Word of Paul's ministry to the Gentiles had reached Jerusalem ahead of Paul and had created quite a stir among the legalistic and traditional Jewish Christians. The elders advised Paul to join in "purification rites" so he would secure the respect and confidence of his Jewish brothers in the Jerusalem church (vv. 23–24). They had also taken it on themselves to make a "decision" regarding practice of the faith by Gentile believers (v. 25; cf. 15:23–29).

3. *Praying for the sick.* This responsibility is defined in James 5:14. Evidently the elders were to be so deeply involved in the individual lives of the congregation that they were aware of any physical or emotional distress among members of the body of

Christ. They were to respond to that need by visiting the sick individual as a group, at which time they would anoint the person with oil and pray for his or her healing.

4. *Solving doctrinal controversy.* Acts 15:1–6 records that when a major controversy regarding Gentile believers enveloped the early church and threatened to tear its fiber apart, the council of elders and the apostles who were in Jerusalem called a special session to decide among themselves what should be done. It is clear that the elders of the congregation were involved in hearing and settling this doctrinal dispute (see vv. 23–29). Eventually the apostles would leave Jerusalem to fulfill their divine commission. In their absence, the church elders were responsible for answering false rumors, combating doctrinal errors of interpretation, and protecting the flock from false teachers and prophets.

The elder is seen throughout the pages of Scripture as an important office of ministry leadership. Whether in the Old Testament community or in the New Testament church, elders were to be people who were above reproach in the eyes of the local community of believers because their lifestyle demonstrated a commitment to biblical standards of conduct and instruction. They were to have a consistent walk with God, and their commitment to serve the local body of believers flowed out of their desire to serve him.

An elder was qualified for service based on issues of character quality, not on such purely outward characteristics as prestige, financial success, or political influence. He used his influence in the spiritual development of the local church through acts of sacrificial kindness, prayerful diligence, protective guardianship, and by providing wise counsel. Both pastor and elder served as team members in the overall ministry. Each position was to be blended together to form a foundation on which the church would be firmly established and strengthened.

Deacons

The word *deacon* comes to us from the Greek *diaconus*, which literally means to serve. It carries the idea of belonging completely and unequivocally to one's master. The early church saw the role and function of a deacon as exemplifying total commitment to serving the risen Christ who was his Savior and Lord. The *diaconus* form of servanthood was that of a house slave, someone with a more intimate relationship with his master than the workers who tended the crops or cared for the master's cattle. In many respects it was a "voluntary" position, rather than a forced or coercive relationship.

The term for "deacon" in the New Testament appears in three forms. The verb form *(diaconeo)* appears thirty-seven times, with various translations in our English Bibles. The noun form *(diaconia)* denotes a service being rendered. This form is used thirty-three times and appears in English Bibles as "ministry," "ministering," "service," "serving," or "doing service." The personal noun *(diaconus)* occurs thirty times and is usually translated as either "servant" or "minister." These references provide us with a broad base to understand the qualifications and responsibilities of a deacon in the early church.

In view of the designated qualifications, the deacons would share the same concerns for the congregation as the elders and pastor and, under the guidance of these overseers, would help in relieving varied needs as they were able.[3] Deacons shared in the leadership of the church's ministry, with each office (pastor/elder/deacon) serving in its proper role and function. This harmony of ministry positions provided the basis for consistent spiritual growth and edification of the local congregation.

Qualifications

The qualities required of a deacon are similar in nature and scope to those for church elders. Deacons, like all church leaders, are expected to set a good example to others and be "worthy of respect." The clearest teaching on their specific qualifications comes from Acts 6:1–7 and 1 Timothy 3:8–13, and these include:

Personal Qualities
- Dignified (respectable attitude and behavior)
- Not double-tongued (consistency in what is communicated)

- Temperate (not addicted to wine)
- Not fond of sordid gain (can't be improperly influenced)

Family Life
- Husband of one wife (pure marriage relationship)
- Good manager of household (leadership in family life)

Relationships with Others
- Good reputation (respected by both Christians and non-Christians)
- Full of wisdom (exhibits godly wisdom, as seen in James 4:14–17)
- Sincere (trustworthy)

Spiritual Maturity
- Full of the Holy Spirit (at full disposal to the will of God)
- Tested (not a recent convert, proven faithfulness)
- Holding to the mystery of the faith (consistent spiritual maturity)
- Clear conscience

Responsibilities

While we do not know all the details of a deacon's role, we can determine a general list of responsibilities from Scripture and early accounts of church history. For example, deacons were expected to:

1. *Respond to the physical and spiritual needs of others.* As commanded by Jesus (Matt. 25:34–45), deacons would seek out those in need and provide for their welfare by giving food, drink, or clothing; extending shelter; and visiting prisoners or those who were sick. They were to exemplify servanthood, both within the community of faith and outside the church.

2. *Be generous with their own possessions.* Deacons were to "excel in this grace of giving" (2 Cor. 8:7) and thereby express their thanksgiving to God (2 Cor. 9: 6–14). It was for this quality that

the apostle Paul commended people like Phoebe, who was "a great help to many people" (Rom. 16:2), and others who "devoted themselves to the service of the saints" (1 Cor. 16:15).

3. *Administer and distribute offerings* (Acts 6:1–4; 2 Cor. 8:18–21). Because deacons were trustworthy members of the congregation, they could be depended on for the proper handling of financial matters in the church.

Deacons were closely aligned with the overall ministry of the local church. They were aware of congregational needs and were actively involved in the church program so that the pastors (who were apostles during the earliest period) were free to devote themselves to studying Scripture, communicating the Word of God, and praying for the fellowship. Deacons worked alongside the pastor and offered their services wherever needed. As in the case of church elders, deacons were part of a ministry team that joined together to provide for the diverse needs they identified in the community at large and within the local congregation.

Trustees

Since a growing number of modern churches are incorporating a trustee board into their organizational structure, it would seem beneficial to mention this office in a general way. Forty-five percent of the churches in my survey had a board of trustees. In almost every case, this committee had fewer members than the elder or deacon board. Since the Bible provides no specific instructions regarding "trustees," it must be assumed that such an office transcended the parameters of church practice at the time the New Testament was recorded.

This is not to say that such a position is unbiblical or unwarranted. Such is also the case for a number of specialized ministry roles seen in our churches today, such as children's pastor, youth pastor, singles' director, Christian-education director, sports and recreation director, Sunday school superintendent, and so on. In general, ministry positions that are not filled by members of the pastoral staff require a moderate degree of spiritual maturity and the character qualities expected of a deacon. For positions that are more closely aligned with shepherding responsibilities, non-academic requirements parallel those for a pastor and/or elder.

A church usually has a special purpose for establishing a trustee board. For example, the trustee board may consist of the senior pastor, the chair of the elder board, the chair of the deacon board, the church clerk, and church treasurer. Generally speaking, trustees are included in the structural composition of a church when the elder board and deacon board become unable to care for all the diverse ministries within the church and still confront the many other issues that face a church in our contemporary culture. Trustees have traditionally coordinated the business, contractual, and legal matters of the church, which allows the elders and deacons more time for interpersonal ministry responsibilities. Each church board plays a part in maximizing the contribution of the others.

Implications

The office of elder, deacon, or trustee is a high calling and should not be entered into without careful self-analysis. Spiritual leaders in the congregation will face a stricter judgment from God than will the members at large, both now and in the future. Because board members are selected on the basis of specific qualifications, they have the important responsibility of furthering the kingdom of God through teaching, counseling, serving, and guiding the congregation in a host of essential areas. Church officers should never view themselves as an appendage to the pastor, but as a vital component in the process of ministry within the body of Christ.

As a pastor, I have seen the offices of elder, deacon, and trustee in action and have sat for long hours into the night with church boards to pray and decide important matters in the life of the congregation. I am convinced that the average parishioner does not realize the awesome responsibility involved in being a church board member. These servants sacrifice much to contribute to the needs of their church and local community. Working with them has been one of my greatest sources of joy. It is thrilling beyond words to watch them feel empowered to share the vision and work of the ministry.

However, I must also admit that there have been times when working with a board has caused me great frustration. When individuals get sidetracked by insignificant matters, political maneuvering, or prideful disputations, the loss of manpower is enormous—and the same can be said about pastoral staff as well.

When those who have been gifted for ministry are channeled into suitable avenues of service, the end result will be growth and harmony in the body of believers (Eph. 4:11–16). It is my prayer that those who serve as church board members will see themselves as essential team members in the total ministry of the church. In the end, God's standard of measure will not be role, position, or status but faithfulness within our areas of calling.

Questions for Discussion

1. Do you believe that the offices of elder and pastor are synonymous?
2. What distinctions do you see between the offices of elder and deacon?
3. If your church has only one board, what would be the advantages/disadvantages of expanding to a two-board form of church governance?
4. How can the average parishioner be made more aware of the valuable contribution that church board members make in their church?
5. If you were to comprise a list of qualifications for a church board member today, what qualities would you include that were not listed in the passages cited in this chapter?

For Further Reading

Beckwith, David. "Sharpening Our Focus: A Biblical Study of New Testament Leadership." Position paper presented to the board of deacons at Woodbridge Community Church, Irvine, Calif., 1989.

DePuy, Norman R. "Responsibility and Authority in the Church." *The Christian Ministry* 18, no. 2 (Mar. 1987).

Gangel, Kenneth O. *Feeding and Leading*. Wheaton: Victor Books, 1989.

Hiebert, D. Edmond, "Behind the Word 'Deacon': A New Testament Study." *Bibliotheca Sacra* 140, no. 558 (April–June 1983).

Knight, George W. "Two Offices (Elders/Bishops and Deacons) and Two Orders of Elders (Preaching/Teaching Elders and Ruling Elders): A New Testament Study." *Presbyterion* 11 (Fall 1985).

Leuke, David. *New Designs for Church Leadership.* St. Louis: Concordia, 1990.

Nayburn, Robert S. "Three Offices: Minister, Elder, Deacon." *Presbyterion* 12 (Fall 1986).

Naylor, Robert. *The Baptist Deacon.* Nashville: Broadman Press, 1955.

The Ministry of the Deaconess

s it appropriate for women to serve the church in an official leadership capacity? This issue has been debated for countless decades within denominations and individual churches. Those in support of providing more leadership opportunities for women point to the ministry roles of women throughout the pages of both the Old and New Testaments. Others hold a more conservative view, agreeing that certain women have been used by God for ministry, but primarily because properly qualified men were either not available or willing to serve. Churches in which the latter view prevails will probably not include the office of deaconess in their structure. However, forty-nine out of a hundred churches surveyed for this book had a deaconess board, with an average of seven deaconesses per board.

It is not my intention to present here the substantive arguments for and against the office of deaconess. (A survey of background materials that will assist the reader in this regard may be found at the end of the chapter.) However, after studying the New Testament passages at length, I have concluded that the office is both biblically documented and particularly needed in our churches today. This chapter will illustrate how a deaconess board might be organized and what service to the church such a board could accomplish.

Historical Development

The office of deaconess has been traced back to the writings of the apostle Paul: "I commend to you our sister Phoebe, a servant of the church in Cenchrea. I ask you to receive her in the Lord in a way worthy of the saints and to give her any help she may need from you, for she has been a great help to many people, including me" (Rom. 16:1).

Although most translations refer to Phoebe as "a servant," the Greek word used to describe her is *diakonon*, which is where we get our English word *deacon*. The Revised Standard Version translates her title as "deaconess," since the word may be either masculine or feminine. ("Diakonissa," from where we get the word *deaconess*, is found only in classical Greek and is not found in the New Testament.) It would seem that Phoebe was held in high esteem by Paul for her partnership with him in the ministry of the gospel. He testifies of her good deeds and her service to those who were in need. She evidently was devout in her commitment to Christ, faithful in her service to the church, and known to many as someone with leadership capabilities.

The office of deaconess was evident in the church as early as A.D. 104, when a Roman administrator and author by the name of Pliny the Younger referred to two women who were called female ministers.[1] The office seems to have been restricted primarily to widows, although virgins were not absolutely excluded. Their duties were to care for the sick and the poor, to minister to martyrs in prison, to instruct female catechumens, to assist in the baptism of women, and to exercise a degree of supervision over the other women in the congregation.[2]

The modern deaconess movement probably began in 1836, when the Lutheran pastor T. Fliedner founded a Protestant women's community in Germany that was devoted primarily to nursing. The idea spread rapidly throughout the Protestant church. In the second half of the nineteenth century, deaconesses were established in the Church of England, the Methodist Church, and the Church of Scotland. In this capacity, the women served as assistants to the pastor.[3]

The concept of a deaconess varies according to denominational distinctives. As with the offices of trustee, elder, and deacon, what is normative in one church may be quite different in another. In general, however, deaconesses perform acts of service (baptism, communion, prayer support), compassion (helping people in need, hospitality, visitation), and leadership (teaching, counseling) in their local church.

Qualifications

Although Scripture has no clearly prescribed list of qualifications for a deaconess, it would seem obvious that she should meet the same general requirements as a deacon, where applicable. Deaconesses should be spiritually mature in the faith, able to work with others in a cooperative manner, and "worthy of respect" (1 Tim. 3:5). They should understand the concept of team ministry and seek to assist the church as members of the body of Christ, using their unique gifts for service. The other qualifications of a deaconess, most of which parallel those already cited for deacons, include the following:

Personal Qualities
- Dignified (respectable attitude and behavior)
- Not double-tongued (consistency in what is communicated)
- Temperate (not addicted to wine)
- Not fond of sordid gain (can't be improperly influenced)
- Modest in appearance (clothing, jewelry, make-up)

Family Life
- Wife of one husband (pure marriage relationship)
- Good helpmate in household (submission in family life)

Relationships with Others
- Good reputation (respected by both Christians and non-Christians)

- Full of wisdom (exhibits godly wisdom, as seen in James 4:14–17)
- Sincere (trustworthy)

Spiritual Maturity
- Full of the Holy Spirit (at full disposal to the will of God)
- Tested (not a recent convert, proven faithfulness)
- Holding to the mystery of the faith (consistent spiritual maturity)
- Clear conscience

Some churches may have additional qualifications for deaconesses, based upon related passages of Scripture, denominational distinctives, and preferences of the membership. These requirements should be clearly communicated in the by-laws of the church constitution and the job description for deaconess.

One important note that should be made at this point concerns the practice in some churches of making the deacons' wives automatic members of the deaconess board. This may help fill some vacancies, but it has serious disadvantages. For example, the fact that a particular man is spiritually gifted for ministry as a deacon is certainly no guarantee that his wife is qualified to serve as a deaconess. If she is, she should be elected to that office on the basis of her own individual merits and not those of her husband. Otherwise, a wife may reluctantly agree to serve as a deaconess only so that her husband can become a deacon. If her position is attained in this manner, it is likely that her level of motivation for service will be low, and the church will suffer by not having enough deaconesses who are truly willing to carry their share of the responsibilities. Furthermore, other members of the deaconess board will probably resent any woman who is merely coasting through her obligations. These tensions can be avoided if the qualifications for selection as a deaconess are the same for everyone.

Responsibilities

The role of a deaconess will vary according to the needs of the church. Deaconesses generally assume a variety of responsibilities related to administrative leadership, hospitality, communion, baptism, visitation, worship, and counseling. Each of these areas is explored in detail below.

Administration

Positions of administrative leadership for a deaconess would include chairwoman, vice-chairwoman, and secretary for the deaconess board. The chairwoman of the deaconess board may also be a member of the church council or board of deacons. In this capacity, she is able to act as a liaison between the two boards and the senior pastor. The leader of the board of deaconesses is responsible for coordinating the board's activities, delegating duties to other deaconesses, and supervising their service. She may also see her position as an opportunity to mentor or disciple the members of her board. The chairwoman usually reports to the chairman of the deacon board or the senior pastor. In some churches, the chairwoman or vice-chairwoman also teaches candidates for baptism and/or church membership.

The secretary of the deaconess board is usually responsible for keeping the minutes of the meetings, writing a monthly article for the church newsletter, and keeping accurate financial records.

Hospitality

The deaconess who serves in this capacity arranges for providing meals and services to individuals in the congregation who find themselves in temporary need (such as after the death of a family member, coming home from the hospital with a new baby, or losing a job) and those who are disabled by age or chronic illness. Services could include sending cards of encouragement, housecleaning for shut-ins or new mothers, recruiting someone to do lawn work or car repair for an elderly person, providing child care for a single parent who must work. If you have ever been on the receiving end of such assistance you know how important this ministry can be.

Communion

The deaconess in charge of communion maintains adequate stock of communion supplies, sets up the elements (except in

churches where this is done by the pastor), and cleans the uten-
sils after their use in the service.

Baptism

If a deaconess is placed in charge of baptism at the church, she
maintains the baptismal gowns in proper care, secures the site if
the church does not have one of its own, and is responsible for
preparing the baptismal certificates for pastoral signature. She usually assists the candidates before and during their baptismal
experience.

Visitation

This includes visiting hospital patients and infirm or elderly
shut-ins at home and in institutions. The deaconess responsible
for this ministry makes sure that the needs of those she visits are
taken care of as completely and promptly as possible. She communicates to the senior pastor any special issues and concerns that
she may be made aware of as a result of her visit. This person—
and anyone who assists her in visitation—should have a heart for
listening, a love for those in need, and a patient compassion.

Worship

This area of responsibility may not be assigned to a deaconess
if the church has a worship committee. However, if the church
does not, the deaconess in charge of worship will be responsible
for the ordering, placement, and care of the flowers in the sanctuary. Many churches are using silk flowers now, in which case the
deaconess rotates the arrangements on a weekly, monthly, or quarterly basis. For special services (Christmas, Easter, Mother's Day,
graduation, etc.), she will select the appropriate floral displays.

In some churches, this deaconess is also responsible for the
acquisition and maintenance of altar coverings and pastoral robes.
She must make special note of all the seasons and special days in
the church calendar and use the appropriate colors and arrangements for both the coverings and the robes.

Counseling

A deaconess involved in counseling should have a heart of compassion and a listening ear, but she need not be specifically gifted

in this field or hold a counseling degree. When serious issues arise, a lay counselor should be prepared to make the necessary referral to a trained professional. In general, this woman has the responsibility of advising female members of the congregation who find themselves in need of direction. For example, these may include women who have been or are currently being abused at home or work and don't know what to do about it, or they may be victims of rape and/or incest who need guidance about the next appropriate step. This deaconess may also counsel women who come forward after a worship service for help with a spiritual problem or who want to join the church. Most senior pastors will agree that there are times when a woman in extreme emotional pain needs to talk with a spiritually mature sister in the faith, rather than with a male counselor, such as a pastor or deacon. In small churches where there is no director of women's ministries available, a deaconess usually answers this important need in the church.

Implications

Holding the office of deaconess is an important ministerial responsibility. Since the early days of the church, deaconesses have served as spiritual leaders. They have provided the senior pastor with valuable assistance in areas of service, compassion, and administration. Together with the board of elders and/or deacons, the deaconess board makes a valuable contribution to the daily life of the church.

Questions for Discussion

1. If your church does *not* have a deaconess board, what are the reasons for this decision? Do you feel these reasons are valid today?
2. If your church has a deaconess board, what areas of responsibility do they fulfill in your church that have not been mentioned in this chapter?
3. How are members of the deaconess board chosen? Do you feel that this is an appropriate manner of selection?

4. How closely does the board of elders and/or deacons work with the deaconess board at your church?
5. How closely does your senior pastor work with the deaconess board?
6. Are there any changes that you feel should be made in the way the deaconess board functions at your church?

For Further Reading

Giltner, Fern M., ed. *Women's Issues in Religious Education*. Birmingham, Ala.: Religious Education Press, 1985.

Howe, Margaret. *Women and Church Leadership*. Grand Rapids: Zondervan, 1982.

Hurley, James. *Man and Woman in Biblical Perspective*. Downers Grove, Ill.: InterVarsity Press, 1981.

Knight, George. *The Role Relationship of Men and Women*. Chicago: Moody Press, 1985.

Kobobel, Janet. *But Can She Type?* Downers Grove, Ill.: InterVarsity Press, 1986.

Maxwell, Leslie. *Women in Ministry*. Wheaton: Victor Books, 1987.

Mickelsen, Alvera, ed. *Women, Authority and the Bible*. Downers Grove, Ill.: InterVarsity Press, 1986.

Spencer, Aida. *Beyond the Curse: Women Called to Ministry*. Nashville: Thomas Nelson, 1985.

A Historical Overview
of Deacon Ministry

here can be great benefit in looking back before pushing ahead into the future. Soon after starting any new job, I always made an effort to interview the employees I worked with to gain their perspective of where the organization has come from and glimpse their view of the future. Knowledge of the past helps us appreciate our heritage. We learn to value those who came before us and paid a price to get us where we are today. It also helps us determine whether or not we have stayed on course toward the goals that the early developers envisioned. Gaining a historical perspective on the office of the deacon can serve each of these purposes.

The Early Church

The historical development of the office of deacon can be traced back to the early days of the Jerusalem church. Like most church traditions, it began from an element of practicality. In their haste to serve the needs of an ever-growing church (over 3,000 members within the first week), the apostles were undoubtedly overwhelmed by the task of both ministering to every believer and winning new converts. They knew little about organizational principles and had few resources to help them in their duties. Things were not going the way they had envisioned. In fact, even after Christ's ascension, they were still expecting their Lord to come and set up his earthly rule at any moment (Acts 1:6). I think it's safe to say that the needs of this new church ministry were at times overwhelming to its leaders. This new church was experiencing some of the pains of its rapid growth.

It was in the midst of these busy days that Grecian Jews who had become members of the Jerusalem church waged a complaint about how the ministry was being handled. (Even the first church had its share of internal problems!) These individuals had a Greek heritage, yet they were living in a community that wanted to preserve the Jewish culture and customs. It comes as no surprise that the widows among them were not receiving a fair share of the welfare benefits. Apparently the Hebraic widows were given a disproportionate amount of the daily food distribution. This caused a sharp disagreement within the congregation.

When news of this discord reached the apostles, they called a meeting to consider a fair and just response. The apostles decided that they should prioritize their time and place their primary emphasis on "the ministry of the word" and offering of prayer (Acts 6:4). In essence, they saw their basic responsibility as one of spiritual development for both themselves and their congregation. To concern themselves with welfare distribution would only compromise the time they needed for prayer and for studying and interpreting Scripture.

Since the problem was being reported by a select group of individuals within the church, it seemed appropriate that these same individuals be allowed the opportunity to create their own solution. Obviously, these people would need a degree of authority to carry out their responsibilities, so the apostles told the congregation to choose from among themselves seven men who met several critical criteria. These individuals had to be filled with the

Holy Spirit and have a public reputation for wisdom, honesty, and integrity (v. 3).

Seven men were presented to the apostles for their blessing (v. 5). By laying their hands on these lay leaders as an act of public consecration, the apostles established the office of deacon. The result of this conflict resolution was fourfold:

First, it established the principle that the primary function of the apostles was to study and interpret Scripture, pray, and arbitrate conflict in the church. This responsibility was theirs alone, but other tasks of ministry could be just as well performed by designated members of the congregation.

Second, it helped the congregation understand that, although they could share in the governance of the church, Spirit-filled living was a prerequisite for church leadership. In times of difficulty, the members would be consulted before major decisions that affected them were made.

Third, it confirmed that conflict resolution in the church is to be a mutually shared process that involves the pastor (apostle, in this case) and the deacons. Together they will address the issues and discuss an appropriate response.

Finally, it provided evidence that church growth and harmony in the congregation will occur when the pastor and the deacons perform their individual responsibilities as a team. Although Acts 6:1 states that "the number of disciples was increasing" even before the controversy broke out, verse 7 shows that "the word of God spread" and "the number of disciples in Jerusalem increased *rapidly*" after it was resolved.

Establishing a deacon board to assist the pastor was a pattern in many of the early churches. In Paul's first epistle to Timothy, dated approximately A.D. 60, the apostle's instructions concerning the selection of deacons indicate that deacon ministry was one of the foundations of church ministry in early Christendom.

From sources of this period, including Cyprian, Eusebius, and Hermos, we find more specific information about the office of church deacon. These early deacons, whose ministry was based on acts of love and compassion, had responsibilities related to charity, administration, education, and worship. Their duties were extensive, since many of the churches during this time were experiencing persecution and were filled with homeless and needy believers.[1] "They visited martyrs who were in prison, clothed and buried the dead, looked after the excommunicated with the hope of restoring them, provided for the needs of widows and orphans, and visited the sick and those who were otherwise in distress."[2]

Materials found in *The Ante-Nicene Fathers, Apostolic Constitutions,* and *Antiquities of the Christian Church,* which date back to the period of the early church, reveal that deacons played a significant role in the worship service as well. They assisted in administering the Lord's Supper and baptism. In addition, they were responsible for keeping order. They exhorted those who caused distractions by laughing, talking, or unnecessary movement and made sure that everyone sat in a proper place during the service.[3] Deacons were expected to train new converts to the faith and help them identify and develop their spiritual gifts within the congregation. They were also involved in matters of church discipline, following the guidelines presented by Jesus in Matthew 18:15–20.

The earliest accounts of ordaining deacons come from the third century. These sources indicate that deacons were expected to be exemplary members of the community, which meant they were to guard themselves from misconduct and model a pure and holy life. If a breach of conduct took place, they were severely disciplined. Whenever it was determined that a deacon was derelict in his duties, he was removed from office.[4] Serving as a deacon during the period of the early church was a ministry that was not taken lightly. Important responsibilities were assigned to them, and strict accountability was required.[5]

The Middle Ages

For the most part, there had been little change in the office of deacon up to the end of the fourth century. The patterns of service established during the initial church period were observed for a few hundred years, but significant changes began to develop during the Middle Ages (about A.D. 500 to 1500).

These changes continued to occur throughout the next ten centuries, and the influence of the Catholic hierarchical organization profoundly impacted the use of volunteers for ministry. As power became centralized within the structure of the Catholic establishment, consultation between the clergy and the lay leaders in the church took place at decreasing intervals. The clergy believed that since they were ordained by God to lead the church, only they were vested with the authority to make decisions affecting the body of believers. Shared governance was gradually replaced by autocratic leadership.

As the separation between clergy and volunteer leaders widened, involvement in the life of the church decreased for the average church member. Pastors lost touch with their congregations and seemed more concerned with matters of control and authority than with meeting individual needs. Because people became less inclined to give financial support to the church, its leaders had to resort to using such "incentives" as guilt, manipulation, and absolution of sins to sustain revenue collections. The end result was a growing intolerance for volunteer leaders on the part of the clergy—and a hatred for the hypocritical lifestyles of the pastors on the part of their congregations.

In most churches, the office of deacon was seen as a stepping-stone toward a more legitimate position, such as pastor, bishop, or even cardinal. Generally speaking, only those who were progressing through the priesthood pursued the office of deacon. This thousand-year period of church history had several consequences for deacon ministry.

1. *The relationship of pastor/deacon became adversarial.* Joint decision making was generally abandoned. The clergy saw themselves as having authority over subservient "employees" known as deacons.

2. *The clergy lost touch with the genuine needs of the congregation.* It was the deacons, who lived among the people, who had formerly brought such needs to the attention of the pastors.

3. *The hierarchical division of "clergy" and "laymen" began to undermine the teamwork dimension of ministry.* Decisions were made and passed down with little opportunity for dialogue and discussion. Mutual resentment and suspicion between the two groups were both cause and effect.

4. *Power struggles grew to the point that ministry lost its original meaning of "service."* Competition for influence, prestige, and material benefits eventually led to secularization of the religious establishment. Authoritative roles such as pope and archbishop began to divide and fragment the ministry.

5. *This emphasis on power had important implications in the secular world.* For obvious political reasons, religious leaders with the most power were placed in positions of civil authority as well.

The office of deacon, as we know it today, was all but lost during the Middle Ages. These were indeed dark days for those who wanted to serve and use their spiritual gifts in the church without making a lifetime commitment to the priesthood. Volunteerism had sunk to an all-time low. In fact, anyone who worked in ministry was viewed with disdain by the general population and even by many within the church.

The Reformation Period

The body of Christ had suffered for a thousand years under bureaucratic leadership. Lay members and some of the clergy were ready for a fresh breath of God's Spirit to move among them. Those who began these changes came from within the church. As men like Martin Luther, John Calvin, and John Knox studied the Scriptures, they came to the realization that the church had veered off course when it delegated only menial tasks to its deacons. They understood Paul's teachings concerning spiritual gifts and concluded that if God had gifted every believer for service, the church had a responsibility to train and equip these individuals for ministry.

Martin Luther, and others like him, began to teach the masses what salvation through Christ implied about the nature of the church. They instructed the people about "the priesthood of all believers," how they could glorify God though not ordained, and why every member was important in the life of the church. Enlightened pastors taught deacons about the biblical role of service to the widows and homeless, about living holy and godly lives, and about practicing the spiritual disciplines. In this period of great awakening for the church, pastors and volunteer leaders came together to form bonds of shared service. Mutual respect began to develop, and once again the church began to expand in response to a team approach to ministry.

There was still a division of responsibilities between pastors and deacons. Pastors were the preferred individuals to administer the Lord's Supper, perform marriages and baptisms, and conduct Bible teaching. However, deacons were now allowed to do more than simply take the morning collection and read passages from the Gospels and Epistles during the worship service.[6]

The Church in the New World

The discovery of America and its subsequent exploration created a difficult challenge for the church. Pastors were needed to serve the early colonists and to establish churches on the new frontiers, but the demand for clergy was far beyond what the schools could provide. As a result, the role of deacon became more important. In the newly settled western lands, one pastor would have to handle the official duties of performing marriages, burials, and baptisms for several churches spread throughout many miles of rugged terrain. Most new towns had to rely on a group of lay spiritual leaders in the community to carry on the work of ministry in the pastor's absence. The office of deacon grew in influence and responsibility. Deacons began to exercise strong leadership in the local churches and were often called on to decide matters of a spiritual nature in the community. Because these men were deeply respected, they were usually consulted on important decisions that affected the life of the entire town. However, the main emphasis of the deacon board was centered around the day-to-day operation of the church. As a result, the concept of deacon as administrative decision-maker was firmly established in the North American church.

Over time, the ministerial training institutions caught up to the demand for professional clergy, and churches began hiring full-time spiritual leaders. These pastors found themselves serving with established deacon boards that were used to making decisions for the church and local community. Members of the clergy who worked as a team with their deacons enjoyed a healthy, growing ministry, but there was tension and turmoil for those who did not.

Contemporary Settings

As churches grew in size and number, they began to hire additional pastors to carry the burden of ministry. In the early twentieth century, the position of associate pastor was created to assist the senior pastor in such church responsibilities as calling on the sick, administration and training of volunteer workers, counseling those in distress, and so on. Each church formulated its own specialized job description for this new pastoral position. Many churches in the 1950s added a youth pastor to their paid staff to oversee ministry to those between the ages of twelve and eighteen.

From the period between 1960 to 1990, a host of specialized pastoral staff positions has been developed to answer diverse needs within a church and the wider community. Job titles such as Children's Pastor, Singles' Minister, Business Administrator, and even Minister of Sports and Recreation are not uncommon in the contemporary church. Except in very small rural churches, one pastor cannot possibly handle so wide a range of responsibilities.

The possible negative effect of these pastoral appointments is that deacons in many churches will be left out of former avenues of service. Some lay leaders, if intimidated by the graduate level of training among the professional staff, may feel unwanted or demeaned. Care must be taken not to communicate to volunteers that they are not needed and that "real" ministry can only be performed by the paid pastoral staff.

Both deacons and members of the professional staff need to have clearly defined responsibilities. Each should have a written job description (see chapter 6) that clearly delineates the scope of his or her ministry. Without these documents, it is easy for deacons to feel out of place and for the pastoral staff to assume an increasing level of authority.

The church of the twenty-first century must be characterized by shared governance based upon patterns clearly established in the Jerusalem church. Although pastors should be seen having final responsibility for *spiritual* matters in the church, this does not mean that deacons are free to make all other decisions. Such a misguided approach assumes that such matters as budget allocations, building programs, and constitutional policy do not affect spiritual ministry. (More will be said on this matter in chapter 9.)

Implications

A glimpse back at the manner in which the needs of congregations were served during the early church period is a reminder to us in a later time that ministry should be a team effort. Pastors and deacons shared responsibilities for the welfare and spiritual health of the fellowship. Deacons were not arbitrary policy makers, but neither were they removed from the needs of those in the congregation. The deacons were expected to bring ministry concerns to the attention of the pastor, and *together* they made decisions that resolved church problems. Such an example should be established and maintained in every congregation across America. Although church history reveals mistakes made by pastors, denominational administrators, and volunteer leaders as well, each of us has much of positive value we can learn by looking back at those roots. Such knowledge will enable us to contribute toward a healthy and prosperous future for the body of believers.

Questions for Discussion

1. How has the office of deacon changed in your church since the church was first established?
2. Are there needs in your church (like those brought to the attention of the apostles in the Jerusalem church) which are currently not being met?
3. Is there an attitude of mutual respect between the professional clergy and volunteer church board members? If not, what needs to be done to help foster a healthier climate between the two groups?
4. Does each deacon know his spiritual gift? Take out a piece of paper and make a list of those represented on the board. What areas/gifts are missing in representation?

5. What kind of training activities are done at your church to help deacons learn their areas of responsibilities? Who teaches the training program? Do you feel that it has adequately prepared you for your leadership role? If not, what additional training would you recommend?

For Further Reading

Hardy, Edward R. "Deacons in History and Practice." In *The Diaconate Now,* edited by Richard T. Nolan. Washington: Corpus Books, 1968.

Howell, R. B. *The Deaconship: Its Nature, Qualifications, Relations, and Duties.* Philadelphia: American Baptist Pub. Society, 1904.

Naylor, Robert. *The Baptist Deacon.* Nashville: Broadman Press, 1955.

Webb, Henry. *Deacons: Servant Models in the Church.* Nashville: Convention Press, 1980.

Job Descriptions for Church Officers

As churches began to grow and expand across the known world, it was important for local pastors to develop leaders who could assist them in their work. It had been God's plan from the beginning that all of his people would become involved in some form of service to the body of Christ. In fact, that is why each believer received one or more spiritual gifts that could in some way contribute to the ministry of the church.

Over time, a distinction arose between paid servants (clergy) and volunteers (laity). Each group had a specified role to fill and related responsibilities to perform. Those who were paid were expected to give most of their time to the work of the ministry. The laity generally provided what assistance they could with the time they had available. This approach has continued until today. Most lay leaders have full-time careers in the secular world but donate a portion of each week to serving the church. In most cases, this service is directly related to their spiritual gifts (at least it should be).

However, since many of these volunteers have neither served

previously in a church setting nor received formal training for ministry, there has always been a need to direct their activities so as to maximize their contributions while at the same time maintain a degree of order and cohesion. Only when this is done will the work performed by the lay leaders be profitable for the church and enjoyable for the volunteers themselves. Job descriptions help ensure just that.

Ever-changing technologies and cultural expectations have affected the world of employment, especially as it relates to the so-called service industries. Some job categories that were once considered necessary in the 1960s are now virtually obsolete. For example, when I was a child and my parents drove into a gas station, four men would come running out. One would check the air in the tires, another would check the oil and water, a third would pump the gas, while the fourth would wash all of our windows. Today, most gas stations are manned by one person who sits in a cubicle and takes money through a slot in the window. The job has changed substantially.

Positions in the church have changed as well. What may have once been the responsibility of the pastor may now be performed by a deacon. What is a deacon's job in one church may be the job of an elder in another. Other duties may be assigned to a trustee or a deaconess. Some churches have a "church clerk," while others have a "secretary" who performs the same job. A congregation may find that when it hires a "director of Christian education," it no longer needs the position of "Sunday school superintendent." As the church adds new staff members, existing job descriptions may need to be revised, both for paid professionals and volunteers.

It is important to understand that it will not be possible in this chapter to present a job description for a "board member" that can be used at all churches. There are clearly too many differences between big churches and small ones, between independent churches and ecumenical ones, between inner-city churches and suburban ones. No one job title and description could apply to every congregation.

For this reason I prefer to provide you with guidelines that will help you as a pastor or board member to either modify an existing job description or prepare one for a new position. Many different kinds of volunteer workers in the church need their responsibilities so defined: deacon, deaconess, elder, trustee, ruling elder, clerk, secretary, treasurer, missions and worship committee members, chairpersons of those groups, and so on.

The Value of Job Descriptions

Why have job descriptions for church board members, who are almost exclusively volunteers rather than paid professionals? The same reasons that make a job description invaluable when dealing with hired personnel apply to volunteer workers. A sampling of those reasons includes the following:

1. *A job description establishes clear lines of authority and responsibility.* It lets everyone know without any doubt whether the person giving an order or making a purchase has the authority to do so. Because it documents who is responsible for certain activities, the congregation also knows who should be held accountable if things go wrong. When something needs to be done, a job description guides the leadership team in the selection of who should do it.

2. *A job description eliminates unwritten expectations.* A fair amount of writing has been done about the ramifications of entering a new job. Great conflicts can arise over expectations that were never clearly communicated. Speaking of this reality in church life, Richard Hansen writes, "Churches want their pastors to be both cloistered, contemplative scholars and aggressive, decisive administrators. Other churches expect their pastors to have specialized skills (preaching or counseling youth work) and yet be generalists competent in all areas."[1] Although many of these expectations are never verbalized, they are nevertheless just as real as those that are. A written job description helps to clearly distinguish fantasy from fact.

Marshall Shelley lists nine separate functions that a senior pastor is expected to fulfill: (1) servant-shepherd; (2) prophet-politician; (3) preacher-enthraller; (4) teacher-theologian; (5) evangelist-exhorter; (6) organizer-promoter; (7) caller-comforter; (8) counselor-reconciler; (9) equipper-enabler.[2] And we wonder why there is so much confusion in the church today among new pastors who are called to serve in the church!

3. *A job description helps to match authority with responsibility.* In management terms, this is known as the principle of parity. It means that if a person is assigned responsibility for a certain action, he or she must also be allowed a corresponding degree of authority to accomplish it. If the two are not given in equal amounts, the employee is set up for failure. Robert Karasek, a specialist in job stress at Columbia University, states, "The greatest stress occurs in jobs where the individual faces heavy psychological demands, yet has little control over how to get the work done."[3]

For example, if a youth pastor is assigned the responsibility of organizing an upcoming retreat but lacks the authority to reserve housing accommodations without a vote from the deacon board, the youth pastor lacks "parity" in his work. Church boards are notorious for handing out miles of job responsibilities but only inches of authority. For the worker, the result is a loss of self-respect, low motivation, miscommunication over expectations, and feelings of inferiority. A good job description is written in such a way that it upholds the principle of parity.

4. *A job description facilitates strategic planning.* For example, if an associate pastor is being added to the staff because the congregation has decided to begin a ministry to the inner-city population around them, that responsibility can be written into the job description of the new position before the screening process begins. The church leaders will then be searching for an associate pastor who knows the goal coming in and has the ability to accomplish it. Although some individuals on the selection committee may be tempted to suggest their own personal agenda for the new staff member, the final job description should clearly represent agreement as to what will be expected of the candidates and therefore what qualifications are needed.

Writing a Job Description

There is no perfect formula for writing a job description for a volunteer office. The hundreds I have seen over the years differed in style and terminology, but most of them accomplished the same purpose. A church should have the freedom to construct job descriptions that suit its organizational structure. Some use denominationally produced documents to achieve consistency among associating churches, while others prefer to develop their own particular wording. Use what works best for you, but follow the same format for each of the positions throughout the church. Include the following elements:

JOB TITLE. This may seem obvious, but never underestimate the power of a title! Be sure to give it some thought before setting it down on paper. Many different titles might be used for the same position, but the one you choose should clearly describe the job function. Terms such as "director," "minister," "coordinator," or "facilitator" each communicate something different.

QUALIFICATIONS. One of the first things that must be documented is a list of qualifications. This facilitates the selection process and also allows potential candidates to determine if they have the right background for the position. The list should have several headings, including education, previous experience, personal qualities, and spiritual maturity.

RESPONSIBILITIES. You may find it helpful to list the job responsibilities in separate categories. For example, in a job description for "chairman of the deacon board," you could itemize them as follows: responsibilities to the general membership, responsibilities to the board, and responsibilities to the pastor and staff. Arranging the material in this way will organize and (in some cases) prioritize the church's expectations. It will also help ensure that nothing important gets forgotten.

REPORTS TO WHOM? Don't neglect to clearly state who (if anyone) is responsible for overseeing the work of this individual. For example, the church clerk might be told to report to the chairman of the deacon board. That way, he or she knows where to go to solve any job-related problems that arise. When in doubt about this matter, consult the church's organizational chart and try to maintain existing lines of authority (see chapter 8).

TERM OF SERVICE. Few church positions are permanent, since appointments are usually rotated every few years. So there are no misunderstandings about the length of expected service, the job description should clearly state how often rotation takes place.

BENEFITS. Most volunteer positions have no material benefits. However, a denomination may expect an officeholder to participate in a regional conference or national training seminar. In that case, the job description should include information about the event and what the church will do to assist with expenses. If known, the dates of the conference and whether or not the spouse is included should be stated.

COMMITTEE RESPONSIBILITIES. Most churches have committees of one kind or another. Some churches prefer to call them commissions, but they work along the same general lines. If the officeholder is automatically assigned to chair or serve on a particular committee, this should be stipulated.

EFFECTIVE DATE. This date, usually at the end of the document, shows when the job description was written or updated. For obvious reasons, if the job description is more than a few years old, the reliability of the information should be evaluated. It is always a good idea to review job descriptions every two years and make minor adjustments to keep them current.

Some Practical Suggestions

This next section is presented to assist the pastor or lay leaders in formulating job descriptions for the church.

Suggestion #1. Be as specific as possible when constructing job descriptions, but be careful to leave room for personal initiative on the part of the person who will be performing the job. Chris Tornquist, an Evangelical Free pastor writes, "The challenge is to prepare a job description that is neither too restrictive nor too general and unspecific."[4] For example, rather than have a deacon's job description say, "Keep in touch with the missionaries supported by the church," be specific: "Write three letters each month to missionaries who are supported by our church, indicating our concern, prayer support, and love for them."

Suggestion #2. Be sure to develop an administrative manual that provides the worker with a great deal more information than can be included in a job description. For example, this manual should clearly state not only who is responsible for church property (e.g., a church van), but also what procedures and deadlines are to be followed for reserving and securing the property when needed. This manual should summarize all the policies and procedures of the church that have been established by the board and pastoral staff.

Suggestion #3. Job descriptions tell new officeholders what will be required of them, and those same expectations should be used to measure their performance and contribution to the overall ministry of the church. Periodic evaluation of performance is both biblical and necessary. The timing and nature of the review process should be communicated to a volunteer in writing. This can be included in the job description or administrative manual, or handled through personal correspondence.

Suggestion #4. Larger churches may want to delegate the formulating of job descriptions to a subcommittee or pastoral staff member. It is difficult to write a job description with a dozen people, all with preconceived ideas about what the position should entail. To facilitate the process, it is more expedient to assign this responsibility to a smaller group of individuals. The final document might be brought before the governing board, pastoral staff, or congregation for a vote. The latter approach will take considerably less time, yet it allows for input and control by those involved in the selection process.

About half of the churches I surveyed while writing this book used written job descriptions for church board members and testified to their value. Experience has shown that these documents play an important role in the effective operation of a church's ministry. Good job descriptions can not only save the senior pastor and governing board a good deal of time and energy, but such open forms of communication and accountability are greatly needed in the church today.

The sample job description that follows uses the material presented in this chapter and will help you conceptualize this kind of document and/or compare it with the one your church currently uses.

Job Title: Chairman of the Deacon Board

Reports to: Senior Pastor

Qualifications (see Acts 6:3, 7; 1 Tim. 3:8–13)

Personal

Blameless and above reproach in the community
Dignified and respectful of others
Not given to a double tongue
Not given to substance abuse
Not given to bribery

Family Life

Husband of one wife with pure marriage relationship
Good manager of household
Demonstrates spiritual leadership in the home
Children are under control

Relationship with People

Able to get along with others without difficulty
Respected by both Christians and non-Christians
Demonstrates wisdom and sound decision making

Spiritual Maturity

Full of the Holy Spirit
Experienced in spiritual leadership
Demonstrates consistent godly living
Clear conscience before God and other people
Strong knowledge of God's Word and its application to personal living and church leadership

Responsibilities

In Relation to the Church

1. Regular personal prayer for the pastor and church
2. Maintain a mind-set of looking out for ministry concerns in the church and community
3. Sensitivity to church-related issues, such as:
   a) Relation of board to church
   b) Relation between senior pastor and church
   c) Job satisfaction of pastor and church staff
   d) Pastor's family life
   e) Relationship with deaconess board
   f) Financial health and accountability
   g) Denominational relations
4. Assist the senior pastor by:
   a) Letting him know who are undergoing trials
   b) Helping church workers heading for burnout
   c) Keeping him accountable for personal growth
   d) Meeting one-on-one with him each month
5. Regular and consistent attendance at worship services, prayer meetings, and board meetings
6. Make a conscious effort to meet new visitors and learn the names of church members
7. Keep lines of communication open between the church and the deacon board

8. In conjunction with the senior pastor, mediate in conflicts, where appropriate
9. Write an article for the monthly newsletter
10. Chair deacon board meetings and set agenda in consultation with the pastor
11. Oversee the development of the annual report

In Relation to the Church Board

1. Encourage and affirm board members so that they
   a) grow spiritually
   b) are effective in their areas of service
   c) are accountable
2. Assist board members who need help

In Relation to the Pastor and Staff

1. Work with the senior pastor to build a meaningful relationship with the staff
2. When possible, attend staff meetings
3. Mediate conflicts between senior pastor and staff

In Relation to Church Committees

1. Troubleshoot committee problems in conjunction with the senior pastor and staff
2. Periodically attend meetings of other church committees to maintain communication and a free flow of ideas
3. Encourage and affirm the deaconess board and provide any needed assistance

Benefits

Each August, the denomination's regional conference is held. The chairman of the deacon board is expected to attend with his wife to represent the church and its ministry. Conference and travel expenses will be provided by the church.

Term of Office

According to the church constitution, each deacon will serve a three-year term. A deacon is elected by the other deacons to serve as chairman for a one-year term. This term may be renewed for another year, but he may not serve as chairman for more than two of his three years on the deacon board.

Effective Date: January 1, 1994

Questions for Discussion

1. Can you identify any values for having written job descriptions that were not included in this chapter?
2. In looking back over your years of church service, can you think of any conflicts that might have been prevented by having an accurate job description for a particular position?

3. When was the last time your church's job descriptions were reviewed and revised?
4. What positions in your church currently need a job description?
5. What individual or group formulates job descriptions at your church? Should this arrangement be changed?
6. Is the principle of parity considered when preparing job descriptions for your church?
7. Who at your church must approve job descriptions for volunteer offices? For staff members?

For Further Reading

Davey, James A., and Bird, Warren. "They Like Me, They Like Me Not." *Leadership* 5, no. 3 (Summer 1984): 74.

Jacobsen, Wayne. "Who Decides What Deacons Do?" *Leadership* 4, no. 3 (Summer 1985): 67–71.

Klos, Sarah. "A Mutual and Shared Ministry." *Clergy Journal* 66, no. 1 (Oct. 1989): 2–3.

Zimmer, Chip. "The Ministry of Mediation." *Leadership* 7, no. 4 (Summer 1990): 90–96.

Part *Two*

Mastering the Art of Serving Others

Developing an Effective Mission Statement

I t has been said that if you aim at nothing, you will be sure to hit it—and that if you fail to plan, you are planning to fail. Although such generalizations may seem somewhat trite and simplistic, they represent a sizable degree of truth. Many of our churches could testify to their validity, which is exactly why every church needs a clearly understood mission statement.

If you want to know whether or not your church has such a statement, simply take an informal survey among a dozen members of your church. Ask them, "What is the essential purpose of our church?" If you get a variety of answers, representing a broad range of opinions, don't be surprised. Rarely would a church find a majority of those dozen people responding in a similar fashion.

The mission statement, also called a statement of purpose, proclaims officially the basic reason why your church is in existence. You might think this would be obvious, given the teachings of Scripture, but in most congregations it isn't clear at all. Most congregations are too busy trying to maintain their programs and match expenditures with income. The thought of projecting direction and purpose into the future seems to go beyond their comprehension.

The church leaders who responded to my survey were asked, "Does your church have a mission statement?" Although the majority said "yes," it was clear by their responses to the next question that they were not all in agreement regarding why one was needed. When asked, "How often does your church revise the mission statement?" the responses included "never," "not very often," "seldom," "every week," "monthly," "every 10 to 20 years," and even "I wrote one, but it was rejected."

In a recent national survey of two hundred churches across America, lay leaders from these churches were asked, "Why does the church exist?" The responses were amazing! About 89 percent responded with something like, "The purpose of the church is to take care of me, my family, and our needs." Obviously, very few of these church leaders thought the purpose of the church is to win the world for Christ. However, when the survey was given to the pastors of these churches, the response was just the opposite. Only 10 percent said the church's purpose was to care for its members, while an overwhelming majority said their purpose was to win the world for Christ. No wonder there are so many conflicts in our churches—we are unable to agree on the most basic of issues!

The mission statement of a church should seek to answer two critical questions. First, "Why are we here as a church?" and second, "What is our unique contribution to the kingdom of God?" These questions serve as the foundation on which a church's reason for being is established. Any church that cannot agree on the answers to these fundamental questions will have a difficult time growing in a consistent and purposeful manner. Any growth that does occur will most likely be sporadic and without design. That kind of growth in a physical body is usually defined as "cancer."

Why Have a Mission Statement?

If a church does not know (or care) where it is going, how it gets there will not matter. Being intent on solving only today's problems and issues prevents us from looking into the future. Then we run the risk of being blind to whom we want to be tomorrow. Simply stated, who we will be tomorrow is largely determined by the decisions we make today. Put from a biblical perspective: "Where there is no vision, the people perish . . . " (Prov. 29:18 KJV).

There are several fundamental reasons why a church should have a clearly defined mission statement:

1. *A mission statement encourages church growth.* Experts in the field of church growth have spent many years studying the common denominators among churches that are experiencing rapid growth and development. They have also studied churches that are in decline. The goal of this research is to determine whether there are recognizable trends, patterns, or themes among each of these types of churches. Without exception, one of the characteristics of growing churches is the existence of a clearly articulated mission statement that explains their basic purpose and the unique niche in ministry that they want to fill.

2. *A mission statement helps people think from a biblical and theological perspective.* A properly worded statement of purpose should be based on a detailed study of Scripture. Those preparing this statement should have a broad base of theological understanding concerning such doctrines as the character and nature of God, his plan for mankind, the meaning of Christ's sacrificial atonement on the cross and his subsequent resurrection, the nature of the church as one body, the spiritual gifts of all believers, the Great Commission, and the end times and final judgment.

This is not to imply that it takes a team of theologically astute Ph.D.'s to prepare a mission statement for your church. But it does reflect a concern that this statement be based on clear biblical teachings. The church must be seen as God's instrument for impacting the world and should therefore fulfill his purposes as well as our own.

3. *A mission statement helps people develop a biblically based world view.* When we see the world as God sees it, there will be a degree of compassion and urgency in our mission. Such a perspective will influence everything we do, including how we treat our neighbors and vote for public officials. For example, Scripture clearly teaches that God has a special place in his heart for widows and

the homeless. A knowledge of this characteristic of God's nature should influence the manner in which we respond to all those who are less fortunate than ourselves. Proclaiming the purpose of a church should force its people into detailed study of scriptural truths.

4. *A mission statement builds enthusiasm for the work of the church.* A clearly defined statement of purpose will focus the congregation's sense of direction. Having a unified objective gives people a sense of meaning and well-being. Simply maintaining the status quo will not motivate a church to action and response. Rick Warren, pastor of Saddleback Community Church, one of the fastest-growing churches in America, states, "Churches do not split over doctrine; they split over strategy." When the members are united in their strategy for reaching the world for Christ, there is an enthusiastic spirit. Morale is high and people join together to accomplish their stated purpose.

5. *A mission statement encourages church leaders to concentrate their energies on ministry planning.* The apostle Paul stated to the church in Philippi, ". . . I press on to take hold of that for which Christ Jesus took hold of me. . . . Forgetting what is behind and straining toward what is ahead, I press on toward the goal . . ." (Phil. 3:12–14). Paul was single-minded in his ministry because he had a clearly defined statement of purpose. Because this allowed him to decide what was important and what was not it gave him a standard by which to measure his opportunities and accomplishments.

6. *A mission statement attracts cooperation.* Every program within a local church should reflect its long-term goals. The overarching statement of purpose serves as a base of operations for establishing and coordinating ministries within the church body, with each part contributing toward the achievements of the whole. For example, if the mission statement emphasizes evangelistic outreach in the community, each program developed within the church should reflect that objective, and departmental leaders will set their agendas accordingly.

7. *A mission statement provides a standard by which the church can evaluate its ministries.* I have pastored in churches with as many as four thousand members and as few as a hundred. In none of

them was there a shortage of activities. Regardless of their size, most churches in America have schedules packed with educational programs, opportunities for fellowship, and general happenings. But the question must be asked at some point, "Are *all* these activities really necessary?"

Developing criteria for evaluating the ministries of a church has long been a source of frustration for pastoral staffs and church boards. But a mission statement allows the leadership team to measure each program's effectiveness with some degree of accuracy. If a church states officially that its primary purpose will be evangelism in the community, this provides a criterion to be applied to all church programs. Those ministries that do not contribute toward outreach are either eliminated or brought under discussion. They are not allowed to continue without accountability or critique.

A mission statement provides the church with an objective, an agreed-upon standard of direction for its programs. It helps both the leaders and the general membership know the difference between what is important and what is not. (More will be said about this in chapter 11.)

8. *A mission statement guides in the distribution of church resources.* Ideally, the budget will be designed around the mission statement. If, for example, your church has stated that the primary reason it exists is to be a sending agency for people called to the mission field, this purpose should be generously acknowledged in church budgeting. If you determine the percentage of funds being set aside each year for missionary efforts, it will become quite obvious whether or not yours is truly a sending church. If it is not, and the church is still committed to its statement of purpose, changes may be needed in the allocation of resources and structure of the budget.

The Evolution of a Mission Statement

Understanding why a mission statement is important is far easier than setting it down on paper. The following suggestions may help your church write such a statement or revise one already in existence.

Step One. Involve the congregation in a comprehensive study of the character and nature of God. The church is meant to be an extension of God's work on earth. As such, its members must understand his character, his divinity, and his purposes. If God is forgiving, compassionate, and tenderhearted, his church must also exhibit those qualities. If God is divine, he is all-knowing and all-powerful, which means we must look to him for ultimate truth and guidance. If God's purposes include the salvation of the lost, that must be affirmed in the church's reason for being.

Step Two. Lead the membership in a survey of the scriptural basis for the church. The names given to the church in the Bible— for example, "bride of Christ," "body of Christ," "army of God"— represent God's desire for his people and should therefore be reflected in the church's concept of ministry. A survey of the parables of Jesus would also be beneficial in understanding the church's role in furthering God's kingdom principles.

Step Three. Look at the past before pushing into the future. It is helpful for church members to review their heritage and see how close they are to living out the dreams of their predecessors. Many churches have wandered from the objectives of their founding fathers. Current events, trials in the life of the church, demographic changes in the community, and a host of other factors may have caused a church to veer from its original course. This is not to say that a church must remain fixed to the vision of its forefathers. In fact, many of the factors cited above should cause a church to rethink its mission and purpose. However, knowledge of the past can provide a church with the bearing by which it will move ahead.

Step Four. Gather input from the general membership. The mission statement of a church should represent a general consensus within the congregation, not just the ideas of the pastoral staff. Although pastors come and go, the congregation remains behind to continue the work that caused it to be established in the first place. This is not to say that the pastor and pastoral staff should not have a say in framing the mission statement. Indeed, pastors are expected to *lead* the congregation in the direction they have been called by God to pursue. A balance needs to be found in this regard, however.

Getting the congregation's input may be done in several ways. Some churches call for discussion at an open business meeting for this purpose. Another approach that has been used with some degree of effectiveness has been the "town hall" meeting, which brings the members together to solicit their thoughts, feelings, and opinions. This is not meant to be a free-for-all, but is designed as a time to gather information on a predetermined subject.

A third method could be a mailed survey. This allows for confidential input from all the members, even those who do not regularly attend meetings or services. If you choose this approach, be sure to provide a stamped, self-addressed envelope for returning the survey. This will increase the number of surveys returned and minimize the time it takes to get them back.

However it is done, it is critical that everyone be given an opportunity to express an opinion. Obviously, not all these comments can be incorporated into a concise statement of church purpose. Nevertheless, it is important for the members to feel that those who actually prepare the document spend an adequate amount of time considering their views. To do anything less will be inviting trouble once the statement is presented to the congregation for approval.

Step Five. Commission a representative body to prepare the statement. Some churches try to save time by having the board of elders or deacons handle this responsibility, but I do not advise such a practice. Preparing the document requires a sizable amount of discussion, and assigning the job to an existing body will place an undue amount of pressure on people who already bear a heavy load of responsibilities.

I prefer to call this representative group a task force, since the title indicates its temporary status. Once the committee's task is completed, it will disband. Knowing this may make the difference for people who are asked to participate but might be reluctant to take on a long-term assignment.

Who comprises the task force will be a matter for the governing boards to decide. Review the church bylaws for possible guidelines. If nothing has been stated in the constitution regarding such a group, consider ways to gain a diverse and broad sampling of the congregation. A member of the elder board and/or deacon board should be included, also a member of the deaconess board (if your church has one). The senior pastor and pastoral staff should have representation, of course, but the majority of the task force members should be selected from the congregation. Include new parishioners, those who have been around for many years, and people who represent the fringes of the church's demographic distribution. Don't just select those who are part of the vocal majority or who represent the largest population of the church. The main criterion for assignment to such a committee is inner character, not prestige, power, or influence. When the apostles were selecting a replacement for Judas, they prayed, "Lord, you know everyone's heart. Show us which one of these two you have chosen" (Acts 1:24). Let this prayer be yours as well.

Select individuals who are spiritually mature and who have a genuine walk with God. As to character, a suitable candidate would be someone who:

Is a known believer. Romans 8:7 says, "The sinful [unsaved] mind is hostile to God. It does not submit to God's law, nor can it do so." For this reason, it is critical that all members of the task force be Spirit-led individuals.

Is not given to disputation. Paul also states, "Don't have anything to do with foolish and stupid arguments, because you know they produce quarrels" (2 Tim. 2:23). Prideful people who like to debate for the sole purpose of winning arguments should not be assigned to this committee!

Has a lifestyle commitment to prayer. A venture of this nature requires a considerable degree of prayer, not just at the beginning of each meeting (although that is important), but throughout the process of discussion. "But in everything, by prayer and petition, with thanksgiving, present your requests to God. And the peace of God which transcends all understanding, will guard your hearts and your minds in Christ Jesus" (Phil. 4:6–7). If ever there was a need for a group of people to have their minds guarded by God, it is for those who are writing a mission statement for a church.

Is able to get along with others. A task force of this nature will produce a certain degree of tension and disagreement among its members. This is the nature of the democratic process. However, it is essential that you select individuals who can separate an opposing idea from the person who is stating it and who can remove themselves from their own opinions long enough to listen respectfully to the views of others. "Do nothing out of selfish ambition or vain conceit, but in humility consider others better than yourselves. Each of you should look not only to your own interests, but also to the interests of others" (Phil. 2:3–4).

Once the members of the special task force have been selected and a spokesperson has been elected, the committee should begin sorting through the surveys, notes, and materials that have been collected during the input stage (Step Four).

The process involves crystalizing the essence of the church's ministry. From the major themes should flow statements about why the church exists and what its primary emphasis will be. Statements may begin with a phrase such as "Our purpose is to . . ." and continue with:

reach the community for Christ (evangelism)

reverse the declining moral fiber of our society (social activism)

build up and strengthen the body of Christ (edification and growth)

send and support those who serve Christ (world missions)

serve those who are needy (community service)

meet together to praise and adore our Creator (worship)

Once the essential areas of concern are identified, they can be expanded to include areas of broader interest. The statement should be written in full and complete sentences. Later, it could be condensed into a catchy motto or phrase to help people remember it.

Examples of mission statements from three churches are included for your interest and review.

Our church exists to glorify God by making disciples who love Christ, love one another, and live to reach our world for Christ.

The purpose of our ministry is to provide a comprehensive ministry to children, parents, and the family unit so that each individual might have the opportunity to receive Christ as Savior and grow in Christian maturity.

As a church: we exalt the Savior by providing a biblical climate for worship that includes preaching, music, prayer, testimonies, ordinances, and offerings.

As a church: we actively equip Spirit-filled saints for service in our fellowship by instructing and encouraging all Christians to concentrate on serving and obeying God and to discover and use their spiritual gifts.

As a church: we evangelize the unsaved by being active disciples who through local outreach, attract unbelievers to faith in Christ and identification with a local body of believers.

Each of these statements reflects the essence of a church's vision for its ministry. By clearly highlighting the reason it exists, a mission statement provides the congregation with clear direction and purpose.

Revising the Mission Statement

Your church may have a mission statement that has been around for many years. When originally formulated, it was reflective of those who attended the church, the demographics in the community, and the vision of pastoral staff members at that time. However, perhaps your church needs to look carefully at that statement and decide whether it is still reflective of those elements. If not, a review is in order.

A frequently voiced question in this regard is: "How often should the mission statement be revised?" The answer is multifaceted. I would recommend that a church review (and possibly revise) its mission statement under the following circumstances:

1. *Whenever a significant chronological period of time has transpired.* The mission statement is a point of reference on a map that gives purpose and direction for future progress and development. This milestone need not be moved every year. The process is time-consuming and too costly in terms of energy to be done that often. Every five years should be adequate as a minimum interval.

2. *Whenever there is a period of transition in pastoral leadership.* It is at this critical time in the life of a church when serious intro-

spective analysis should take place. If the senior pastor left because of philosophical or doctrinal disagreement, the mission statement should be reviewed to see if changes are needed *before* the church calls another pastor.

It can be very helpful to pastoral candidates to know if the mission statement of the church has been recently revised. If so, this tells a candidate in what direction the members want to go, and the statement can be used as a point of reference to determine whether the candidate is able and willing to take them there. If it has been revised just prior to the pastor's selection, the new pastor would do well not to try to change the statement until he has been at the church long enough to build credibility and support for such a change.

3. *Whenever significant demographic changes within the local community or the church membership have occurred.* Population shifts from rural to urban settings, moves from inner city to the suburbs, and/or ethnic changes in the surrounding area will impact the size and characteristics of a congregation and therefore its primary needs. Without a corresponding change in direction for their ministries, many churches will find it difficult to survive. For example, the programs of an inner-city church may need to be radically altered when most of its members have moved to the suburbs and now commute to church only on Sunday. Any such transitional factors within a church should precipitate a review of its mission statement.

4. *Whenever there have been structural changes within a church.* When several churches merge together or a large church divides into two or more smaller ones, a mission-statement review should be conducted. A church that has begun several satellite churches in response to its rapid growth may now view its contribution to the kingdom of God from a new perspective.

Implications

Commitment to a unified purpose and mission is critical to the effectiveness and growth of a congregation. It will influence the way the church's leaders design ministry models, develop programs, allocate space and funding, and measure its impact on the community. Preparing or revising a mission statement requires a large investment of time, energy, and church resources. However, the effort expended on this venture is worth the price to be paid, since the document will be the basis for so much of what will happen at the church for many years to come.

Questions for Discussion

1. Can you quote the mission statement of your church from memory?
2. How is the mission statement communicated to the members of your congregation?
3. Do you feel that the average person in your congregation is familiar with the mission statement?
4. How is your church's mission statement used throughout the year to guide and keep the church on target in its programming activities?
5. Is the mission statement used as a measure of evaluation for church activities?
6. What percentage of the budget is directly related to fulfilling the mission statement?
7. Has the mission statement of your church been revised recently? Do you feel that it needs to be examined again? If so, why?

For Further Reading

Harton, Michael. "Helping Your Church Have a Mission That Matters." *Church Administration* 34, no. 5 (Feb. 1991): 22–23.

McCourney, David G. *Pastoring the Single Staff Church*. Nashville: Convention Press, 1990.

Malphurs, Aubrey. *Developing a Vision for Ministry in the Twenty-first Century*. Grand Rapids: Baker Book House, 1992.

Marrs, Ross W. "Planning for the Future: How to Develop a Mission Statement." *The Clergy Journal* 67, no. 4 (Feb. 1991): 45.

Ramsden, William E. "Building a Spiritual Foundation." *The Clergy Journal* 66, no. 10 (Aug. 1990): 910.

Organizational Structures in the Church

O   bserving the natural world will convince us that God is the author of order, because nothing happens in nature without a purpose. The way the universe is held together and functions reveals the magnitude of God's incredible design. Likewise, Scripture clearly teaches that God wants his church to be operated in an orderly manner (1 Cor. 14:26–39). This is not to say that all churches are to be identical, any more than all creatures and all forms of plant life are identical. Although God is the author of order, he has also created diversity.

Designing organizational structures for church ministry should reflect this diversity. No one organizational structure will work for all churches. There are too many differences to support such a rigid approach. Each local church is unique in theology, geography, ethnography, and demographic distinctives. Even a cursory look at the churches described in the Book of Acts reveals many differences among them. The church in Antioch did not replicate the structure of the Jerusalem church. Christians in Ephesus did not pattern their church after the church in Philippi. The church in Corinth certainly had a way of doing things that was unique to their particular fellowship! What is important about a church's structure is not whether it looks like another church down the road, but whether the structure facilitates its ministry and outreach in the local community.

It may be important at this point to draw a distinction between order and organization. From its earliest days, the church has had to consider the question of order, and this is still a vital issue of concern for the church today. *Order* is seen in an established plan and agreed-upon guidelines specific enough to keep any group from chaos, yet set it free for growth. Order is a unified purpose that acknowledges commonly accepted means toward recognized ends. Order assigns and limits responsibility, but it also defines and limits authority. *Organization* is the way that a particular group keeps its procedures orderly—for example, by selecting a chairperson, secretary, or treasurer.[1]

A Survey of Common Organizational Patterns

There are almost as many different ways to organize church governance as there are churches. Some denominations express a preference for one type of structure for all affiliated churches. Other denominations allow churches within their fellowship enough autonomy to create their own design. It might be helpful for church board members who are somewhat new to this topic to survey the more common ways that churches organize themselves and identify some of the advantages and disadvantages of each approach.

Ecumenical Model

Certain denominations, such as Catholics, Lutherans, Methodists, and Episcopalians, have an ecumenical (worldwide, general) approach to structuring their churches. There are, however, a good number of denominational distinctives within this pattern. Bruce Jones writes: "In its original form, it was a monarchial concentration of power in one bishop over a local church. Later it developed into the position of diocesan bishop who presided over a territory of local churches, called a diocese. It is based on the doctrine of apostolic succession (Catholic) or historical succession (Episcopalian)."[2]

Bishops are indeed characteristic of Catholic, Orthodox, and Episcopalian churches, but not necessarily descriptive of all Methodist or Lutheran bodies. Lutherans in the U.S., for example, may combine regional synods (see next category) with a congregational structure, hence more autonomous, type of government. And Methodists—at least those in the United Methodist Church—may have bishops, or superintendents, but this is not a priestly office, as it may be in some denominations in this category.

Advantages

Greater degree of stability since change is seen within the context of long historical context. In essence, this church does not easily fall prey to sudden changes in doctrine, leadership, etc.

Broad base of denominational support since the diocese or denominational body can provide resources in time of temporary need.

The bishop can place a pastor in a church who can preach/lead according to the need without fear of being removed by the congregation for preaching against sin.

The pastor is not likely to be a respecter of persons in the church or show partiality toward a select few in leadership since the diocese or bishop holds the pastor accountable, not the local congregation.

Disadvantages

Slow to change since new programs to meet changing community needs may not reflect the desires of those in denominational leadership.

Those in denominational leadership make many of the critical decisions for the local congregation even though they may be far removed geographically or ethnically.

Due to large denominational government structure, placing clergy in local churches can become highly political rather than based on local needs.

Many large denominations, in an effort to appease large sections of special interests, are forced to compromise their doctrinal distinctives. The result is a slow erosion toward biblical relativism.

Republican Model

The "representative" approach is demonstrated in the Presbyterians' form of church organization. This denomination groups its churches (General Assembly) into "synods," or a collection of churches within a specific geographical region (e.g., Southwest Synod). Each synod further divides itself into "presbyteries," which are local associations of churches within a smaller territory (e.g., San Diego County). Within each presbytery are a number of churches, and that will vary according to density of population in the district. For example, a rural presbytery may have fewer churches than a suburban presbytery, even though the former may cover a larger geographical area. (See figure 1.)

Fig. 1. "Republican model" of organization

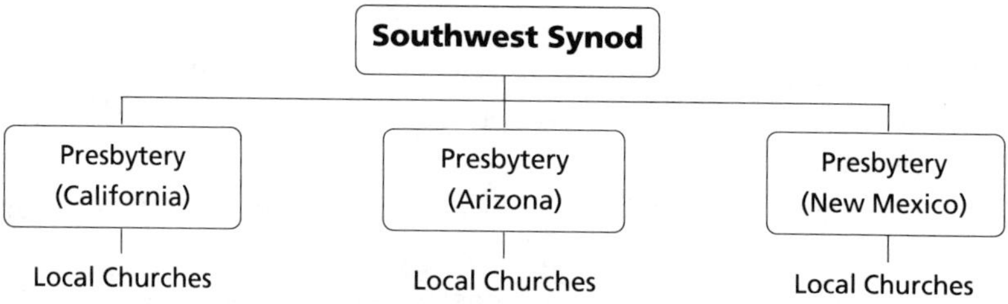

```
                      ┌──────────────────────┐
                      │   Southwest Synod     │
                      └──────────────────────┘
         ┌──────────────────────┼──────────────────────┐
┌──────────────────┐  ┌──────────────────┐  ┌──────────────────┐
│    Presbytery    │  │    Presbytery    │  │    Presbytery    │
│   (California)   │  │    (Arizona)     │  │   (New Mexico)   │
└──────────────────┘  └──────────────────┘  └──────────────────┘
         │                     │                     │
   Local Churches        Local Churches        Local Churches
```

A Presbyterian church will have one or more pastors, a board of elders, and a board of deacons. The latter boards may have both men and women in representation. The board of elders, sometimes referred to as ruling elders, are laypersons who are elected by the congregation. The teaching elders are usually ministers who preside over the presbytery.[3] The board of elders and the pastor serve as joint administrators of a church and together with the co-pastors form a "session."

The senior pastor is the "moderator" of the session. There is also a "clerk of the session," who, next to the pastor, holds the position of greatest responsibility. This person acts as the chairperson of the executive committee of the session.

In this form of church structure, the session is central. The pastor's position as moderator of the session provides one of the greatest opportunities for prophetic leadership. Pastors who have the session on their side—not by Machiavellian manipulation, but by genuine sharing of leadership though common study, candid discussion, and farsighted policy-making—are likely to enjoy a long and fruitful church ministry.[4] An illustration of the structure of a typical Presbyterian church is shown in figure 2.

Fig. 2. Organization within a Presbyterian church

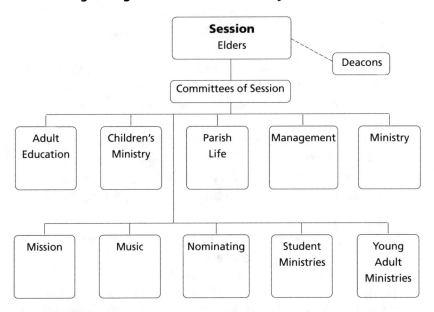

Advantages

This type of structure allows a consistent philosophy to be followed throughout all the churches of a denomination. Members who relocate can find a similar approach to church ministry as long as they remain in the denomination.

In Presbyterian polity, pastors (teaching elders) are called by local congregations. Their call is subsequently confirmed by the presbytery. There is shared governance between the church and the denomination, based on mutual communication.

Denominational distinctives and publishing materials can be shared between churches, thereby keeping costs lower.

Denominational representatives can speak with some degree of certainty for their entire denomination. In such matters as morality, social injustice, and politics, the denomination has a stronger voice than an individual church.

Disadvantages

When the geographical area for a presbytery is quite large, it can be difficult for denominational representatives to have an accurate knowledge of the needs of each church. (Effective leadership requires shepherds to be in touch with all their people.)

Pastors may sometimes care more about pleasing denominational representatives than about the members of their congregation. (This is a danger found in any denominational setting.)

Confirmation of a pastor to a local church can sometimes become a political issue among the denomination's leaders.

Denominations, by their very nature, can become entangled in bureaucracy, making change very slow, if not impossible.

Corporate Model

Sometimes referred to as the board-control model, this organizational design takes a business approach to decision making. Many churches in America have board members who are influential in the business community. They are used to the nomenclature and procedures of board settings and carry this mentality into their church leadership. In the corporate model, the church's board of elders/deacons serves in the same way as members of a corporate board. It can hire and fire the senior pastor (CEO) and decide the long- and short-range direction of the church. The board of elders/deacons sets the goals that the church staff is hired to execute and serves as the policymaker for the church. The board is responsible for handling most financial, legal, or ethical decisions and then communicates those decisions to the church staff and congregation. An example of this type of church structure is depicted in figure 3.

Fig. 3. Corporate model
of church governance

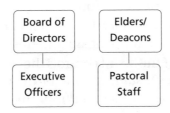

One very significant problem with this approach warrants some discussion. If the pastor is controlled by a lay board, fear of losing his job may make him reluctant to speak openly as the church's spiritual leader. In a 1975 study of Church of Christ pastors who had left the ministry, 60 percent of them said that an unsatisfactory relationship with church board members was the reason. It was the opinion of one denominational leader that the authoritarian role assumed by elders to hire and fire ministers was the root problem.[5]

Advantages

The board-control model allows for quick decision making during times of crisis and church conflict.

Since one body speaks for the entire congregation, there are fewer occasions for a breakdown in communication over policy.

Authority and responsibility are clearly centralized in one body. There is parity between these two important management functions.

Pastors can be held accountable for professional competency. In the event that termination is needed, the governing body can make the decision with a minimum amount of denominational or congregational struggle.

Disadvantages

Although this form of governance works well in a business setting, it has little biblical support. The deacons mentioned in the Book of Acts were *not* elected to tell the apostles how to conduct their ministries!

The board can become so entrenched with political maneuvering that it determines the direction of the church with little regard for spiritual input.

This approach to church leadership does not allow for shared governance between the board and the pastoral staff.

The chairperson of the board controls the church and the members of the church staff, in spite of the possibility that this leader may possess little (if any) spiritual training.

Presidential Model

In this leadership format, the pastor reigns supreme in his church. As chief executive, he sets policy and makes decisions that the church boards and staff are directed to implement. A presidential pastor is able to configure his own "cabinet" or church staff. Churches that operate in this approach allow a newly selected pastor to fire all staff members who are currently serving at the church and replace them with his own team. Because it is stated in the church constitution that the pastor has such executive powers, staff members who are brought on board should be aware that their term of service may end when the pastor leaves. An example of this form of church organization is shown in figure 4. Cabinet members of a president would be analogous to the pastoral staff of a church.

Fig. 4. Presidential model

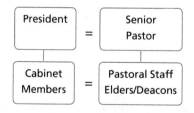

Advantages

Since church staff and board members have very little power or authority in this model, they do not need a great deal of training for leadership.

Very large churches that have pastors with a great deal of personal charisma can operate smoothly with this form of governance because the senior pastor "rules the roost."

The presidential pastor has such strong control over decision making that the church can respond to demographic trends and changes with little effort.

A presidential pastor is able to build a team of assistants who support his personal philosophy of ministry. Little time need be wasted on trying to convince staff members to accept his way of doing things.

Disadvantages

This leadership formula is clearly not the servant-leader approach modeled by Jesus in the New Testament.

If all members of the church staff may be forced to resign when the senior pastor leaves, chaos or loss of momentum in ministry objectives is often the result.

There is very little accountability required of the senior pastor in this model. Since the board is seen as a "rubber stamp," its members may not have the courage to confront the pastor on a questionable policy.

The effectiveness of this type of governance depends a great deal on the personal charisma of the "president." Senior pastors with this quality are difficult to find. Continuity of leadership is broken when the senior pastor leaves.

Balance-of-Power Model

This model views the congregation as the power base for the church. The congregational form of governance has both Puritan and Baptist roots dating back to the colonists who separated themselves from the Church of England and sailed to America where they could practice their own form of religion without denominational control. The congregation selects the senior pastor, members of the pastoral staff team, and each board member. Since major decisions are made primarily by vote, a general business meeting may be needed each month. The church moderator, who usually serves as the chairman of the church board, directs the proceedings of these meetings.

In this approach to church governance, the board of elders/deacons takes care of the administrative activities of the church, such as budgeting, purchasing, legal contracts, hiring and firing staff, and maintenance of buildings, grounds, or church equipment. The pastoral staff attends to spiritual matters: preaching, teaching, evangelism, and counseling. Staff members (who are usually not trained in administrative management) do not get sidetracked in their ministries by trying to handle business matters. A diagram of this approach to church structure is seen in figure 5.

Fig. 5. Balance-of-power model

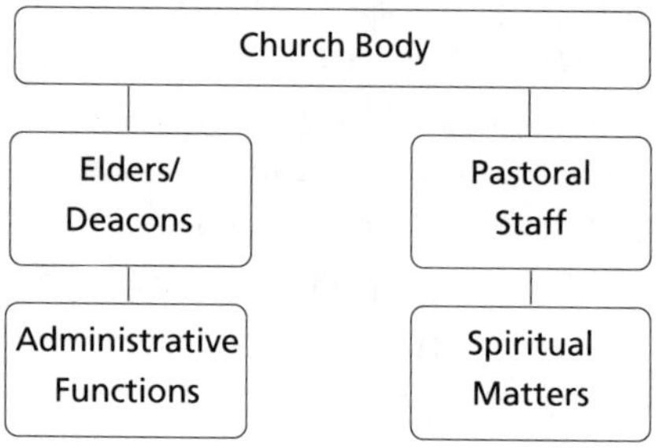

```
                    ┌─────────────────────────────┐
                    │         Church Body         │
                    └─────────────────────────────┘
                            │                │
          ┌──────────────┐                  ┌──────────────┐
          │   Elders/     │                  │   Pastoral    │
          │   Deacons     │                  │     Staff      │
          └──────────────┘                  └──────────────┘
                  │                                  │
          ┌──────────────┐                  ┌──────────────┐
          │Administrative │                  │  Spiritual    │
          │  Functions    │                  │   Matters     │
          └──────────────┘                  └──────────────┘
```

Advantages

Each congregation controls its own destiny. Parishioners can select their spiritual leaders and decide how long their term will be.

Free from denominational constraints, church members are able to select a curriculum that best meets their individual needs.

The congregation is given the authority to discipline its own members. It can follow biblical patterns of church discipline without having to comply with denominational procedures that could slow the process.

Each congregation has the ability to direct the affairs of the ministry to reflect local resources, cultural patterns, and demographic trends.

Disadvantages

This approach assumes that administrative functions and spiritual matters are separate. Such a distinction is clearly not biblical. One area greatly influences the plans of the other.

Sometimes a democratic vote in the congregation does not truly reflect the mind of God. The Spirit does not always abide by majority decisions!

Some churches, in their desire to support majority opinion, opt for consensus decision making. Where this occurs, an entire congregation's plans can depend on one person's vote. If that person is not being led by the Spirit of God, the whole body suffers. Consensus voting could become minority rule.

This approach assumes that the congregation is spiritually mature enough to make important decisions. It can negate the influence of the senior pastor and pastoral staff in spiritual matters.

Team Ministry

A newer idea that is becoming increasingly popular among churches in America is a team-ministry approach to structuring the church.[6] In this model the board of elders/deacons and the pastoral staff form a leadership team and work together to make the administrative and spiritual decisions of the church. When the leadership team meets, all the elders, deacons, and members of the pastoral staff share their ideas or concerns and participate in problem solving and decision making.

No one body has authority over the other. The board members know that their control over the spiritual leaders of the church is limited. At the same time, members of the pastoral staff recognize that the board members will probably remain at the church years longer than they will and that these lay leaders have been elected by the parishioners to represent their interests. (Those who serve on church boards have a unique perspective that is usually not possible for a member of the pastoral staff.) An example of how this team ministry model looks is seen in figure 6.

Fig. 6. Team-ministry model

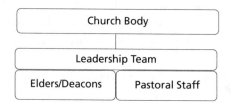

Advantages

Team ministry is clearly a biblical approach to church leadership. It allows for mutual accountability and shared governance. The more all members of the team share in the knowledge that serves as a basis for a decision, the more they will share in implementing that decision.

It allows for group decision making, as opposed to denominational hierarchy. As Proverbs 11:14 states: ". . . many advisers make victory sure."

It provides members of the congregation more opportunity to get involved in leadership. They are able to use their gifts of wisdom, knowledge, faith, and prophecy to build up the body of Christ.

The church staff members are allowed to share in the decisions that will ultimately impact their area of ministry.

Disadvantages

This approach would probably not work in large churches that have many elders, deacons, trustees, and pastoral staff members.

Sometimes information is shared in the context of a leadership team meeting that should be held in strict confidence. Not all staff members need to know the details of everything being discussed about church matters.

The more people involved in the decision-making process, the more difficult it is to arrive at a decision that is agreeable to all the voting members.

Having other church staff members at the leadership team meeting may take away from the authority of the senior pastor.

Speaking of the team approach to church leadership, Bruce Jones writes: "Certainly the biblical model of eldership in principle authorizes at least an equal status for the pastor with his board. Although there may be no real relationship between structure and church growth success, many contemporary churches feel equal eldership is the biblical model because it has proven effective in their own ministries."[7]

Staff Participation in Board Decisions

The final model mentioned above highlights an important issue that merits separate discussion: Should associate pastors, sometimes referred to as co-pastors, be allowed to attend church board meetings? This question is receiving increasing attention as more and more associate pastors have earned graduate degrees and feel qualified to share in the decision-making process at their churches.

There are a number of advantages and disadvantages to allowing associate pastors to play an active role at board meetings of elders and deacons:

Advantages

Team management requires that all those involved in leadership be present at the same meetings. Anything less than that does not truly communicate team ministry.

Having all pastors present reduces the possibility of conflicts of interest arising between board members and staff members.

It safeguards against the feeling of autonomous ownership that can develop among members of the pastoral staff regarding their area of ministry.

When associate pastors participate in decision making, there is a proportionate increase in commitment and cooperation toward goals.

It prevents resentment from growing among members of the pastoral staff about a decision that was made without their participation or vote.

Because, biblically speaking, pastors are "worthy of double honor" and should be obeyed (1 Tim. 5:17; Heb. 13:17), they are meant to be an integral part of the leadership team.

Disadvantages

Certain pastoral staff members may be dictatorial or domi-
neering during the decision-making process.

The absence of a staff member who will be affected by a decision may facilitate more open discussion about the issue.

Since pastors can lose their objectivity about an issue, having
them in the meeting can create emotional tensions.

Professional leaders sometimes tend to overpower and intimidate volunteers.

Associate pastors might try to bypass the supervisory role of
the senior pastor by appealing directly to the board.

These advantages and disadvantages should be weighed carefully by the senior pastor and church board(s). Obviously, once it
is decided to include associate pastors in board meetings, it is very
difficult to reverse this policy without creating hurt feelings and
mistrust.

Creating a Church Organizational Chart

The best way for a church to illustrate its structure and governance principles is by creating an organizational chart that clearly
depicts lines of authority and internal relationships. Because one
glance at the chart will show who has authority in each area of
responsibility (and who does not), much miscommunication and
poor decision making can be eliminated.

If your church does not already have such a chart, it is best to
first construct one that illustrates how the church is *currently* functioning in terms of working relationships. Each officeholder and
group should be included. If your church is associated with a
denomination, the chart will probably take into account denominational preferences concerning the assignment of ministry
responsibilities. For example, you might choose to classify your
groups as "committees" or "commissions" or even "departments."
The terms you use are not as important as getting each area of
responsibility represented somewhere on the chart.

Ken Gangel's excellent book, *Leadership for Church Education,* provides four principles to help guide the church in the formation of an organizational chart and also presents four examples.[8] The principles and charts are as follows:

1. Chart the church as it presently exists.
2. Circulate it among all the teachers and leaders.
3. Construct another chart with suggested changes to improve the organization and administration.
4. Continually update the chart.

Chart 1
Functional Chart—Board Control

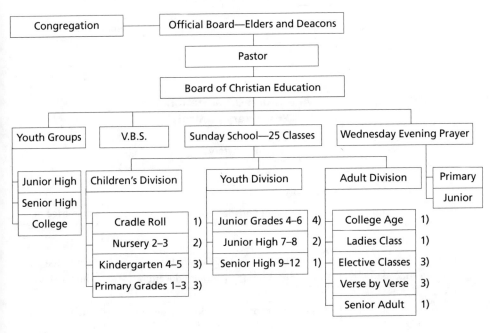

Implications

To some people, the very nature of organization and administration is seen as contrary to the leading of the Holy Spirit, but that is because they are uninformed about all that the Bible teaches on the subject of order and organization. God himself is the author

Chart 2
Functional Chart—
Congregational Control

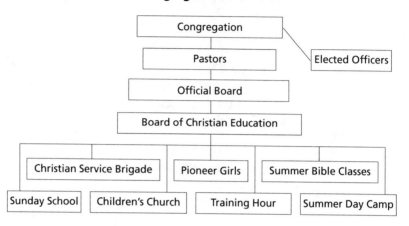

Chart 3
Age-Group Organization—
Presbytery Control

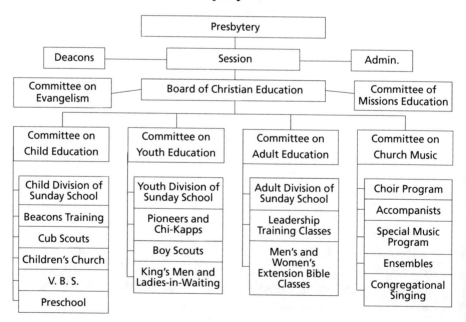

Chart 4
Functional Chart— Director of Christian Education

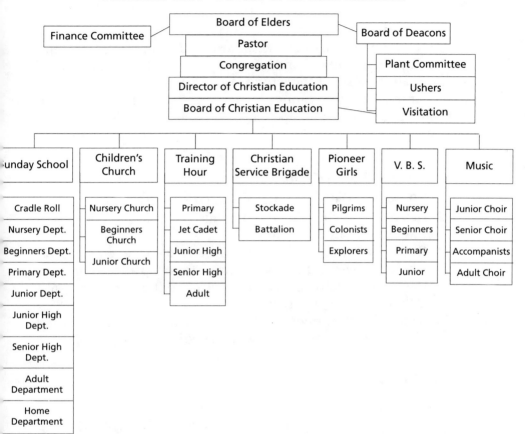

of order, and it seems only logical that he would desire his church to function in an orderly manner. To accomplish this, the leaders of the church must decide together which approach to organizational structure is in the congregation's best interest. Since the New Testament does not present a clearly defined pattern of structure that must be replicated throughout the universal church, we can assume that God allows differing structures in different settings. There is great danger in demanding allegiance to only one way of organizing ministry when the New Testament does not teach such an approach.

The goal of organizational structure in a church is to facilitate more effective distribution and stewardship of the resources with which God has entrusted us. The most critical factor is not the structure itself but the personalities represented. Having the right person for every job can make almost any organization work efficiently. On the other hand, a smooth and concise church structure can fall apart if the wrong leadership team comes into the equation. Finally, it cannot be overstated that an emphasis on prayer is the essential component in the effectiveness of any church structure.

Questions for Discussion

1. What organizational pattern does your church follow?
2. Has your church adopted or modified a particular model that was depicted in this chapter?
3. Other than the ones listed in this chapter, can you think of any advantages and/or disadvantages to your particular model?
4. Does your church allow associate pastors to attend church board meetings? Why or why not?
5. If your church currently has an organizational chart, how long has it been since this chart was revised?

For Further Reading

Anthony, Michael J. (ed). *Foundations of Ministry: An Introduction to Christian Education for a New Generation.* Wheaton: Victor Books, 1992.

Gangel, Kenneth O. *Feeding and Leading.* Wheaton: Victor Books, 1989.

Graendorf, Werner. *Introduction to Biblical Christian Education.* Chicago: Moody Press, 1981.

Perry, Lloyd M. *Getting the Church on Target.* Chicago: Moody Press, 1977.

Perry, Lloyd M., and Norman Shawchuck. *Revitalizing the 20th Century Church.* Chicago: Moody Press, 1982.

Team Ministry: *The Biblical Ideal*

*Y*ear after year, the Super Bowl, the NBA championship, the World Series, the Stanley Cup, the college bowl games, the NCAA basketball title, and many other sports competitions are won, not by players, but by teams. Interviews after championship games frequently show team members giving credit for their own outstanding performance to other members of the team, coaching staff, or even the team's owner. Rarely, if ever, will you hear a player say, "You're right. I was pretty good this season. I guess I'm the reason this team made it all the way to the top." Besides lacking credibility, someone like that deserves little respect. What's even more significant is that often a lower-placing team had greater talent, but failed to come out on top because individual players were more concerned about their own achievements, statistics, or notoriety. This caused internal dissension and poor team performance on the field.[1]

Functioning as a team doesn't come naturally. It takes a great deal more to create a genuine team effort than it does to form a group. This is especially true in ministry, where the motivational techniques used in corporate, athletic, or institutional settings are absent. The leverage of a potential pay raise, promotion, or transfer is very effective in convincing team members of the need to function as a unit!

The church has few such direct incentives toward team performance, especially in regard to its lay leaders, The fact is, getting a group of volunteers to sacrifice their individual goals and work together to fulfill group aims is a major feat. The larger the church, the more difficult the challenge, because then not only does the senior pastor have to keep the laity motivated, he also has the task of keeping several staff members pulling in the same direction. When multiple boards are added to the scenario, it is easy to understand why team effort is often the exception instead of the norm. It doesn't have to be that way. It is possible to gather a group of church leaders together—both paid staff and volunteers—and get them to operate as a team if you understand some basic rules and guidelines. Obviously, these guidelines can be modified to fit the denomination, size, geographic setting, ethnic variance, and cultural distinctives represented in a particular church. However, there are some common principles that can be applied in most churches to help its leaders work together efficiently.

The Biblical Basis of Team Ministry

As with most chapters in this book, I have found it best to start with the biblical teaching and then explain its relevance in the church today. That way, we lay a solid foundation of truth before attempting to decide how and in what areas Scripture can be applied to contemporary church settings.

The Old Testament

Volunteerism was virtually nonexistent in Old Testament times. Nobody filled out a job application for the office of "high priest." That position was determined on the basis of gender, tribe, and birth order. There was no guessing who the next high priest would be (see Lev. 8–10). The role simply followed in succession from Aaron.

It was basically the same for others who ministered in the tabernacle, or later in the temple. Leadership in those areas was clearly designated for men from the tribe of Levi. There were strict provisions laid down in the Old Testament about who was qualified to serve in ministry and who was not (Deut. 18). The penalty for violating these conditions was death (Num. 18:7). Even entering the temple without meeting these qualifications was a serious transgression, if not a fatal mistake, which explains why Nehemiah refused to hide in the temple from those who sought his life (Neh. 6:10–13).

However, that doesn't mean that all forms of ministry were conducted only by those from the tribe of Levi. There are numerous examples in the Old Testament of people other than Levites being involved in spiritual leadership. On the advice of Jethro (who realized the tremendous burden he was bearing by holding court for the entire nation of Israel), Moses selected "capable men from all the people—men who fear God" to assist him in hearing disputes and deciding important civil and religious matters (see Exod. 18:13–24). These men formed a team to lead the nation in the application of God's laws.

Likewise, Boaz went to the elders at the city gate to secure a contractual land arrangement that would allow him to marry Ruth (Ruth 4:2–11). Because elders were authorized to rule on legal and governmental matters that involved the town, important decisions were to pass through this team of men before they became law. Village elders were seen as the local spiritual leaders. They were known for their wisdom, piety, and ability to provide counsel for those who were in need of guidance and direction.

The New Testament

There are a number of New Testament examples of spiritual leaders forming teams for the purpose of effective ministry. The creation of the first deacon board fulfilled this purpose (Acts 6:1–7). In addition, Barnabas and Saul (Paul) went to Antioch as a ministry team for a full year to confirm the faith of this new church and see that it was firmly established in the correct doctrine (Acts 11:19–26). This same team was later sent by the church at Antioch on a journey to spread the gospel to the gentile world (Acts 13:1–3).

Paul later formed a ministry team with Silas, while Barnabas formed another with John Mark, for the same purpose: missions to the gentiles. In each of the churches these men visited, they sought to establish a team of elders and/or deacons to carry on the work of the ministry in their absence.

Probably the best New Testament prototype of team ministry is found in the analogy that Paul draws between the physical body and the spiritual body of Christ:

> For even as the body is one and yet has many members, and all the members of the body, though they are many, are one body, so also is Christ. For by one Spirit we were all baptized into one body, whether Jews or Greeks, whether slaves or free, and we were all made to drink of the one Spirit. For the body is not one member, but many. If the foot should say, "Because I am not a hand, I am not a part of the body," it is not for this reason any the less a part of the body. And if the ear should say, "Because I am not an eye, I am not a part of the body," it is not for this reason any the less a part of the body. If the whole body were an eye, where would the hearing be? If the whole were hearing, where would the sense of smell be? But now God has placed the members, each one of them, in the body, just as He desired. And if they were all one member, where would the body be? But now there are many members, but one body (1 Cor. 12:12–20 NASB).

The apostle Paul wanted the members of the church to realize that each one had been given a spiritual gift (see v. 7) that made him or her an important part of Christ's spiritual body, the church. When all members contribute according to their gifts, the church becomes a healthy, fully functioning body. In essence, no one gift, or part, is more important than another. Whether your leadership position calls you to teach, counsel, serve, give, or any number of other options, your ability is an essential part of the team's total performance. All team members must be willing to contribute toward accomplishing the goals of the body.

Those new to lay leadership may be unaware of this scriptural teaching. Even some pastors need to be reminded of its importance. One senior pastor writes, "After preparing for four years in pre-theological schools, spending four years in seminaries, and devoting three years in a doctrinal program, I noticed something about spiritual gifts: The subject was absent!"[2]

The nature and purpose of spiritual gifts demands total member involvement. Each gift provides an essential ministry that the body of Christ needs to fulfill the Great Commission (Matt. 28:19–20). No one person in a church, including the pastor, has all the gifts. Pastors are usually gifted in the ability to teach the Scriptures, and some are gifted in a variety of other talents, such as counseling and administration. But because no one pastor can do it all, a pastor needs each member of the congregation to discover his or her own unique area of giftedness and then use that gift to further the growth of the church.

There are many good books available to help a church leader understand the nature and scope of spiritual gifts. Some of these are listed at the end of this chapter, but your pastor or Christian bookstore dealer will be able to guide you in selecting further material on this important principle of team ministry.

Reasons for Team Ministry

There are many good reasons why viewing ministry from a team perspective makes sense. Not only is it biblical, but it is also highly effective within the context of contemporary ministerial practice. Rod Wilson, a teaching elder in a Brethren church, discusses four reasons why team leadership is advantageous for the church:

1. Team leadership allows for the contribution of various gifts. If elders are called out of a community to serve as a leadership group within that community, then presumably those elders have various gifts and strengths for the different areas in which God has ordained them to work.
2. Team leadership allows for the sharing of wisdom. The Bible tends not to discuss the expertise of individual, autonomous people. Rather, it lays more of an emphasis

on the principle of Proverbs 11:14, "For lack of guidance a nation falls, but many advisers make victory sure."

3. Team leadership allows for mutuality. In team leadership, within the context of the local church, interaction, blending, and mutuality allow for a base of unity, rather than pride and power-tripping.

4. Team leadership allows for representation within the church. One person at the top of a governmental structure won't be able to represent the entire church to the same degree that a team would.[3]

Clearly, there are many benefits of operating a ministry as a team venture. In addition to those listed above, there is also a shared sense of ownership in the ministry, accountability in decision making, and freedom for idea sharing, all of which provide the church with more creative approaches to programming. Team ministry also lightens the burden of overworked staff members, helps the average person in the pew understand the importance of serving the Lord by serving his people, and provides all members with a degree of recognition for their contribution and help.

Causes of "Team Fractures"

Considering all the advantages of team ministry, one would think that more churches would adopt this approach. However, achieving a genuine team spirit is not easy. There are a number of reasons why team ministry does not always work as intended. Success will require the total commitment of the entire congregation, especially on the part of its leaders. Otherwise, there will be "team fractures" that can cause dissension in the body of Christ and undermine the church's effectiveness within the local community.

Perhaps the primary cause of team fractures can be traced to the hesitancy of some people to get involved in ministry at their church. Those who grew up in a traditional church are often willing to let the pastor do all the work. After all, wasn't that why he went to seminary? Dale Wicker, a Southern Baptist pastor, states that "a departure from the traditional concept of ministry might be met with skepticism and, for a few, the hint of hostility."[4] The team approach to ministry, although it has been around since the Reformation, requires a change in mind-set for some, and (as we know all too well) change does not come easily for many people in our churches.

A second cause of team fractures is found in the arrogance and pride of individual members. When team players begin to believe their own press reports, trouble is not far behind. Paul warns, "So, if you think you are standing firm, be careful that you don't fall!" (1 Cor. 10:12). Pastor Calvin Miller writes, "Much of the unrest in church staffs is born in the ambition of staff members who begin to compete with each other for congregational prestige. This kind of strife is not usually sparked by the senior pastor. Indeed, it usually catches him by surprise."[5] Care should be taken to delineate clear lines of organizational authority, especially in the pastor's absence. Some bickering is unavoidable because human nature tends to be self-serving, so senior pastors and board chairmen will have to maintain vigilance in this area.

A third cause of breakdown in team solidarity is a spirit of criticism. Excessive faultfinding, whether on the part of an individual on the pastoral staff, a board member, the general congregation, or even the senior pastor, is extremely destructive to the work of the ministry. For example, if you are more critical than supportive of the pastor's work, chances are that you are in the process of losing respect for him.[6] A critical attitude is contagious and needs to be dealt with as soon as possible. Discovering the source of the criticism is the first step in working out what can be done to correct it. (Some criticism may be justified, or it may be caused by poor communication within the church.)

Fourth, the very nature of our culture can contribute to the fracturing of team relationships. We live in a highly competitive world where getting to the top seems to call for aggressiveness in occupational performance. Most church members understand this climate all too well, but we don't expect to find it in the body of Christ. However, it is there, and it can certainly affect team cohesiveness. Since each staff member's responsibility is usually specialized (children, youth, single adults, etc.), it may be hard to climb any form of career ladder in the church. This, in turn, can lead to a sense of frustration over apparently being locked-in, with no place to go.[7] Eventually, this type of discouragement breaks down staff morale and performance of the entire team.

A final reason for team fracture is the structural ambiguity created by organizational charts and job descriptions that are either inadequate or outdated. Power struggles between the pastor and the board(s) are often the result. With unclear lines of authority, debates over ownership of responsibility are inevitable. For example, board members may assume that they are responsible for staff hiring and termination when the pastor feels that should be his responsibility alone. This is one of many areas that needs to be specified in writing (see chapter 6).

Although these are a few of the more prominent causes of team fractures in a local church, they are by no means the only ones. Each church may have a few more to add to the list, based on its unique organizational structure, the characteristics of its members, and its context in the community.

Transforming a Group into a Team

Without doubt, one of the most difficult tasks a pastor has is changing a *group* of believers (congregation, board, and staff) into a cohesive *team*. In the midst of personal issues and ministry-related pressures, the pastor-shepherd is called on to assume the role of coach as well. Forming a group is not that difficult. Any pastor who is strong in communication skills, personal charisma, and various other leadership qualities can muster a band of believers. The real work lies in trying to transform that group into a team. In fact, this is usually where stress, crises, and wildfires erupt in the lives of the pastor and every board member.

The first step in the transformation process is making sure that the church has a clearly formulated mission. (See chapter 7.) This mission, or statement of purpose, needs to be written down and communicated on a regular basis so that all team members understand the destination. They might not know how they are going to get there, but they must be in agreement concerning the end result. This statement becomes the goal to which the energy and resources of the church will be directed. As simple as that seems, it is amazing how many churches do not have a mission statement that is concise and clearly communicated. Henry Waller, manager of human resources at World Vision writes, "A team isn't an accident. It grows as each member becomes involved in and feels a part of the process that aims to reach a good goal."[8]

Once goals have been set, the next important step is to identify the roles of the team players. In football, for example, there must be a coach, a quarterback who calls the plays, team members who have specific responsibilities, and support personnel. Each position is essential. A church team is no different in this regard. The pastor, board members, staff personnel, and congregation all have roles to fulfill. Job responsibilities should be clearly defined and then agreed on according to procedures outlined in the church's constitution. Once approved, they become a foundation for future activity and performance, although they should be reviewed periodically and changes made to keep them current.

The third step in the team-formation process involves nurturing a positive attitude. By far, the most difficult thing to achieve in any group of people is a unified and optimistic frame of mind. First, of course, the entire team must be in agreement about goals and convinced that the ministry is headed in the right direction. Next there must be an understanding of how team objectives will be achieved and who will be the key leaders. Above all, there must be an expectation of success. When any of these elements are missing, one or more members may develop a "critical spirit," which will jeopardize the desired outcome. Waller suggests seven "team-building attitudes" that will help maintain harmony:

1. Attack the problem, not the person.
2. Verbalize feelings—don't act them out.
3. Forgive, in place of judging.
4. Give more than you take.
5. Let love rule your life.
6. Humble yourself in the sight of the Lord (and of men, too!)
7. Finally, always take courage from the Word of God.[9]

If these attitudes sound familiar, it is because they are inspired by a popular passage of Scripture: Philippians 2:2–3. "Ministry coaches" would do well to review these verses with the entire team on a frequent basis. Ultimately, it is up to God to change a person's attitude. Although there are some things that a pastor or board member can do to facilitate the process, overly critical people who refuse to change should be removed from positions of leadership to prevent their negativism from causing further dissension and division within the team.

A fourth transformational technique calls for establishing open communication between all players on the team. When decisions are made, they should be understood by every concerned party. Whether it be done in an inter-office memo, the church bulletin, the monthly newsletter, or the annual report, decisions that affect other people must be publicized and explained. Without this safeguard, there will be hurt feelings, misunderstandings, wasted resources, and fractured team morale. Discussing ideas and creative methods in an atmosphere of trust and mutual respect will foster a team spirit and discourage power plays.

Another essential element in team building is accountability. The maverick minister who makes every decision by himself and is not held responsible for the outcome may seem effective for a brief period of time, but eventually the same "free spirit" that allowed him to shine momentarily will also be the cause of his downfall. This same principle applies to every other team member. The church constitution should clearly identify the procedures for maintaining accountability, and these procedures should be diligently followed.

A sixth transformational step is to inspire confidence in the leadership style of the pastor and board chairman. If these individuals are not modeling servanthood, neither will the rest of the team. Workers feel more confident when their leaders actively demonstrate how and why the work should be done. In essence, leaders who can say with humility, "Follow my example," will face fewer team fractures. Hard work and commitment to a common goal should be demonstrated at all levels of decision making.

Finally, no group will work as a team unless its leaders share praise and merit with all who contribute their time and energy.

Abraham Maslow identified the desire for recognition and status as a basic human need. It is not prideful or arrogant to simply want the satisfaction of knowing that one's contribution to a joint effort made a difference. Giving recognition to those who share in the work of ministry is clearly biblical. Read the last chapter of Romans for an example of how enthusiastically the apostle Paul commended his fellow workers. President Reagan had a plaque on his desk, positioned so that anyone coming into his office would be able to read its message: "It is amazing how much can be accomplished if you don't care who gets the credit."

A major stumbling block in this area is a supervisor's self-doubt and lack of confidence. Wanting to be seen as the person who gets all the glory is the mark of an insecure team player, and this attitude clearly undermines team effort. Those who did the work (and those around them) know which people deserve credit for their ideas and energies, but the pastor and board members should also be willing to honor them publicly. Whether this is done from the pulpit, in the church bulletin or annual report, or at a department meeting will depend on the magnitude of the contribution.

Retiring board members, especially those who have served for many years, should receive public commendation for their contributions. Likewise, staff members who work above and beyond the call of duty to accomplish a church goal should be brought to the attention of the entire congregation. Just knowing that individual efforts made a difference and will be acknowledged can have a very positive effect on team spirit, motivation, and morale.

Implications

Although building a team requires careful planning, the proper attitudes, a great deal of hard work, and long hours, Scripture is clear about the importance of performing as a team in the ministry of the church. Because God understands the difficulty of fulfilling this imperative, he stands ready to provide the leadership of the church with assistance. After all, as the team owner and its head coach, God desires his church to grow and impact the world for Christ, and he will provide the guidance needed to accomplish that purpose.

A wise leader knows his destination and keeps his eyes on the road. The sooner he can spot potential hazards and make minor steering adjustments, the smaller will be their impact. Knowing what could cause team fractures in your church's ministry will suggest ways to prevent them. If breakdown has already occurred, steps can be taken to rebuild the group of believers into a team that will truly further the kingdom of God in your community. (See chapter 18.)

Questions for Discussion

1. Can you identify additional causes of team fractures in a church?
2. What team fractures have occurred in your church in the past?
3. In retrospect, what could have been done differently to prevent this fracturing?
4. What is your church doing now to transform the ministry group into a team?
5. What things can be done differently (or perhaps added) so as to strengthen the team-building process at your church?

For Further Reading

Bradford, Robert C. "Growing Your Own Staff." *Leadership* 5, no. 2 (Spring 1984): 84–88.

Bridge, Donald, and David Phypers. *Spiritual Gifts and the Church.* London: InterVarsity Press, 1973.

Gangel, Kenneth O. *Unwrapping Your Spiritual Gifts.* Wheaton: Victor Books, 1983.

Jacobsen, Wayne. "Seven Reasons for Staff Conflict." *Leadership* 4, no. 3 (Summer 1983): 34–39.

Klos, Sarah. "A Mutual and Shared Ministry." *Clergy Journal* 66, no. 1 (Oct. 1989): 2–3.

McKee, Tom. "Roadblocks and Guardrails for Visionaries." *Leadership* 6, no. 2 (Spring 1985): 74–79.

McRae, William. *Dynamics of Spiritual Gifts.* Grand Rapids: Zondervan, 1976.

Morrison, Jim. "Building Team Spirit Among the Church Staff." *Church Administration* 31, no. 4 (Jan. 1989): 27–28.

Sheffield, Jimmie. "Who Cares for the Staff?" *Search* 3, no. 3 (Spring 1990): 22–28.

Starr, Eileen. "Shared Accountability: A Fresh Look at Coordinating Christian Education." *Christian Education Journal* 10, no. 2 (Autumn 1991): 73–81.

"Teamwork Isn't Everything: It's the Only Thing: A Conversation with Ridge Burns." *Leadership* 7, no. 1 (Winter 1986): 42–46.

Wagner, C. Peter. *Your Spiritual Gifts*. Glendale: Regal Books, 1979.

Effective Leadership in Ministry

hroughout the pages of Scripture, God reveals that he ordained certain people to communicate his nature and purposes to the world. Those biblical leaders were an amazingly diverse group of individuals. Men and women, rich and poor, educated and illiterate, brave and cowardly, young and old, healthy and weak—all were used by God to teach his truths to others and serve them in his name. If there is any one common theme in both the Old and New Testaments, it is that God has called leaders to represent him throughout the history of mankind.

Some churches have spent decades trying to identify the ideal pastor! In search of the ultimate leader, they have exhausted every resource known to man. Although it might be said that leadership isn't what it used to be, the study of leadership qualities and what contributes to their development has been around for many years. We have learned a few things about what good leadership is and is not, but we are still in need of answers to some important questions.

A Brief History of Leadership Research

The serious study of leadership began in the mid-1800s, motivated in part by the desire to discover "the ideal man." This early research focused on identifying the traits characteristic of proven leaders. Because it was assumed that effective leaders were born with certain character qualities (or personality traits), it seemed logical that an organization could save time in leadership training by simply locating people with the appropriate traits and then promoting them into positions of higher responsibility. Since literally hundreds of so-called leadership traits were identified, this method of study was abandoned.

The idea that leaders all have certain traits in common later gave way to the situational view of leadership, which stated that a leader who was effective in one set of circumstances might not be as effective in another. Therefore, the key to leadership development was to match a person with the right area of responsibility.

By the mid-1900s, it was widely accepted that leadership was multidimensional. That is, leadership called for balancing an emphasis on interpersonal relationships with an ongoing concern for production. Since both were seen as critical to good leadership, the effective leader was a person who could maintain this dual point of view in all decision making.

The Primary Leadership Styles

In more recent years, as a broadened perspective has replaced the idea that any one style of leadership is correct, it is generally agreed that flexibility is the key to effectiveness as a leader.

Secular studies have identified three primary leadership styles: autocratic, democratic, and laissez-faire. Although I have found over twenty other styles mentioned in secular literature, most of them are variations of these three basic patterns. Each style has a distinct set of characteristics and warrants a brief review.

Autocratic Leadership

These leaders see themselves as correct under all circumstances. When in doubt about which direction to follow, ask an autocratic leader and he or she will be more than willing to tell you the way to go. These people are strong-willed, opinionated, forceful in dialogue, and controlling of others to the point of being aggressive and manipulative. They have little patience for failure or even mild incompetence and generally have enormous egos.

When placed in a church setting as a pastor or board member, autocratic leaders do not like to discuss alternatives to their own plan of action. They often insist that they *know* what God's will for the church is, so they will be confrontive (even combative) during board meetings if the discussion is not going their way. Although quick to offer criticism, they have difficulty accepting any that is directed their way. Because autocratic leaders are self-oriented, they use terms such as "I," "me," and "they," when discussing ministry issues.

Democratic Leadership

This leader believes in shared governance. Decisions are arrived at by consensus rather than through decree. Democratic leaders are open to discussion and, in fact, encourage frankness and active debate before arriving at a conclusion. Because they believe that the feelings of others are important, they will want to determine what the group wants before pushing ahead.

In church settings, this type of pastor or board member takes the time to explore all options and alternatives, not because he or she does not know which direction to take but because of commitment to the group process. These leaders know that any decision not "owned" by the group will not be supported by the group, thereby undermining its implementation. They are easy to get along with and enjoy interpersonal relations with others around them. They use terms such as "we," "us," and "the team," to describe the ministry.

Laissez-Faire Leadership

Contrary to popular opinion, these people are not completely removed from what is happening all around them! The stereotypical picture of a laissez-faire leader is someone who is a few years away from retirement and does not want to do anything to "rock the boat," but he or she can be found at all levels of an organization and with various levels of education, experience, and age. The laissez-faire leader likes to maintain the status quo and prefers not to make a scene about anything. It may not be the best way of doing something, but as long as it works, why try to change it? This person's motto is, "If it isn't broken, don't fix it." He or she prefers to stay out of the spotlight and avoid giving direction. Although available if a question or problem arises, these people don't go looking for trouble. They are generally soft-spoken and cordial, but they prefer to work alone in their office, far removed from the action.

A pastor or board member with this leadership style does not give advice or direction and usually encourages others on the team to select their own course of action. Laissez-faire leaders are non-confrontive and "go with the flow." Although not known for dynamic communication, they can relate to people well in small-group settings. These people are seen more as kindhearted chaplains than commanders of the troops. They use sentences such as "Whatever *you* like is fine with me," "What do *you* think we should do about this?" and "If *you* have any problems, *you* know where to come for help" to describe their approach to ministry.

I found it interesting in my survey of senior pastors and their board members to discover that when the senior pastors were asked what leadership style they felt they demonstrated, they responded as follows:

7%	autocratic
60%	democratic
7%	laissez-faire
26%	other

Yet, in the view of board members, the leadership style of their pastor was:

20%	autocratic
61%	democratic
15%	laissez-faire
4%	not sure

It would appear that most of the senior pastors saw themselves as "democratic" (some of the terms in the "other" category also fit that description). While many board members saw their pastor as "democratic," more of the board members than the pastors themselves described the pastoral style as either "autocratic" or "laissez-faire."

On the other hand, when board members were asked to describe their own leadership style, the percentages were:

7%	autocratic
91%	democratic
2%	laissez-faire

It would seem from these differing opinions that there is room for a healthy dialogue between pastors and their board members regarding their respective leadership styles.

Leadership Style and Church Growth

Some people believe that one particular leadership style is more effective for ministry than another, at least in terms of church growth. Research in the field, however, indicates that this is not true.

A few years ago I conducted a survey of over 130 pastors (ministers of Christian education) to determine if their leadership style was related to the growth rate in their church. Some of these churches were experiencing an explosive rate of growth, some were static, and a few were in decline. To my surprise, the pastor's leadership style apparently had no bearing whatsoever on their church's growth.[1] A few years later, I conducted a similar survey to determine if a senior pastor's level of charisma (autocratic style) could be correlated with his church's growth rate. Once again, the answer was an unequivocal "no." Some highly persuasive pastors had a fast-growing church, yet others faced a declining membership. Some pastors with low levels of personal charm had a growing church; others did not.

I have concluded that the leadership style of the pastor does not determine the success of a church's overall ministry. The best leaders have the ability to be flexible in their approach.

For example, if a church has been experiencing immoral behavior, it may be appropriate for a newly arrived pastor to take an authoritative stance—in essence, to declare, "Thus saith the Lord." A strong form of leadership may be the best way to correct the problem and guide the church through a turbulent period of transition. However, no church can survive under dictatorial leadership indefinitely. Once stability is established, this new climate of security will provide an atmosphere conducive to leadership development. Now the pastor should demonstrate a shared-governance approach, one that allows others to assume a higher level of responsibility and partnership in the ministry.

Perhaps, down the line, this once-troubled church may experience years of growth and a fruitful ministry shared by the pastoral staff and lay leaders. The membership has eventually been educated in how ministry should be done and now demonstrates mature decision making. At this point the pastor may want to take a "hands off" approach, especially if the lay leaders are taking additional training and demonstrating an ownership of the ministry. Supervision by the pastor can now be minimal, since each person knows his or her area of responsibility and strives for excellence in its accomplishment.

Myron Rush suggests that an autocratic style of leadership is called for under the following circumstances:

During extreme emergencies or crises

When people's lives are at stake

When severe disciplinary action is needed

When employees consistently misuse their authority

When organizational rules/regulations are violated[2]

While these lists use terms that seem more applicable to the business world than to the church, the generalizations are relevant to church leadership. The appropriate time and place for democratic leadership would include:

As people become competent in their responsibilities
During organizational planning sessions
During organizational evaluation sessions
Motivating people who become stifled with routine assign-
ments[3]

I suggest that a laissez-faire style of leadership is recommended
in these situations:

When directing people in their own area of expertise
If one's technical competence is less than subordinates'
When one's subordinates are already highly motivated
If one must be away from the work site for lengthy periods of
time

Ministry effectiveness isn't a matter of which leadership style
is better than another. It comes down to the context in which
leadership is needed, how long a particular pastor has been at the
church, the qualifications of staff and lay leaders, and the general
atmosphere within the congregation.

There were times when biblical leaders were very forceful in
their approach (e.g., Joshua's response to the sin of Achan, Jesus'
cleansing of the temple and criticism of the religious leaders, or
Paul's censure of the church in Corinth for its immorality). There
were also times when biblical leaders shared their responsibilities
with others around them. Such leadership teams as Moses and
Aaron, Jesus and his disciples, or Paul and Silas functioned efficiently in a spirit of mutual respect and partnership. I believe it
can be said with some degree of certainty that no one style will
be appropriate in all circumstances and that flexibility and sensitivity hold the key to effective leadership.

Character Qualities vs. Leadership Styles

Although much has been written by Christian authors on the
subject of leadership styles, I find relatively few passages in Scripture that deal with this topic as it relates to the church. However,

the Bible is filled with references to the *character qualities* of an effective leader. I believe this emphasis is missing in much of our discussion about church leadership today. It is here where we must take a divergent course from what secular studies of leadership have to say.

The Bible clearly teaches that men and women who assume leadership positions in the church must possess certain character traits, and I believe that these qualities are far more important in ministry than one's leadership style. Of the many Christian leaders who have fallen from their high positions in the past few years, most of them fell because of a serious character flaw.

Space limitations prevent a comprehensive discussion of every essential leadership quality (see chapters 3 and 6 for additional material on this topic), but four of them are foundational: servanthood, integrity, empathy, and love.

Servanthood

Jesus chose as his symbol of leadership not a scepter, but the towel with which he dried his disciples' feet. He saw the needs of his followers as far more important than his own. True leaders do not see themselves as authority figures, but as models of servanthood. They minister to the body of Christ solely because any service offered in Christ's name is a way of paying homage to Christ himself. Serving others may not bring public recognition, prestige, political clout, or affluence, but the only meaningful reward for a disciple of Christ is "Well done, good and faithful servant" from the master. Nothing else provides as much satisfaction. Material gain seems insignificant compared to the privilege of serving the King of kings. Biblical passages on the subject of servanthood include:

> "You know that the rulers of the Gentiles lord it over them, and their high officials exercise authority over them. Not so with you. Instead, whoever wants to become great among you must be your servant, and whoever wants to be first must be your slave—just as the Son of Man did not come to be served, but to serve, and to give his life as a ransom for many" (Matt. 20:25–28).

"You call me 'Teacher' and 'Lord,' and rightly so, for that is what I am. Now that I, your Lord and Teacher, have washed your feet, you also should wash one another's feet. I have set an example that you should do as I have done for you" (John 13:13–15).

Do nothing from selfishness or empty deceit, but with humility of mind let each of you regard one another as more important than himself; do not merely look out for your own personal interests, but also for the interests of others. Have this attitude in yourselves which was also in Christ Jesus, who, although He existed in the form of God, did not regard equality with God a thing to be grasped, but emptied Himself, taking the form of a bond-servant, and being made in the likeness of men (Phil. 2:3–7 NASB).

Be shepherds of God's flock that is under your care, serving as overseers—not because you must, but because you are willing, as God wants you to be; not greedy for money, but eager to serve; not lording it over those entrusted to you, but being examples to the flock (1 Peter 5:2–3).

Integrity

The word *integrity* comes from the Latin term for "wholeness." Our mathematical term *integer* has the same origin and refers to a number that cannot be divided. When applied to character, "integrity" means that the person lives according to what he says—there is unity or consistency between his words and his actions.

People with integrity are often described as honest, credible, and upright. They have a high standard of moral conduct and are above reproach by those around them because they are never guilty of misconduct.

When 1,500 managers from across the country were surveyed about what character trait they valued or respected most in their superior, the number-one response was integrity.[4] The Bible has much to say about this important character quality, including:

"I know, my God, that you test the heart and are pleased with integrity. All these things have I given willingly and with honest intent" (1 Chron. 29:17).

My integrity and uprightness protect me, because my hope is in you (Ps. 25:21).

The man of integrity walks securely, but he who takes crooked paths will be found out (Prov. 10:9).

"Teacher," they said, "we know you are a man of integrity and that you teach the way of God in accordance with the truth" (Matt. 22:16b).

In your teaching show integrity, seriousness and soundness of speech that cannot be condemned (Titus 2:7b–8a).

Empathy

Because Jesus was a leader who knew how to empathize with those around him, it is not surprising that he won the trust of downtrodden and hurting people. Most of the religious leaders of the day were characterized as callous-hearted and apathetic toward those in need. Jesus was able to touch the world with his Father's love because he was willing to get involved in people's lives and share their pain. In fact, that is one of the main points of the parable of the good Samaritan.

Empathy is the ability to participate in another person's feelings—to walk a mile in another person's shoes so you can experience his joys and his sorrows and fully understand the burdens he carries. Effective Christian leaders never remove themselves so far from their congregations that they lose touch with their needs and concerns. As Robert Sheffield writes, "Since being a leader involves inspiration and influence, a leader cannot be dispassionate and be an effective leader. If the leader doesn't care, the followers likely will not care either."[5]

Spiritual leaders are often referred to in Scripture as shepherds who must know the sheep and care for their needs:

> "Woe to the shepherds of Israel who only take care of themselves! Should not shepherds take care of the flock? You eat the curds, clothe yourselves with the wool and slaughter the choice animals, but you do not take care of the flock. You have not strengthened the weak or healed the sick or bound up the injured. You have not brought back the strays or searched for the lost. You have ruled them harshly and brutally. So they were scattered because there was no shepherd. . . . [therefore,] I am against

the shepherds and will hold them accountable for my flock. I will remove them from tending the flock so that the shepherds can no longer feed themselves" (Ezek. 34:2–5, 10).

"I am the good shepherd. The good shepherd lays down his life for the sheep. . . . I am the good shepherd; I know my sheep and my sheep know me—just as the Father knows me and I know the Father—and I lay down my life for the sheep (John 10:11, 14–15).

Love

Perhaps no other character quality is as important in a leader as love. To love others is to forgive their mistakes, to think the best of them, and to provide sacrificially for their needs. After discussing the value and purpose of spiritual gifts in 1 Corinthians 12, the apostle Paul states that he will show the church an even better way to serve the body of Christ: a ministry grounded in love, which is the motivating influence that empowers the gifts of the Spirit. Paul says that even the most miraculous gifts and abilities are wasted if they are practiced without love:

> Love is patient, love is kind. It does not envy, it does not boast, it is not proud. It is not rude, it is not self-seeking, it is not easily angered, it keeps no record of wrongs. Love does not delight in evil but rejoices with the truth. It always protects, always trusts, always hopes, always preseveres (1 Cor. 13:4–7).

Church boards would do well to read this passage of Scripture before every business meeting. A loving attitude would foster friendlier discussions and set the climate for a more biblical approach toward interpersonal relationships.

The Word of God confirms that it is more important for spiritual leaders to develop exemplary character qualities than to focus on which leadership style is "correct." Any leadership style can be abused without the right attitude, but demonstrating servanthood, integrity, empathy, and love can cover a multitude of mistakes on the part of any pastor or board member.

Implications

Clearly, the Scriptures teach that effective leadership in ministry is not the same as leadership in the secular world. Those who were selected as spiritual leaders in the Old and New Testaments probably did possess qualities that a business or civic organization would value today. However, the distinct difference they had was the enabling power of the Holy Spirit, which is why studying secular leadership styles is inadequate in explaining what is required of those who serve in the body of Christ. When filled by the Holy Spirit and overflowing with character qualities that reflect respect, care, and concern for others, Christian servants will demonstrate leadership in a flexible manner and according to the direction that God provides.

Questions for Discussion

1. How would you describe your leadership style (as a pastor or board member)?
2. How would you describe the leadership style of your senior pastor?
3. Do you feel that it would be appropriate for you (or your pastor) to adjust your (his/her) leadership style? If so, why? If not, why not?
4. What form of leadership style do you feel your church currently needs from its pastor and board members?
5. Besides those mentioned, what other character qualities are important for a church leader to demonstrate?

For Further Reading

Balswick, Jack, and Walter Wright. "A Complimentary-Empowering Model of Ministerial Leadership. *Pastoral Psychology* 37, no. 1 (1988): 3–14.

Carter, James. "Building Personal Integrity Into Your Ministry." *Church Administration* 32, no. 6 (Mar. 1990): 17–19.

Clinton, J. Robert. "How to Look at Leadership." *Theology, News and Notes* (Fuller School of Theology Newsletter), June 1990, 4–7.

_____. "The Emerging Leader." *Theology, News and Notes* (Fuller School of Theology Newsletter), June 1990, 25.

Habecker, Eugene B. *Leading with a Follower's Heart.* Wheaton: Victor Books, 1990.

Luecke, David S. *New Designs for Church Leadership.* St. Louis: Concordia, 1990.

Means, James E. *Leadership in Christian Ministry.* Grand Rapids: Baker Book House, 1990.

Muck, Terry; Paul Robbins, and Harold Myra. "A Biblical Style of Leadership? An Interview with Larry Richards and Gene Getz." *Leadership* 2, no. 2 (Spring 1981): 69–78.

Osborne, Larry W. *The Unity Factor: Getting Your Church Leaders to Work Together.* Waco: Word Books, 1989.

Shawchuck, Norman. "Are You a Flexible Leader?" *Leadership* 12, no. 2 (Spring 1991): 89–93.

Planning and Goal Setting

$\mathcal{A}$ nyone who has served in a church as a pastor or board member knows how difficult it is to plan very far into the future. The problem usually isn't a lack of good intentions or ideas. All too often, church leaders must face "the tyranny of the urgent." How does one find time to forecast five or even two years ahead when Mrs. Adams is in the hospital and needs to be visited this morning, the air-conditioning unit has just broken (it's 103° in the education building), and there are homeless people in the secretary's office who need immediate assistance? On top of all that, the bank has just called and said that the church is overdrawn on its line of credit. Five-year plan? Most churches are just trying to get through the day!

Sound familiar? If it does, you are not alone. Planning ministry into the future is not easy. It involves a good deal of groundwork and preparation before plans can even be made. In simple terms, planning is merely the application of common sense to whatever goals have been set. It is not trying to predict the future, but involves taking an intelligent look at what the future may hold and then developing a strategy for dealing with it in an efficient manner.[1] This chapter is designed to help those in the leadership of the church identify the obstacles to long- and short-range planning, decide who should be in charge of the planning process, and understand how a strategic plan should be incorporated into the life of the church.

The Biblical Basis of Planning

One of the first problems a church faces when making long- or short-range plans is the opposition of well-meaning people who are not convinced that planning is biblical. They believe that trying to mold the future somehow leaves God out of the picture—as if dreaming about (and planning for) what we want to do for the kingdom of God goes against our faith that "God will provide." But nothing could be further from the truth, as Scripture makes very clear.

From the beginning of time, God had a plan. Scripture says that "he chose us in him" before the foundations of the world were laid (Eph. 1:4). Now that's long-range planning! Speaking of the nation of Assyria, God declares, "Surely, as I have planned, so it will be, and as I have purposed, so it will stand" (Isa. 14:24). Seeking to encourage the Jews in exile, God says through Jeremiah, "For I know the plans I have for you . . . plans to prosper you and not to harm you, plans to give you hope and a future" (Jer. 29:11). God developed and followed a plan for the creation of the world and for his intervention in human history. And he has laid out a plan for the future of his church.

Planning in the Old Testament

Not only does God plan, but he wants his people to plan ahead as well. Those who served him in Old Testament times followed plans, some that God provided and some that the leaders he chose developed under his guidance.

Moses followed a set of plans for the preparation of the tabernacle (Exod. 25–28); Joshua had a plan for conquering and dividing the land of Canaan; Gideon had a plan when he destroyed the Midianites (Judg. 7); David was a masterful military planner; Solomon laid out very elaborate plans for building the temple and his palace (1 Kings 6 and 7) and even his stables (1 Kings 10:26–29); Ezra used extensive planning to prepare for the rebuilding of the temple (Ezra 1–3); and Nehemiah inspected the broken walls of Jerusalem to determine how to repair them (Neh. 2:13–16).

A brief summary of the importance of planning is provided in the following Old Testament verses:

> Plans fail for lack of counsel, but with many advisers they succeed (Prov. 15:22).
> Make plans by seeking advice; if you wage war, obtain guidance (Prov. 20:18).
> But the noble man makes noble plans, and by noble deeds he stands (Isa. 32:8).

Planning in the New Testament

In the New Testament we find that Jesus practiced and taught the principles of good planning (Luke 14:28–30), and that he presented to his disciples a strategic plan for evangelism (Acts 1:8). Likewise, Paul laid out a plan for some of his missionary journeys (Rom. 15:22–25; 1 Cor. 16:5–8), and John tells us God's plan for the future of the church in the Book of Revelation.

Notice the strong emphasis on planning in these two passages:

> "Suppose one of you wants to build a tower. Will he not first sit down and estimate the cost to see if he has enough money to complete it? For if he lays the foundation and is not able to finish it, everyone who sees it will ridicule him" (Luke 14:28–29).
> If anyone does not provide for his relatives, and especially for his immediate family, he has denied the faith and is worse than an unbeliever (1 Tim. 5:8).

Obstacles to Church Planning

The survey I conducted among pastors and board members indicated that about half of their churches had written long-range plans that covered, on average, a five-year period. In most of these churches, plans were reviewed every one to three years. However, as these results show, not everyone in ministry likes to plan very far ahead. In fact, many church leaders refuse to plan! The following statements are often made by pastors and/or board members to explain why they choose not to make plans for their ministry:

1. "Planning isn't spiritual." These people are ignoring the preponderance of Scripture passages that teach the importance of planning—both in one's personal life and in the life of the church.

2. "God alone can determine the future, and it is presumptuous for the church to try to do so." This observation could be true in some churches, especially those under autocratic leadership. Certainly, one of the greatest dangers in ministry planning lies in the temptation to leave God out of the process. But it doesn't have to be that way. Planning can and should be a team effort that reflects the guidance of the Holy Spirit and the rational decision making of Spirit-filled men and women.[2]

3. "We don't have the time to plan." It is true that proper planning requires many hours of hard work. But cleaning up the mess caused by inadequate planning will take even more time. Although most church leaders have pressing demands weighing on them, and responding to all of them requires a great deal of energy, it can be disastrous for a church not to project its ministry into the future.

4. "Planning controls my future activities and I like to be spontaneous." Robert Bingham writes in his book *Traps to Avoid in Good Administration* that "any good fool can draft a five-year plan. It takes creative leadership to be able to make day-to-day adjustments as crises arise."[3]

5. "I like things the way they are, and if we make a lot of plans, those things will change." Change is inevitable! We either allow it to happen and then respond to it or—we prepare for it in advance and control its influence in our lives. Planning allows a church to do the latter.

6. "If we make a lot of plans but don't accomplish them, people will know that we have failed." Nobody likes to fail, especially in public. But planning is worth the risk. Besides, failure can be a stepping-stone to success. Some of the greatest inventions were developed because an earlier plan failed. As a result, the inventor learned a lesson that helped him take an entirely different approach.

These "excuses" for not planning are apparent in many of our churches, and they permeate ministry at all levels. Once these obstacles are recognized and addressed, progress can be made toward projecting purposeful and goal-oriented objectives into the future.

Setting the Right Climate for Planning

Before a serious attempt can be made toward effective long- or short-range planning, a foundation must be laid to support the process. These brief suggestions may help:

Establish a general direction and purpose for the church. This should be done through the use of a mission statement that outlines the church's overall philosophy, emphasis, and reason for being (see chapter 7).

Prepare and encourage the entire membership to support the planning process. If the congregation does not already see the need for planning, groundwork will be needed to create an atmosphere of acceptance for the process. People should be prepared for change; it should not be sprung on them without warning.

Clearly identify the church leaders and obtain their commitment to a planned ministry. The pastor and governing board should foster an atmosphere of stability, strength, and unity. For example, it is a mistake to begin making long-range plans if the pastor is in the midst of a serious disagreement with the lay leaders of the church. If the pastor leaves in the middle of the process, the whole experience will need to be shelved while the search for a new shepherd is underway. The planning process will be productive to the degree that it is done in a spirit of harmony, good will, and hopeful anticipation.

Develop ways to ensure healthy interpersonal communication between all levels within the church organizational structure (see chapter 8). It is important that there be an openness about church policy and goals, and about the intentions of the leadership. The congregation and pastoral staff should feel free to express their opinions to the senior pastor and board(s), and board members should be able to dialogue—even disagree—with each other and with the pastor without fear of censure.

The Process Itself

Once the aforementioned foundational areas are covered and the church leadership senses the freedom to move ahead into some long- and short-range planning, the following principles may prove helpful. Keep in mind, however, that there is no fool-proof planning formula. The process that works for other churches may not work for yours. Whoever has the responsibility for planning should feel free to modify or change any of the steps outlined below.

Developing Long-Range Plans: Setting Goals

Long-range plans for ministry generally cover five to ten years in the life of the church. Large churches often plan for ten years or even longer, but most small churches find five years to be an appropriate period for them.

Step One. Spend a significant amount of time praying for guidance from God. Never lose sight of the fact that he is the one who provides the resources that make ministry possible. It is *his* ministry, and we are simply stewards of whatever he provides.

Step Two. Conduct an assessment of the surrounding community. Look at demographic trends, economic predictions, ethnic variance, housing or other building projects, and so on. Each of these factors will tell you something about the current and future needs represented in the local area. Every community is different and is also ever-changing. For example, towns with nearby military bases will have different needs from those that are heavily industrialized. Communities with several apartment complexes will have more single adults, single parents, and elderly than communities with mainly private homes. The local chamber of commerce can provide you with helpful demographic information. Don't overlook interviewing people who must keep informed about local issues (e.g., school boards, civic clubs, city government, political party representatives, marketing directors in local corporations). There are also many books on planning that provide worksheets to organize your data. (Some of these resources are listed in the "For Further Reading" section at the end of this chapter.)

Step Three. Determine the areas of concern for which your church could (and could not) provide a ministry. No one church has the resources for meeting the needs of its entire community. Since most churches in America have less than two hundred people in attendance, it is obvious that priorities have to be set. For example, not every church needs a ministry to single adults. Or, if your church has a large number of senior citizens, an extensive AWANA (youth) program may not be realistic. Don't feel as if your church must do it all. Find out what other local churches are doing and plan to work together to provide a balanced perspective of ministry in the community.

Step Four. Gather information about what is needed from a variety of sources in the church. Although not everybody's ideas can be incorporated into a long-range plan, all members should at least have the opportunity to provide their input. This can be done through church meetings, mailed surveys, or phone interviews.

Step Five. With all of the above information in hand, and having spent considerable time in private and corporate prayer, identify the general areas where your church could impact the community in the years to come. Then set some specific goals about staffing, training, programs, space requirements, and so on. Prioritize this list according to which long-range objectives are appropriate, given what is known about your current staff, budget, buildings, and number of members—and how those factors might change in the immediate future. These goals need to be stated in such a way as to be measurable and attainable. Don't make them unrealistic, but don't be afraid to dream a little!

Step Six. Prepare a document itemizing these long-range goals in order of priority. Circulate this proposal among the pastoral staff, the various boards, committees, and departments that will be initially affected. Gather their input and make any needed revisions.

Step Seven. Present the long-range plan to the congregation for their review and endorsement. Be willing to correct any serious omissions. Obviously, not everyone is going to "buy into" the document, especially those whose suggestions were not deemed realistic or appropriate. If you don't expect to please everyone, you won't be disappointed when you find out that you didn't. The idea behind this step is to try to satisfy the majority at all levels: congregation, staff, and board(s).

Notice that I have not said anything about who is to coordinate the research and serve as the clearinghouse for preparing the long-range planning document. This is the subject of discussion in many churches. Some believe that the primary church board should have this responsibility or that the denominational headquarters should lead the way, whereas others feel it is the prerogative of the professional church staff. A fourth option would be to form a long-range planning committee, or task force.

Each church needs to determine which technique is most appropriate for its organizational structure. However, if a separate committee is formed, it should be representative of all bodies within the church (and possibly the denomination). The senior pastor must be included, as well as representatives of the various boards (elders, deacons, deaconesses, etc.).

Developing Short-Range Plans: Establishing Objectives

Once the long-range goals for the church have been adopted and prioritized, the next step is to identify shorter-term objectives for each of these goals. Some goals, such as building new educational facilities, involve several years of work. Progress should be planned in no greater than one-year increments, using statements that are detailed regarding expectations and responsibilities. "Objectives" are much more specific and measurable than the goals themselves, as is illustrated below.

Long-Range Goal #1: To establish a day-care center at the church within the next five years.

Year One

The associate pastor will begin assessing the demographic needs related to starting a day-care center that would serve families within a fifteen-mile radius of our church. This study will be presented to the board of elders prior to the end of the next calendar year.

Year Two

The associate pastor will interview the directors of the day-care centers located within fifteen miles of the church to determine what unique contribution our day-care ministry could make. He should look for ways in which our program will meet needs that are not currently being met by existing programs in our local area.

The associate pastor will explore staffing options in the community, neighboring community colleges, and the church itself.

A financial feasibility study will be presented to the finance committee prior to the end of the fiscal year.

Year Three

The church board of elders will appoint a committee to prepare the policies, budget, procedures, structure, and guidelines for a day-care center. This committee will also secure state licensing for the program.

The day-care committee will hire a part-time director and the appropriate number of assistants to staff a program for no more than twenty children between the ages of three and five.

The church will begin the day-care program when all facilities and necessary staff are in place.

Year Four

Upon completion of Long-Range Plan #4 (a new educational building), the church will expand its day-care program to bring the total number to fifty children between the ages of two and five.

When a church matches its long-range goals with a corresponding short-range agenda, that church will be able to determine what progress has been made toward the completion of its master plan. However, to be of any value, the short-term objectives must be clearly measurable and assigned to a specific individual or group. Day-to-day activities of the church should not be sacrificed to short- or long-range planning, but—even in the midst of routine activities—progress can be made toward plans that transcend the immediate cares and concerns of the congregation.

All goals and objectives should be reviewed on a regular basis (annually for goals, and quarterly for objectives). Never be afraid to discard a goal or rewrite an objective that now seems inappropriate. It is better to plan and later change your mind than never to have planned.

Keep in mind that people change, church personnel come and go, board leadership rotates, and the community never remains constant. Changing the plans of the church is not a major sin, but it should be done with careful thought and for good reason.

Implications

Long- and short-range planning facilitates harmony and healthy growth within the body of Christ. By setting clear and measurable standards of achievement, church leaders communicate their expectation that the membership will move in an agreed-upon direction that affirms the mission statement of the church. Well-conceived goal setting should be the basis for documenting an agenda that is specific as to the assignment of responsibilities, thereby minimizing the need for staff and leaders to make day-to-day decisions that might distract from the overall ministry and outreach. It is biblically correct to plan for the future of the church, so long as its representatives seek the counsel of God and others in establishing their objectives. Above all, plans must be flexible enough to allow the Holy Spirit to intervene anywhere along the way.

Questions for Discussion

1. What changes in your church's climate will need to take place before long-range planning can be initiated?
2. Who do you feel should lead the long-range planning process—the senior pastor, the board of elders/deacons, or a special committee? Why?
3. If your church already has a long-range planning document, how long has it been since it was reviewed?
4. What changes do you feel should be made in it at this time?

For Further Reading

Beal, Will. "Planning Through Church Staff Meetings." *Church Administration* 65, no. 2 (Nov. 1988): 29–31.

Dayton, Edward R., and Ted W. Engstrom. *Strategy for Living.* Glendale: Regal Books, 1979.

Hagerty, Donald D. "Directing Everyday Activities Toward Long-Range Goals." *The Christian Ministry* 20, no. 5 (Sept.–Oct. 1989): 11–13.

Hunter, Joel C. "Questioning the Obvious." *Leadership* 7, no. 2 (Spring 1986): 72–75.

Noyce, Gaylord. "Administration as Ministry: Taking the Long View." *The Christian Ministry* 18, no. 2 (Mar. 1987): 13–15.

Ramsden, William E. "Strategic Planning for Growth." *The Clergy Journal* 67, no. 4 (Feb. 1991): 2–3.

Richardson, Marilyn. "How Our Church Benefited from Long-Range Planning." *Church Administration* 32, no. 8 (May 1990): 12–14.

Rush, Myron. *Management: A Biblical Approach.* Wheaton: Victor Books, 1983.

Schaller, Lyle E. "Three Different Planning Models." *The Clergy Journal* 67, no. 6 (April 1991): 34–38.

Resolving Interpersonal Conflict in the Church

esus made it very clear that if there was to be any one characteristic by which the world would recognize us as his disciples, it was to be our profound love for one another (John 13:35). Although this was certainly his ideal for the church, another characteristic is more readily noticeable in the church—conflict! It seems as though lurking in every corner of God's kingdom is an element of strife and discord. Even most of the overseas mission organizations I have visited have personnel who are at odds with other members. Para-church groups in North America, too, have their share of employee stress and strain.

One observer writes, "The cold fact is that churches are made up of imperfect people who are being made perfect. Because of imperfection, a person expects churches to have conflicts among and between people in the congregation."[1] In my survey of pastors and board members, I asked the senior pastors if they involved their board members in the resolution of interpersonal conflicts

156

in the church, and if so, how often. To my surprise, 85 percent of the pastors said that they called on board members in such matters and did so more than half of the time. In other words, anyone serving as a board member in a local church can expect to have to deal with conflict resolution several times during his or her term of service.

The Benefits of Conflict in the Church

Even the most dedicated servants of the kingdom of God do not always agree with each other. Although we are created in the image of God, we still have the nature of imperfect man inside. That is not to say that all conflict is counterproductive and to be avoided. In fact, a certain degree of discord can be beneficial for the church. For example, some disagreements force us to examine established beliefs and traditional methods of doing ministry. In essence, conflict can help us address the need to change and keep abreast of changing trends in our church and community.

Another benefit derived from conflict is that it motivates the sharing of opinions and feelings between people and groups. Some individuals feel too intimidated or embarrassed to speak out under normal circumstances, so their ideas remain suppressed until conflict brings them to the surface. At that point, the long-awaited solution to a particular problem may emerge and be applied with success.

A third benefit of conflict is that it forces the church to provide a procedure for maintaining order and stability. Finally, conflict can act as a prime agent for bringing the congregation together. It can establish lines of communication that never existed before and encourage those who think alike to get together and discuss ideas.[2]

This is not to say that church members should go out looking for reasons to fight and disagree. However, as in a marriage relationship, after a conflict has been resolved, there is an opportunity for some wonderful making up. Eventually loving relationship can be restored and is usually strengthened in the process. As the old adage says, "A relationship that isn't worth fighting for may not be worth staying together for."

Causes of Church Conflict

In the eyes of most pastors and board members, there seem to be as many sources of church conflict as there are people in the congregation. The longer I am in ministry, the more I discover! In speaking with pastors and board members over the years, I have identified a few causes of strife common in most churches: personalities, power plays, perspective, and purpose.

The first cause of conflict in the church is rooted in *personality* differences. I believe it is accurate to say that wherever there are people there will be conflict. Because every person is unique, no two personalities blend together perfectly. Where there is an assortment of personalities seeking to get along, tension is bound to come to the surface eventually. Perhaps one of the best descriptions of church members in conflict is presented by Marshall Shelley in his book *Well-Intentioned Dragons,* where he writes, "Within the church, they are often sincere, well-meaning saints, but they leave ulcers, strained relationships, and hard feelings in their wake. They don't consider themselves difficult people. Often they are pillars of the community—talented, strong personalities, deservingly respected—but for some reason, they undermine the ministry of the church. They are not naturally rebellious or pathological; they are loyal church members, convinced they're serving God, but they wind up doing more harm than good . . . they drive pastors crazy, or out of the church."[3]

Every pastor or board member who has been in ministry for a few years can attach a name and a face to that description of a conflict-producing parishioner. In fact, according to a survey taken by *Leadership,* 80 percent of the pastors who read the publication said they needed help in learning to handle difficult people in their church. Yet, how unfortunate it was that many never received training in conflict resolution while in seminary.[4]

A second source of conflict in the church is the *struggle for power.* When a pastor comes into a new church, he knows that there are some members who have power by virtue of their office and others who have power because of their reputation, wealth, longevity, demeanor, political influence, or ability to intimidate. A wise leader realizes that not all conflicts are over programs, personnel, or the order of worship. Although one of those items may be the topic that starts an argument, many crisis moments are more about whose ideas will prevail.

Church leaders need to remember the wise counsel of Norman Shawchuck, renowned conflict-resolution author, who writes, "The local church is an association of volunteers 'owned' by all the members, and each feels he controls a portion of decision-making power. They do not perceive a single boss sitting at the top from which power and authority originate. Rather, these originate at the grassroots of the entire membership base."[5] It is for this reason that some church members feel confident enough to voice their opposition to the church leadership. In essence, they feel they have as much right to exercise their power as anyone else. The observation of British historian Lord Acton that "power tends to corrupt and absolute power corrupts absolutely" is as true in the church as it is in the secular world.

Conflict in the church can also erupt if its members have too narrow a *perspective* on its ministry. A Pentecostal pastor observes that "self-centeredness and self-sufficiency surface in many forms. The egocentric person, caught up with himself, says 'I am more important than you are.' Egocentricity is not well understood. It's the attitude that surfaces when we're so engrossed in our task, when our ministries so consume our emotional energy, we forget the legitimacy of what others are doing."[6]

In churches where there is a high level of member involvement, it is not uncommon to find this form of conflict. As members invest themselves in various programs, sometimes from the initial birth stage, they develop a sense of parental pride and protection that causes them to lose sight of the overall work of the church. I noticed this narrow perspective in the music minister of a church at which I was once a staff member. This woman truly felt that her Christmas production, which involved a great number of church members, was more important than anything the pastor had planned for the season. Soon she was able to control all the plans and programs for the church throughout both the Christmas and Easter seasons. The music minister gave the orders, and the senior pastor followed. By allowing this to happen, the church, too, lost its perspective!

A fourth type of conflict within a congregation revolves around *purpose*. If the church does not periodically take the time to assess its mission and refocus its philosophy of ministry, the program with the greatest attendance, flashiest promotion, or loudest supporter soon begins to dominate. Like a ship in a windless sea, the church almost imperceptibly begins to lose its bearings and drifts along, following one current after another. This goes unnoticed until something causes the captain and crew to sense their danger and raise an alarm. At that point, crisis management and damage control are assigned top priority, at the expense of all other activities.

All this chaos could have been avoided if the church leaders had regularly checked the progress of the ministry, making any needed planning adjustments that would help the church reach its intended destination. No organization should expect to stay in the same place year after year. Changes in our cultural environment, economic trends, demographics, and countless other forces push us along in life. A church that does not have alert leadership at the helm will find itself merely reacting to these changes instead of proactively planning for them.

Principles of Conflict Resolution

I have deliberately not labeled this section "principles of conflict management." That title would imply that it is possible to control or regulate the course of a conflict, yet those who have experienced its intensity and aftereffects realize that "control" and "management" are hardly descriptive of what happened. Conflict is usually beyond our ability to control. The best we can hope to do is reduce its destructive power, learn from the experience, and try to initiate healing after the battle.

Principle #1. *Realize that conflict in the church is inevitable.* The biblical record is permeated with stories of discord and strife among God's people. Conflict is as old as the Garden of Eden. The Old Testament religious establishment was riddled with factional disputes, and the New Testament church has not done much better. Even a casual glance at the history of Christianity reveals the perennial nature of human conflict.

If, as a church leader, you acknowledge the reality of church conflict, it will not take you by surprise when it occurs. My seminary students are sometimes amazed when I tell them about disagreements that arose at my church the week before. Some of them actually believe that all Christians love each other and can get along harmoniously in the church. I tell them about the conflicts I face as a staff member because I want them to be realistic about ministry. Conflict will come, and there is seldom anything you can do about it except keep it from catching you unprepared.

Principle #2. *When you have been wronged by a fellow believer, always seek a biblical solution.* If you have business experience, you might be tempted to use methods that you were taught in the corporate headquarters of your company—but don't go that route. The church is not an organization; it is an organism. The body of Christ has a different set of procedures it must follow when it comes to conflict resolution. They are found in Matthew 5:22–26 and 18:15–17. In summary, if you honestly believe that you have been unfairly treated, the Bible says you are to go to the person with whom you have the conflict and endeavor to settle your differences in private. If that does not resolve the problem, you should take one or two other individuals with you and confront the person again. If your adversary still refuses to admit any wrongdoing, the matter should be brought before the entire congregation as a matter of corporate discipline. If at that point the person continues to take no responsibility for his or her actions and repent, that person is to be expelled from the fellowship (see Matt. 18:17). This may seem a harsh measure to take, but in the churches where I have served, only once did the process go as far as removing someone from the church roster. I have usually found that the second step is as far as I ever have to go.

Principle #3. *Identify and deal with conflict before it gets out of hand.* Disagreements usually start small and gradually become larger and more destructive. Wise church leaders keep their ears to the ground with a sensitive spirit. This vigilance allows them to recognize a conflict in its embryonic stage, where it can be handled with a minimum amount of miscommunication, emotion, and pain. Generally speaking, the sooner you identify and confront a conflict, the easier it is to resolve.

Principle #4. *Approach the conflict from a Christian perspective.* Problems and conflicts will always arise in ministry, but God expects a Christian world view to determine our response to them. The biblical principles of mutual respect, graceful speech, and submission to the will of God still apply during the storms of life. God is *still* on the throne, Jesus is *still* sovereign, and the Holy Spirit is *still* able to intercede for mankind. Never let the actions of others take control of your emotions. View a problem as an opportunity to learn and grow. I find it helpful to keep asking myself, "What would Jesus do in this situation?" and then try to respond accordingly. If I were to lose my temper with troublemakers in my church and begin to shout and scream, I might win a few arguments, but I will have sacrificed something far more important—my self-respect and integrity, their friendship, and possibly the spiritual gifts they might otherwise have used to serve the congregation.

Principle #5. *Gather the facts.* In the midst of a heated debate, it is often too easy to argue on the basis of emotions, narrowed perspective, and misinformation. Take the time to investigate the conditions surrounding the conflict. This may mean responding to someone who comes to you with a grievance by saying, "Thank you for bringing that to my attention. I will look into the matter and contact you as soon as I have done so." Then make some phone calls, talk to the original sources, and get to the bedrock security of knowing all the facts. You will be surprised at how many times distorted information, miscommunication, and fragmented sources can feed the fire of conflict. Objectivity increases your ability to experience firsthand the words of Jesus: "Blessed are the peacemakers, for they will be called sons of God" (Matt. 5:9). Peacemaking requires the fine art of asking penetrating questions, collecting information, and investigating allegations. Whether you are directly involved in a conflict, or acting as a third-party mediator, it is difficult to bring about a lasting and meaningful resolution without knowledge of the essential facts.

Principle #6. *Be careful what you say during a disagreement.* Words spoken in haste are impossible to retract, and in most cases they will never be forgotten. One can hardly overemphasize the need to exercise wisdom with words when dealing with interpersonal conflict. The right words can develop understanding, diffuse enflamed emotions, and resolve differences.[7] Knowing when to apply the "tourniquet of reasonable and controlled discussion" is an important lesson for any church leader to learn.[8]

Principle #7. *Don't try to cover up a mistake—it only makes the problem worse.* If you, as a church leader, make a mistake that causes hurt feelings, embarrassment, or pain in the life of someone in the congregation, admit it and confront the aftereffects head on. If you run and hide, or pretend it didn't happen, you will only intensify the conflict. The injured party will begin to collect supporters and may eventually undermine your leadership and authority. It is always better to admit a mistake and apologize for it, even when you aren't sure you've been at fault. That way, you give the person you think you have hurt the opportunity to clear the air and discuss what happened. You also reveal your human weakness. A high degree of transparency can be an asset in times of conflict. And, in the words of Solomon, "A gentle answer turns away wrath . . ." (Prov. 15:1).

Principle #8. *Remember that some battles are of a spiritual nature.* The conflict may not be between you and another individual but between you and the forces of darkness. Satan is able to muster support from people you would never suspect! Just moments after Peter had given testimony that Jesus was "the Son of the living God," Jesus rebuked Satan for raising doubts in Peter's mind (Matt. 16:13–23). It is a mistake to see Satan and his army lurking in every disagreement, for not all conflicts are over spiritual matters. However, be alert to the possibility that there is an element of spiritual warfare present in some of the conflicts you will encounter.

Principle #9. *Keep an eternal perspective on the conflict.* While I was serving as executive director of a Christian camp, my staff blind-sided me with a power play to end all power plays. I had to be away from the office on business for two weeks, and halfway through the trip I was called on the phone and told to find another job. I was never given a chance to explain my side of what was essentially a clash of personalities. Hurt, angry, and frustrated by what had happened, I considered leaving the ministry. I felt that if God could let that happen to me, I didn't want a part in serving him any longer. I threw the biggest pity party in North America, but I invited only myself.

Several weeks passed, and I found myself serving in another Christian camp and slowly recovering from my emotional wounds. Through a turn of divine fate, the director of that organization resigned at the end of the summer and I was asked by the governing board to return the following year as executive director. Remembering what had been done to me earlier, I turned it down. Then the Holy Spirit began a work in me, and I eventually accepted the assignment. The next four summers of ministry at that camp were some of the most fruitful years of my ministry. Looking back from a multiyear perspective has shown me that the hand of God really does work in mysterious ways. Though shattered and depressed by the original incident, I have since come to see God's sovereign hand in all the events of my life. I have learned some incredible lessons, which I now pass on to my students when I teach courses in administration and leadership.

Principle #10. *Don't use your authority as a leader to coerce people into compromising their position.* If the people you disagree with truly feel that they are right—and you feel just as strongly about your own views—just "agree to disagree" and move on. Because some arguments are simply not worth causing bloodshed, I have found it wise to carefully consider the issues over which I will "go to the mat." For me, those issues involve interpretation of doctrine and methods of ministry that affect the health and safety of others. Beyond that, I keep an open mind, and if a few people disagree strongly with me about the way something should be done, I usually let them do it their way. If they are wrong, it will come out soon enough. If not, I will gain respect in their eyes for allowing them to do what they felt so strongly about.

Even if the issue is something as critical as adding a new church building, hiring a staff member, or making a major budget allocation, God is able to intervene in the affairs of men and bring to pass what is truly important to him. Let God fight his own battles! You don't have to feel as though you must defend God's plans. He is more than able to do that all by himself. If he wants a building program to move forward and a member of the congregation seems bent on stopping it, stand back and watch the power of

God at work. Pray for God's help and then relax in the faith that his purposes will prevail. Jesus said, "I [not Peter] will build my church" (Matt. 16:18). Ultimately, it's his responsibility, not yours or mine.

In the words of Marshall Shelley, "Failure is not fatal." Even if a conflict causes the worst thing you could possibly imagine (e.g., you get removed from office, the church goes through a split, etc.), remember that there will be other churches in which you can serve, other people who need and want your ministry. Some conflicts hurt a great deal, and only time can heal certain kinds of emotional and spiritual wounds. Perhaps leaving the church to allow the tensions to subside is the best course of action. A. W. Tozer once said he doubted that God could use any man who had not been hurt deeply. If you have been wounded in the service of God, don't despair. You are not the first—and I can assure you that you will not be the last.

Implications

Conflict among Christians dates back to the early days of the church. In fact, the church was on the brink of a serious split after it had been in existence only about twenty years (see Acts 15). Church leaders are called to guide believers through the storms of strife and internal dissension. Without such experiences, the church would have little need of your leadership! Therefore, when conflict comes, and it surely will, gather together the church board(s) and pastoral staff and begin the process of conflict resolution with prayer. If the conflict involves you personally, seek the godly counsel of others who may have a different perspective and less emotional involvement than you do. Be humble enough to admit when you're wrong and be careful what you say. Always remember to keep an eternal perspective on disagreements and let God defend his church. Sounds like simple advice, but as you will soon discover (if you haven't already), resolving interpersonal conflicts in the body of Christ will be one of the hardest things a church leader will ever be called on to do.

Questions for Discussion

1. Can you identify sources of church conflict other than those presented in this chapter?
2. What kinds of interpersonal conflict are the hardest for you to face and resolve?
3. As a board member (or pastor) do you understand and use biblical procedures for resolving conflicts in your church?
4. What lessons have you learned as a result of a church conflict that you have experienced in the past?
5. How can a church board help mediate a conflict between a member of the congregation and the senior pastor?

For Further Reading

Crowell, Rodney. *Musical Pulpits: Clergy and Laypersons Face the Issue of Forced Exits*. Grand Rapids: Baker Book House, 1992.

Jacobsen, Wayne. "7 Reasons for Staff Burnout." *Leadership* 4, no. 2 (Summer 1985): 34–39.

Leas, Speed. "Rooting Out Causes of Conflict." *Leadership* 13, no. 2 (1992): 54–61.

McSwain, Larry. "Conflict Ministry and Forced Termination." *Search* 21, no. 1 (Fall 1990): 22–29.

McSwain, Larry, and William C. Treadwell, Jr. *Conflict Ministry in the Church*. Nashville: Broadman Press, 1981.

McWilliams, Warren. "Christian Ministers as Problem Solvers." *Search* 21, no. 4 (Summer 1990): 22–26.

Manning, Preston. "The Reconciliation of Parties in Conflict: The Theory and Application of a Model of Last Resort." *Crux* 21, no. 1 (Mar. 1985): 10–18.

Mills, Lavelle, and Frank Rachel. "Small-Church Pastors and Interpersonal Relationships." *Search* 20, no. 4 (Summer 1990): 49–53.

Mims, Gene. "Confrontation Without Conflict." *Church Administration* 32, no. 5 (Feb. 1990): 22.

Moore, Christopher W. *The Mediation Process: Practical Strategies for Resolving Conflict*. San Francisco: Jossey-Bass, 1986.

Osborne, Larry W. *The Unity Factor: Getting Your Church Leaders to Work Together.* Waco: *Christianity Today* and Word Books, 1989.

Wise, Robert L. "When Mindsets Collide." *Leadership* 7, no. 4 (Fall 1986): 22–28.

Zimmer, Chip. "The Ministry of Mediation." *Leadership* 7, no. 4 (Summer 1990): 90–96.

Modeling a Biblical Lifestyle

odeling a godly lifestyle in a secular culture has never been easy to do. Down through the ages, there has always been the possibility that pious people will drift away from their love relationship with God, yet will put so much emphasis on their outward religious activity that nobody asks questions about what is going on inside. Because others simply assume that anyone serving diligently in a position of spiritual leadership must be growing in his or her personal walk with the Lord, the temptation to fool people in this way is nothing new.

"Woe to you, teachers of the law and Pharisees"

The Pharisees ranked high in the religious aristocracy of their day. They were laymen who came primarily from the middle class of society: merchants, craftsmen, traders. Once having passed an initial probationary period of about one year, they joined religious communities led by "scribes," who were professional interpreters of the law. Pharisees were so deeply devoted to God that they remained separated from society to ensure their personal piety.[1] To become a member of this elite group of spiritual leaders, one had to have vast quantities of Scripture committed to memory. Pharisees also had to be very consistent in their prayer life. In fact, several times a day they would stop whatever they were doing to pray. Tithing, too, was obligatory—not just tithing on income, but on everything they consumed, including the food they ate.

However, in spite of all their outward religious activity, the Pharisees were the recipients of Jesus' harshest rebukes, condemnations, and reprimands. Probably no other group of people received as much negative press from Jesus as the Pharisees. Jesus never faulted them for their orthodoxy, but for their hardheartedness toward their fellowman. They had put such a heavy emphasis on the law that they had neglected the concerns of the people whom they were commissioned to serve.[2]

The problem with the religion of the Pharisees was that it was all just a show. Their devotion to God amounted to little more than a ritualistic display for the purpose of impressing their fellow Jews. Despite all their scriptural knowledge and religious activities, they knew little about the meaning of true spirituality. They had developed a disciplined lifestyle filled with strict traditions and a rigid legalism that far exceeded the intent of the Old Testament teachings. These men had a superior head knowledge about God, but they lacked any heart response. Somehow, during all those hours of study about God, they had neglected to form a meaningful relationship with him. The Pharisees' faith was professional, not personal.

There are modern-day Pharisees in the church as well. Although certain religious leaders possess a great deal of knowledge about God, and can even quote the fine points of their denomination's traditions and doctrinal distinctions, they do not truly walk with God on a daily basis. They are practicing "churchianity" instead of modeling a personal commitment to the living Christ.

For several years while I was studying in seminary, I lived with a man who was a Christian attorney. I had no doubts as to the spiritual commitment of this friend, for he went to church several times a week, sang in the church choir, and spent time on Bible study at home. But I learned that there was little connection between his professional life and his personal faith. At night we would discuss the events of the day. I would describe some of the things I was researching and he would tell me about some of his cases. The most interesting dialogues took place when we talked about the ethical issues he faced as a defense attorney.

For example, even when he knew that a client was guilty of rape, drug trafficking, or child molestation, he would defend the man in court with tenacious zeal. My friend was an excellent orator, so when he gave a final summation for the defense, the district attorney had better stand back—because this man could really let the jury have it. He was convincing, even to me, though I had been told the client was guilty.

I once asked him, "How can you as a Christian attorney defend a man who has admitted his guilt?" His response nearly floored me. In essence, he told me that what he did in the courtroom had no relation to his personal Christian life. His job was to present the best case possible, regardless of the client's guilt or innocence.

This man had learned over the years to separate his professional activities from his personal faith. The two simply didn't go together. The mere suggestion that they could be harmoniously integrated seemed too unrealistic under our present legal system. I have no doubt that it can be difficult for a Christian to be an attorney. I have several friends who are attorneys, and I have the deepest respect for the ethical dilemmas that they face. However, I believe that unless our personal faith is foundational to everything we say and do, we are letting expediency, not God, rule our lives.

Causes of Spiritual Compartmentalization

To "compartmentalize" is to separate and spread apart. That is what happens when we isolate some aspect of daily life from our Christian commitment and respond to events around us without giving serious thought to biblical imperatives. At some point we are all guilty of this. For example, when someone cuts in front of us on the freeway while we are driving to work, our first response is usually to ventilate rather unedifying descriptors that are punctuated with fists banging on the steering wheel. What have we done? We have allowed a separation to take place between our Christian beliefs (how we know we *should* respond) and our lifestyle (how we actually *do* respond). What I am describing in this chapter is the tendency for people to operate with a spiritual set of values and behaviors on Sunday and an entirely different set the rest of the week. Obviously, this is not what God intended for us. How can we avoid falling into this trap? The answer to that question lies in knowing some of the causes of spiritual compartmentalization:

1. *An overfamiliarity with the things of God.* As a seminary student I had to wrestle with this on a regular basis. I spent many years studying the Word of God at two Bible colleges and three seminaries. My daily diet included courses in systematic and historical theology, Bible doctrines, Old and New Testament interpretation, church history, Greek, Christian ethics, hermeneutics, apologetics, and the philosophy of religion. After years of studying the Bible and everything related to it, I found myself growing spiritually cold. The words of Scripture no longer carried a special meaning as "thus saith the Lord." Rather, they had become an assortment of cold phrases of dissected Greek words, historically descriptive documents, and archival teachings about God. I had grown so overly familiar with the writings of God that I neglected the person of God.

That may also explain the failure of so many television evangelists and other nationally known members of the clergy. In recent years, dozens of pastors (some of whom are my personal friends) have fallen from their ministries as a result of moral or ethical misconduct. In most cases the transgression was not just a one-time yielding to passion or other temptation. Rather, these men continued their immoral behavior for several years, while at the same time they were preaching and teaching Bible truths. Their churches grew and their ministries expanded at a phenomenal rate. Yet, over the years of their ministry, they had gradually compartmentalized their faith. They had become so knowledgeable about God that they forgot to fear and glorify him. The result was a separation between their professional life as church leaders and their personal walk with God.

2. *Pride over one's status as a church leader.* Although it is often stressful to serve as a pastor or church board member, acting in such a capacity will automatically bring you respect and prestige within the fellowship. Scripture commands Christians to respect those who are in authority (Rom. 13:1; Heb. 13:7). As a leader and spiritual guide for the congregation, you will find that people tend to put you on a pedestal. If you aren't careful, you will find yourself taking pride in your special status. Eventually you may come to expect recognition and privilege and resent anyone who does not show you the honor you feel you deserve. The result is a self-glorification far removed from what God intends for the leaders of his church.

3. *Believing your own press.* This is a danger that pastors and seminary professors face every day. Because church members often regard their pastor as some sort of "super-saint" with special abilities and powers, they may boast about the church they attend. Or they continuously quote a theological expert they have just heard at a seminar or Bible conference. They answer Bible questions with "Dr. So-and-So says . . ." or "Pastor You-Know-Who feels that this passage means. . . ." When religious leaders hear this, they may begin to think they really *are* special and somehow different from the average Christian. This attitude has its roots far back in New Testament times. Paul was condemning such attitudes among the believers in Corinth when he wrote: "I appeal to you, brothers, in the name of our Lord Jesus Christ, that all of you agree with one another so that there may be no divisions among you and that you may be perfectly united in mind and thought. My brothers, some from Chloe's household have informed me that there are quarrels among you. What I mean is this: One of you says 'I follow Paul'; another, 'I follow Apollos'; another, 'I follow Cephas [Peter]'; still another, 'I follow Christ' (1 Cor. 1:10–12).

Even pastors are guilty of this kind of prideful boasting. When defending their theological perspective, they may accentuate a point by saying, "I studied under Chafer at Dallas Seminary," or "I took this course under Feinberg at Talbot Seminary," or "When I was a student under Francis Schaeffer at L'Abri, he said. . . ." It isn't just church members who resort to name-dropping!

Boasting about one's teacher or pastor causes arguments, division, and strife in the body of Christ. But it also leads to pride and ego-trips among church leaders. At first we know we aren't special, so we accept praise with humble gratitude. Eventually, because we are human, we begin to believe the talk that tickles our ears and feeds our egos. Take a lesson from the apostle Paul: Don't look for the praise of men (1 Thess. 2:6). It can slowly creep in and cause us to overemphasize our professional ministry at the expense of our personal faith.

4. *An inability to maintain objectivity.* After King David committed adultery with Bathsheba—and subsequently executed her husband, Uriah—Nathan the prophet was sent by God to tell David a story that would trap him. (It has always amazed me that David did not immediately realize that the prophet's parable closely resembled the king's own life.) Caught in God's judgment, David was confronted by his sin with the force of two trains colliding head-on. But Nathan had to *trick* David into confessing, because the king had lost his objectivity.

It may seem incredible to the average Christian that a person like David, who was clearly chosen by God, could willfully commit such a string of failures that he began to lose touch with reality. Reading through the accounts of recently disgraced pastoral leaders indicates this same type of spiritual blindness. Some leaders begin to think that the rules that apply to others do not apply to them, as though their position and accomplishments allow them special privileges and exemptions from the moral commands of God. People who get so immersed in their own world that they lose touch with God's Word and its universal laws have compartmentalized their faith. They then establish rules, procedures, and methods of doing ministry that are based on a distorted concept of reality. However, when their "Nathan" catches up to them, and surely he will, they will be struck with the shocking realization that they have been living and ministering in ways that are far removed from God's standards.

5. *Using religious activities as a substitute for personal spiritual development.* This particular cause of spiritual compartmentalization is a chronic problem among church leaders of all kinds. Sunday school teachers, seminar instructors, Bible-study leaders, pastors,

and anyone else who is sharing in ministry can be guilty of this lapse. It happens, to some extent, because we are all victims of the fast-paced society in which we live. Because we get over-extended, before we know it we don't have time to develop our personal walk with God, and we rationalize that our religious "busyness" is sufficient to meet all our spiritual needs.

Some people are able to allow their preparation for ministry to replace their personal Bible study for a brief period of time. Perhaps an occasional day or two of ignoring our spiritual health can't cause any significant damage, but a steady diet of only professional development will lead to a starved and malnourished personal faith. Neglecting our own spiritual life because of church-related activities is the equivalent of modern-day Pharisaism.

Integrating Personal Faith and Professional Responsibilities

Due to our fallen nature and the culture in which we live, modeling a biblical lifestyle on a consistent basis is a difficult challenge. Those of us who are serving in ministry will face the causes of spiritual compartmentalization far more than the average Christian in the pew. There are, however, some things that we can do to prevent a fragmentation of our convictions. Careful attention to the following renewing influences can help us keep our personal faith connected to our daily routines.

First of all, it is critical that we keep short accounts with God. By that I mean we need to develop such a strong sensitivity to sin that we can easily recognize its presence in our own lives and go immediately to God for forgiveness. Waiting until the end of the week to unload all our contrition at church is not the way to experience the victorious Christian life. As soon as you see sin creeping into your motives, thought life, actions, or attitudes, admit that this is unacceptable to God and ask him for forgiveness. Keeping short accounts with God will prevent you from becoming so used to seeing sin that you fail to respond to it as God has commanded.

Second, recognize the temptation to compartmentalize your faith and to separate it from daily events. Modeling a biblical lifestyle requires consistent attention to the things of God. It is good to read and study his Word, but faith can't end there. As we have already seen, that was the problem with the Pharisees. Their beliefs were not evident in their actions. Compassion, kindness, understanding, and graceful speech must be characteristic of everything we do. Obviously, that isn't easy. If it was, more Christians would be Christ-like on a regular basis. Such an expectation sets a very high ideal, but Scripture demands excellence from those who hold leadership positions in ministry—it comes with the territory.

Third, maintain a personal quiet time that is separate from any of your commitments in the church, whether they be at Sunday school, a men's fellowship, a board meeting, or a home Bible study. Don't let your ministry responsibilities become a substitute for a consistent devotional life. As a pastor, I know how easy it is for this to happen. Some months ago, I noticed that I had slipped into a pattern of neglecting my daily devotions, so now I get up several hours before anyone else in the house (I do *not* like early mornings) and have my personal Bible study and prayer time with the Lord. My professional development takes place when I get to the office or after I get home at night. By separating these two elements in both time and location, I am able to keep myself from sacrificing one for the other—yet both are integrated in my total lifestyle.

Finally, establish an accountability partnership with someone you trust and can meet with on a regular basis. Many pastors and church leaders do this consistently. Your partner-in-faith may be a fellow church board member, a member of the pastoral staff, or perhaps another believer who does not attend your church. Ensured of confidentiality, you can share the issues that are really important to you without concern that they may get back to someone else.

I used to meet with a graduate student each week for breakfast for this reason, and now I meet with several fellow pastors in the area for the same purpose. We talk about such issues as what we are learning in our quiet time, what prayers God has been answering lately, the condition of our thought life, how faithful we are being with our tithe responsibilities, how well we are balancing our family and ministry responsibilities, and personal health concerns. We constantly ask each other questions to check our motives in responding to ministry opportunities.

I once received a phone call from a long-time friend who was then the executive director of a large para-church organization. Sobbing as he spoke, this man was calling to tell me that he had resigned his position because of a moral failure in his life that had just been made public. He kept saying over and over, "Tell your students to keep accountable to someone. I fell because I didn't have anyone who asked me the tough questions. Please, tell them they have to keep accountable." I tell my students that, every chance I get. Accountability is critical to keeping your life on target.

It is sometimes hard to notice yourself spiritually drifting. Like the captain of a ship in the middle of the ocean, if you have no bearing by which to measure your passage, it is not until you are perilously close to the rocks that you notice how far you've come. Some, like my friend, don't realize the danger until it's too late. A trusted advisor who is willing to ask you the tough questions about the quality of your personal faith is a true gift from God. If the questions sting, you may be tempted to lie so you can avoid a confrontation, but church leaders who are willing to model a biblical lifestyle must be willing to accept this difficult challenge.

The Seasons of Faith

Don't confuse spiritual compartmentalization with the changing seasons of spiritual life. Every Christian I have ever spoken with on this topic agrees that there are times when they go through spiritually dry periods. There are times when it may be difficult to maintain a disciplined Bible study or consistent prayer life. Meditation drifts into daydreaming, and tithing seems more than you can bear.

Take hope in the realization that you are not alone. All those who serve in ministry go through these dry spells in their lives. Sometimes this is related to a medical condition that is affecting their blood chemistry or metabolism and causing cycles of moodiness and depression. For such people, a trip to their doctor would confirm and correct the problem. One pastor I know discovered a physiological basis for his periodic doldrums after over twenty years in ministry, and he now takes a small dosage of lithium to correct the problem.

All Christians go through spiritual seasons in their walk with God, much like the changes that take place in the life of a married couple. Marriage begins with the thrill of a joyous ceremony and a honeymoon. After the initial adjustments common to all young couples, the two people eventually settle into a daily routine that sometimes seems rather dull. Children bring a new phase that mixes turbulence with joys, and with this comes the challenge to communicate on a different level and in ever-changing patterns. Once the children have left home and the parents adjust to the empty nest, a new quality in their relationship begins.

In the same way, most Christians experience changes in their relationship with God. Knowing him may have been truly thrilling at the time of our conversion, but then a brief period of adjustment allowed us to settle into a routine of Bible exploration. Through our spiritually young years, most of us studied Scripture as we discovered that Christian growth involved some turbulent trials and testings. Sometimes those challenges caused us to grow cold and distant from God, especially if we failed to understand their purpose in our lives. However, eventually we settle into a renewed intimacy with the Lord as we realize that our anticipated reunion with him draws closer. Seasons are natural in the physical world, and they are natural in the spiritual realm as well.

Perhaps you are experiencing a dark and chilling winter in your own spiritual life. With that transition comes uncertainty about the future and doubts about your spiritual health. That is not the same as growing so cold in your faith that you no longer model or practice what you know you should as a church leader. Nevertheless, the same renewal techniques I suggested in the previous section will rekindle your faith, so that once again you will experience the warmth of spring and more easily model a lifestyle that will bear spiritual fruit in due season.

Implications

Modeling the Christian life has never been easy, and I doubt that it ever will be. God never promises a free ride in life at the point of conversion. In fact, if anything, he promises hardships and suffering. Christian leaders can expect even more adversity than the average believer, because not only must we persevere during the maturation of our faith, as God has purposed (James 1:2–3), but also Satan will continually try to discourage us from being the leaders that God has called us to be. The more spiritual responsibility you assume, the greater will be the attacks from Satan. He wants to tear you down and disrupt your Christian walk, for he knows that if he can destroy your personal faith, he can probably bring others down with you. The example of a failed and defeated leader often influences others to give up as well.

For this reason, as leaders in your church, you must covenant to pray for one another. Pray for each other's spiritual health, that it might be pure and growing. Pray that you are able to model a biblical lifestyle that is distinctive and will attract the nonbelievers around you. Pray for each other's families and for the strength to live out your faith at home, perhaps the most difficult challenge of all. Establish accountability groups among yourselves or with other believers whom you trust and respect. Be willing to ask and answer the difficult questions that keep you spiritually in tune. My prayer as I write this book is that your lives will make a difference in our world and that you "guard against the yeast of the Pharisees" (Matt. 16:6).

Questions for Discussion

1. What examples of modern-day Pharisaism do you see in the North American church today?
2. In what areas do you find it difficult to maintain a consistency between your personal faith and your professional responsibilities?
3. In what ways do you find yourself compartmentalizing your faith?
4. Other than those listed in this chapter, can you identify some causes of spiritual compartmentalization?
5. What are some of the ways that you are able to keep your faith alive and growing?

6. Would you be willing to begin an accountability partnership on a trial basis for a few months? Who would you choose as a partner?
7. What spiritual season do you find yourself in at this time?

For Further Reading

Barnett, Jake. *Wealth and Wisdom*. Colorado Springs: NavPress, 1987.

Borthwick, Paul. *Leading the Way*. Colorado Springs: NavPress, 1989.

Briscoe, Stuart. *David: A Heart for God*. Wheaton: Victor Books, 1988.

Campolo, Anthony, Jr. *The Power Delusion*. Wheaton: Victor Books, 1983.

Engstrom, Ted. *Integrity*. Waco: Word, Inc., 1987.

MacDonald, Gordon. *Facing Turbulent Times*. Wheaton: Victor Books, 1981.

Rush, Myron. *The New Leader*. Wheaton: Victor Books, 1987.

Sanders, J. Oswald. *Spiritual Leadership*. Chicago: Moody Press, 1980.

MacDonald, Gordon. *Ordering Your Private World*. Nashville: Thomas Nelson, 1985.

Part *Three*

Leading During Crisis Periods of Ministry

Financial Storms in the Church

*T*he need for responsible financial stewardship in the church has never been more obvious than in the past decade. Several para-church organizations have recently come under scrutiny by governmental regulatory bodies and even by the donors themselves. Struck by what is perceived to be unethical (and nonbiblical) methods of managing finances, federal and state agencies, church members, and denominational authorities are closely monitoring how ministries are managing their money.

It isn't just the widely publicized television ministries that are losing their credibility with the American public. Many established churches are in jeopardy of losing the support of their members because of mismanagement of tithes and offerings. Once this takes place in a church, severe consequences usually follow. Ministers lose their jobs, board members suffer public humiliation, and parishioners leave the church in disillusionment. Tightening the standards by which the Lord's financial resources are used in our churches is long overdue.

What is most disappointing about all this is that, in most cases, corrective measures do not require major changes in the way finances are being handled. Many churches simply need a little guidance about their bookkeeping practices, accounting procedures, and/or methods of reporting. It is my hope that every church board member (and, of course, every pastor) will watch this area of responsibility with sharp eyes and a discerning spirit. The credibility of your ministry, and that of the church you serve, depends on your vigilance in this regard. Let's face it, credibility in ministry is not something that is automatically achieved. It must be earned. In fact, you earn it each week by the way you responsibly handle the church's resources. Although it may take several years to establish a high level of credibility for your church, you can lose it overnight.

The contents of the average collection plate have changed drastically over the years. A hundred years ago, it was not unusual for a church member to drop in a watch or some other piece of jewelry. Fifty years ago, the church offering consisted mainly of paper currency and change. Today, the offering is primarily in the form of checks, drawn on local bank accounts. Although the method of giving has changed over the years, the gift still represents a significant transaction between a person and God. In this, the offering has not changed.[1]

This chapter will focus on the crucial role that the church board plays in the stewardship of our God-given financial resources. Mismanagement of funds can seriously disrupt the life of the church. Examples of irresponsible financial practices include wasteful use of money, spending church finances on nonbudgeted items, misappropriation of funds (embezzlement), inaccurate bookkeeping, not paying payroll taxes on time, failing to pay workmen's compensation for nonpastoral staff employees, and unethical fundraising techniques. Any of these issues can create a financial storm in the church, leaving in its path a tremendous destruction of morale, confidence, and respect.

Preventing Financial Mismanagement

Most of the financial storms that can occur in a church are avoidable. A little common sense and a few standard accounting procedures will eliminate a great deal of the pressure in this regard.

The following suggestions should assist church board members in their efforts to be wise and faithful stewards of God's resources.

Suggestion #1. The first step in managing the church's finances is to create a realistic and accurate budget. Until quite recently, few pastors were taught in seminary about how to create a church budget or even how to read one. This is one area where a lay leader can provide some valuable insights and make a significant contribution to the day-to-day operation of the church.

Simply defined, a budget is an itemized statement of expected spending. It translates goals into financial terms by estimating the resources needed by the pastoral staff and lay leaders to maintain and expand their ministries in the coming year. All department heads should have the opportunity to contribute to the formation of the budget within their own areas of responsibility. If a church board member is ultimately accountable for expenditures in a given area, he or she should have the authority to stipulate the budgeting in that area. The person who spends the funds should be the one who says what is needed.

A budget should be a fairly accurate statement of where the monies will be spent, but many churches fall into trouble in this regard. As the end of the fiscal year draws near, it is not uncommon for some budget accounts to be fully spent. Rather than overspend on a given line item, some church leaders simply make the purchase and shift the expenditure to a different line item that still has funds available—on the mistaken assumption that a line item that is "overspent" represents financial mismanagement. However, when a budget is prepared, it is based on both known facts and projected trends. If the predicted patterns change, the expenditures must reflect these changes. At some point, there may be more funds needed in one area and a surplus in another. The correct way to handle such a situation is to go ahead and overspend on a particular item so that you have an accurate measure of what was actually needed. Then, the next time the budget is written, you will be able to make the necessary adjustments in the allocation of funds. Shifting expenditures to other accounts may make the budget look better to the inexperienced eye, but it is not an honest way to manage church finances.

A budget also protects the church staff and board against being charged with misdirection of funds for private purposes. In other words, if all the planned expenditures of the church are clearly stated in writing in advance, and if this budget is followed, the opportunity for inadvertent or deliberate misappropriation is greatly reduced.[2]

Suggestion #2. Review the budget monthly and make necessary revisions. Some churches where I have served on staff evaluated their budget only on a quarterly basis. They might have saved paper and staff hours, but in the long run they created the potential for financial storms. (It did little good for me to know in July that I overspent my budget for classroom supplies in April.) All those responsible for managing a budgeted item must be kept informed on a monthly basis as to the condition of their accounts. If spending is examined regularly, inappropriate practices can be spotted and problems handled *before* they arise.

Suggestion #3. Regulate church finances according to known patterns of income. Most churches do not maintain large bank accounts of contingency reserves, which means they must manage their finances on a cash-flow basis. Donation levels vary according to the time of year. For example, Christmas and Easter are usually the best periods for receiving tithes and offerings, whereas the summer, when people are on vacation, is often the worst season in terms of church income. This means that some expenditures may have to be shifted to months when money is more plentiful. Obviously, congregations should not plan on purchasing a major item like a church van in September—after three months of financial drought—unless they have saved up for it in advance.

One church at which I served used a graph to chart the historical pattern of giving. Once income trends were established, the information was used to determine the best months for making major purchases. Barring any unforeseen changes in income, the church board could realistically plan for capital expenditures.

Suggestion #4. Establish an accounting system that is user-friendly. Let's face it, most people who look at the church budget do not have a degree in accounting or finance. Therefore, if a budget is to be of value to them, it must be something they can understand. It should be:

Easy to understand by the average person

Concise, so as not to bury the reader in obscure detail

All-inclusive of the activities of the church

Able to provide comparisons of the current month with the annual budget, the year-to-date expenditures, and perhaps the previous year's expenditures

Prepared and distributed on a timely basis

Footnoted to explain any important information that is not self-explanatory

Suggestion #5. Have the financial records of the church audited on a regular basis. This audit will provide an accurate assessment of the church's current financial health and indicate any changes in fiscal procedures that the accountant feels should be made. Not all audits are the same, however, so knowing which type of audit you want (or need) is important. A "partial audit" is conducted when the budget sheets are examined to determine the accuracy of the figures. The accountant decides whether there are any mistakes in the reported calculations and provides advice on the basis by which the statistics are formulated. An "external audit" is more comprehensive in nature and requires the accountant to review all the receipts for expenditures and the records of income, and also to calculate church assets and depreciation of resources. This type of audit usually takes several weeks to develop. For the average church, it is usually not needed on an annual basis unless the financial procedures have been radically altered since the previous audit. I generally recommend that a comprehensive external audit be conducted about every four or five years, even though the IRS does not require this for most churches.

The Church Audit

Since the matter of a church audit is so important, it warrants further discussion. Having an independent accountant examine the church's financial records can save the church a great deal of stress and regret. The cost is not prohibitive and well worth the investment.

As already mentioned, the average church should have an external audit conducted every few years. This usually involves having a Certified Public Accountant (C.P.A.) come to the church to review all the church's financial records. However, if the books and files are not too extensive, it may be feasible for a church representative to bring the records to the accountant's office.

A professional auditor knows how to review and assess the financial condition of an organization and is able to draw a conclusion about the accuracy of its records. This person is trained to use commonly accepted accounting principles and auditing standards. Once completed, the auditor's report provides an accurate statement of assets and liabilities. With this document, the church can gain credibility in the eyes of the congregation who observes its operation. The report also has a more practical application, since it provides banks, bond companies, and other potential creditors with a better opportunity to interpret and assess the financial condition of the church.[3] In fact, if your church is about to apply for a loan, don't be surprised if an external audit is required. Banks and other lending agencies are often hesitant to lend money to a church, since it is nearly impossible to collect on a defaulted loan made to a religious institution. An audit is a way of determining the church's ability to repay the loan.

Some church governing boards, realizing the value of a financial audit, have established an auditing committee. A member of the congregation who is a qualified C.P.A. is often willing to serve as chairman of such a group. Other parishioners who could make a significant contribution to the committee would be bankers, bookkeepers, and business executives. These people could serve as a temporary task force at the beginning of the fiscal year to review the previous year's financial records. The committee members could also keep the congregation informed about important financial issues in the church. Their conclusions might seem more credible than the opinion of a member of the pastoral staff or church board, since there is no obvious conflict of interest involved. Current auditing standards require that certain matters related to the conduct of the audit be clearly communicated to those who have the responsibility for the financial reporting process. A church auditing committee can usually serve in this capacity.[4]

One of the most helpful products of an external audit (sometimes referred to as a formal audit) is the auditor's "management letter," which is typically submitted with every report. This document provides the organization's leaders with guidance as to how they can better manage the finances for which they are responsible. Procedures that are not common knowledge to the entire board can be brought out into the open for discussion.

When I was directing a certain para-church organization, we once had an external audit conducted on our books. The accountant discovered that our secretary was keeping all the organization's financial records in the trunk of her car. If her car had been stolen, lost, or destroyed in an accident, those books and files, including all our donation records, would have been gone. Needless to say, this came as quite a shock to the board members, and they immediately had procedures drawn up to correct the problem. Our auditor possibly saved us countless hours of work, embarrassment, and expense with that one simple discovery. That revelation alone was worth the price of the audit!

Professional Fund-Raising and the Church

The use of professionals to raise church revenues for such special purposes as eliminating church debt, building a new sanctuary, or making capital improvements, has been an increasingly controversial subject in recent years. It has also been the cause of financial storms in some local churches. Many church members object to the rather heavy-handed methods used by professional fund-raisers, but some churches have found this an effective way to further their long-term objectives. There seems to be no clear biblical precedent for this practice. To present as unbiased an overview as possible, I will detail several of the more common pros and cons of using professional fund-raisers in a church setting.

Disadvantages of Using Professional Fund-Raisers

The first argument against using professional fund-raisers in the church centers around the lack of biblical evidence for doing so. One does not have to look far in Scripture to find people who made generous contributions to fulfill God's purposes without being pressured! For example, in the building of the tabernacle in the wilderness, the Israelites were expected to give voluntarily (Exod. 25:2). In fact, they had such a desire to give that they actually had to be restrained from giving too much (Exod. 36:6). When the heart of the people is right with God, he is able to motivate them to provide whatever is needed for his church.

Likewise, Scripture tells us that when King David began to make preparations to build the temple, the people got involved in giving as soon as they heard that David was storing resources for the task. Following David's example, the people of God responded in kind: "Then the leaders of families, the officers of the tribes of Israel, the commanders of thousands and commanders of hundreds, and the officials in charge of the king's work gave willingly" (1 Chron. 29:6).

Generous giving is seen in Scripture as an indication of spiritual maturity. People who are strong in their faith will not have to be bombarded with professional appeals for money. Because they know that all their resources come from God's hand, a simple telling of a need is sufficient to prompt their giving. Anything more than that becomes manipulative and coercive.

Luther Powell, in his book *Money and the Church,* writes, "There is something lacking in the spiritual life of the church when secular professional money-raisers have to be employed. One's giving should be a manifestation of his faith, and it seems to be a reflection on the church that the faith it proclaims has not produced the necessary funds for maintaining and extending her program."[5]

A second disadvantage to using outside fund-raisers is that the cost of their services adds to the overall amount that must be raised. These people do not work for free. No matter how dedicated they may be to furthering God's work, they have to meet their operating expenses as well. Some fund-raising organizations charge a modest fee, e.g., just enough to meet their promotional costs and the salaries of those involved in the consulting process. However, others are more profit-oriented and charge an astronomical amount for their services.

There are generally two means of payment for these services. Some organizations set a flat fee, based on the amount of money they are expected to raise. The other approach is to charge a percentage of the amount raised. When the percentage is small, perhaps 1 or 2 percent, it may not appear to impact the fund-raising program. However, when that figure reaches double digits, as it often does, a significant added financial burden is placed on the congregation.

Finally, professional fund-raisers usually employ high-pressure sales and marketing techniques that come straight out of the business world. Most people agree in theory that anyone who raises money for the kingdom of God should not resort to such methods, but "hard sell" has been proven to work. Just ask any car salesman, and he will attest to its success.

Speaking about the danger of using secular methods for biblical ends, Carl F. H. Henry, a leading evangelical theologian writes, "Evangelical ministries need constantly to investigate this dependency on the philosophy of secular professionals. It is understandable that some evangelical administrators readily enlist the expertise of secular fund-raisers and investment agencies. But this practice brings with it great risks. Promotion built on philosophies of the secular world must always be carefully scrutinized; Madison Avenue's most successful commercials, it is said, are those which stretch truth but do it subtly. In transferring financial activities to professional managers, administrators may unwittingly lose control of an organization's destiny."[6]

These professionals will train your stewardship committee in the art of "closing the deal" by teaching them certain phrases to use, such as: "So how much can I put you down for?" and "Are you willing to demonstrate your faith in God by making a pledge to your church's building campaign tonight?" Such phrases imply that a person is unspiritual if he or she does not immediately make a sizable monetary commitment. It is not at all unusual for parishioners to leave a church because of the pressure placed on them by professional fund-raisers. Because a financial pledge represents a decision made between one individual and God, the gift should be anonymous unless the person chooses to reveal it to others.[7]

192

Advantages of Using Professional Fund-Raisers

The disadvantages listed above are but a few of the reasons why some people consider the use of professional fund-raisers an inappropriate way for the body of Christ to meet its financial needs. However, there are some compelling practical reasons why a particular church might choose to go this route.

First, something as important as raising money for God's work requires professional consultation and guidance. An effective fund-raising campaign appears deceptively easy to an untrained observer. As with so many other professions, it may be done so smoothly that it looks like anyone could do it. However, nothing could be farther from the truth. For example, knowing how much a church can realistically raise without jeopardizing its existing programs, staff, and morale is one important consideration. Professionals know how to calculate such equations with care and accuracy. After all, what good does it do to raise the money if the church is destroyed in the process?

Professional fund-raisers are just that—*professionals*. They understand the best way to approach people when it comes to the delicate subject of stewardship. They understand the issue of a church's cash flow and know how long a fund drive should last. They know what time of the year is best to introduce the campaign and how many leaders should be employed to make it successful. They will train the volunteer workers to keep consistent and accurate records. They also have experience in which techniques will work and which will not. In short, they can help the church avoid a great many pitfalls along the way.

Second, using professional fund-raisers avoids placing an added burden on the church staff. Raising a large amount of money is emotionally and physically draining. The stress of having to show even weekly progress toward the goal can be overwhelming, but a successful campaign has to be managed on a *daily* basis. Constant monitoring is needed to be sure that all the many details are ready when needed. Important practicalities such as advance publicity, promotional materials, banquet preparations, training materials, selection of sermon topics, and scheduling of testimonies have to be planned far in advance and evaluated along the way.

Forgetting one item can have long-term repercussions in the life of the campaign. Obviously, someone has to be responsible—and ultimately accountable—for the entire process.

If a church chooses not to enlist the services of a professional fund-raiser, its pastor must then assume additional duties. Even if a lay leader or associate pastor is assigned the primary leadership role in the funding campaign, the senior pastor will still have to take on more responsibilities than if a team of professionals had been enlisted. It is no wonder that so many senior pastors resign during or shortly after a building campaign has taken place in their church! Adding the demands of a funding program to the daily pressures of pastoral responsibilities has destroyed many a pastor's ministry. When a church considers the cost of replacing its senior pastor as a possible consequence of their fund-raising campaign, the fee that a professional organization charges may seem quite small in comparison.

A third practical advantage to using professional fund-raisers is that it adds to the credibility of the project within the congregation. Church members are smart enough to realize that their senior pastor is probably not trained in the techniques of raising large sums of money. Therefore, bringing in a team of professionals for so important a goal establishes confidence on the part of the people.

Professional fund-raisers have sometimes been compared to commissioned sales agents. The average person does not see all that happens behind the scenes to make a transaction successful. For example, homeowners who try to sell their property by themselves will quickly discover just how involved the process is. The art of raising large amounts of money in a short amount of time requires finely tuned skills. Fund-raising may appear to the uninitiated to be a simple task of advertising the need. But once they have had a glimpse of all the steps involved, they will quickly admit to its complexity.

I have served on staff in churches that have employed professional fund-raisers and also in churches that preferred to raise the money on their own. Both were pleased with the results. Under the guidance of its leaders, a church must consider all the factors involved and make its own decision as to how best to reach its financial goals.

Implications

Marriage counselors tell us that financial storms are one of the leading causes of divorce, and there is little doubt that the inability to agree on methods of managing money shatters countless families. Likewise, the lack of clear-cut policies for financial management in a local church can be extremely disruptive. It can even cause pastors to leave and congregations to split. A significant degree of wisdom and humility is needed to manage church finances in such a way as to satisfy the pastoral staff, the lay leadership, and the members of the congregation. Since those responsible for handling church monies are stewards of God's resources, their decisions must be based on biblical principles and the goals of the ministry.

It is your responsibility as a church leader to work with the various parties involved and remain above reproach in the way you manage the finances of the church. Few aspects of your office will affect the lives of so many people as the allocation and distribution of church funds.

Questions for Discussion

1. What financial storm(s) have you seen in church ministry?
2. Which of the suggestions presented in this chapter would have prevented the storm from erupting?
3. Which area should be focused on to make the financial management at your church more effective? What recommendations would you make?
4. How and by whom should these recommendations be implemented?
5. How long has it been since your church conducted an external audit?
6. Do you feel one is needed at this time?
7. What is your view regarding the use of professionals to raise money in your church?

For Further Reading

"Accountability in Fund-Raising." *Christianity Today*, 4 April 1979, 10.

Bassett, William, and Huizing, Peter. *The Finances of the Church*. New York: Seabury, 1979.

Colson, Chuck. "Chuck Colson Interview: Speaking Out on Fund-Raising Heresy." *Christian Advertising Forum*, April–May 1983, 321.

Dulaney, William. "Financial Accounting for Non-Profit Organizations." *Fund-Raising Management* 16 (Dec. 1985): 18–22.

Evangelical Council for Financial Accountability. "ECFA's Seven Standards of Responsible Stewardship." Washington D.C.: Evangelical Council of Financial Accountability, 1987.

Frame, Randall L. "Trying to Tighten the Belt of Financial Accountability." *Christianity Today*, 20 Nov. 1987, 48–50.

Hale, Ashley. "The Lost Art of Church Fund-Raising." *Church Management—The Clergy Journal* 66, no. 3 (Jan. 1990): 10.

McKenna, David L. "Financing the Great Commission." *Christianity Today*, 15 May 1987, 26–31.

Virts, Paul H. "Public Perceptions of Christian Fund-Raising Ethics." *Fund-Raising Management* 18 (July 1987): 36–46.

Walker, Joe W. *Money in the Church*. Nashville: Abingdon, 1982.

Wilmer, Wesley K. "Seeking a Godly Perspective for Fund-Raisers." *Fundraising Management* 18 (July 1987): 60–65.

_____. *Money for Ministries*. Wheaton: Victor Books, 1989.

The Empty Pulpit

eing without a senior pastor can be one of the most stressful experiences in the life of a local church. It seems as though every member of the congregation has the prescription for the perfect pastor and is eager to see progress made in the selection of such a person. However, the time spent without a pastor does not have to be merely a period of tedious searching. It can also be seen as an opportunity for the church to reassess its ministry direction. In fact, it is not unusual for a church to experience consistent growth during the absence of the senior pastor, especially if there was significant tension in the church just prior to his departure.

Stop-Gap Measures

How the church leadership puts together its strategy for filling the empty pulpit is critical to establishing confidence on the part of the membership. The entire congregation needs to know that someone or some group is in charge and that systematic progress will take place in selecting a new pastor. Although a search plan should be formulated as soon as possible after the resignation of a senior pastor, several preparatory steps should be taken by the governing board of the church.

When a pastor leaves a church, its leaders will first have to confront the variety of emotions that will circulate throughout the congregation. Regardless of what precipitated the resignation, there will be a degree of shock, disappointment, and anger, especially if the pastor had been well liked by most of the members. Even under the best of circumstances, some people will be pleased he is leaving! As hidden tensions surface, members who previously remained silent will now speak their mind. As a board member, you may hear such comments as: "I didn't think he would stay long," "He never really fit in that well," and "I saw it coming but didn't say anything." It is advisable to encourage all members to ventilate their feelings in an appropriate manner. Otherwise, they may surface at a less opportune time. In fact, feedback from the congregation—whether positive or negative—will help you establish guidelines as to what kind of new pastor your church really needs.

The lay leaders of the church should next try to meet with the outgoing pastor and gather his input regarding a number of areas: staff competence and work assignments, decisions that cannot wait for the next pastor, existing pastoral commitments that must be met, and the real reason the pastor is leaving, if it is not already known.

The third step is to select a pastoral search committee in accordance with the church's constitution and bylaws. Churches have different procedures, but it is usually advantageous for this committee to include representatives from the various church boards, continuing professional staff, the congregation at large, and perhaps the denominational body.

Meanwhile, a strategy for interim pulpit supply should be established without delay. There are two common approaches to handling this. The first is to locate a qualified person who is willing to fill the pulpit indefinitely—that is, until a permanent replacement has been selected. This temporary pastor might also agree to provide such related services as hospital visitation, staff supervision, and counseling. The main advantage of this arrangement is that it maintains a semblance of order and stability. Fewer items of church business will drop through the cracks, and the pastoral staff will continue to have a degree of accountability. As a result, the church can focus on finding a new pastor with a minimum of distractions. However, as comforting as it is to know who will be in the pulpit each Sunday during the transition period, there are certain disadvantages to using this approach. For one thing, there is always the possibility that the interim pastor will begin to see his position as "official" (or permanent) and therefore try to meddle in the business matters and long-term objectives of the church. In addition, after only a brief period of involvement in the church's ministry, he could become too generous with his "advice" to staff and board members. He might even attempt to influence the search process. Finally, this arrangement can be rather costly, since it often involves drawing up a formal employment contract and including certain fringe benefits. This is seldom necessary when a substitute pastor agrees to serve only once in a while or for a short length of time.

The second way to handle pulpit supply would be to rotate interim pastors on a weekly or monthly basis. As mentioned above, the total cost of acquiring a succession of short-term replacements will probably be far less than arranging for one temporary pastor to serve indefinitely (and such a person may be very hard to find). In addition, it can be very edifying for a congregation to hear different preaching styles and be exposed to a broad range of pastoral insights. On the other hand, the teaching will have little continuity, since one Sunday's preacher will not necessarily know the content of the previous weeks' messages. Another disadvantage to pastoral rotation is that someone else will have to follow up on church business during the week. Sometimes a competent church secretary can do most of this. However, especially if the secretary is not a full-time employee, another person must coordinate the programs and financial affairs of the church. Finally, since each interim pastor will probably bring his best message to the pulpit, a certain level of unrealistic expectations can develop within the membership. As the congregation becomes accustomed to brilliant preaching, it will begin to expect a steady diet of excellence from its next senior pastor, a requirement that can rarely be fulfilled by any one person.

The advantages and disadvantages of either approach must be carefully weighed and an initial decision made about the direction to take. Some churches begin with rotating pastors and then change to a one-person interim assignment if the search process takes longer than anticipated. There is no right or wrong way to handle this. You must do what seems best for your church and give yourself the freedom to change the approach if it doesn't meet your needs.

Search Committee Guidelines

After serving on or consulting with search committees for a number of years, I have learned a few commonsense do's and don'ts. Here are a few of the most important considerations:

Do's

1. *Do pray continually!* Seek God's guidance before each committee meeting and whenever the congregation gathers together. Every step along the way must be bathed in prayer. Choosing a spiritual leader is one of the most important decisions your church will ever make!

2. *Do keep search details confidential.* Information about candidates—and communication with them—must be considered "top secret." The search committee has the power to do severe damage to a candidate if information regarding his qualifications and availability (or lack thereof) is not handled appropriately. Committee members who do not agree to absolute confidentiality about their preliminary findings should be asked to remove themselves from the search process.

3. *Do keep church leaders informed.* All those in the church who have a "need to know" must be kept apprised of progress. This may take the form of periodic reports made by the search committee to the chairman of the elder and/or deacon board.

4. *Do let the congregation know what headway is being made.* The entire membership should receive an update every couple of months as evidence that the process is in motion. It can be very

frustrating for a congregation to go more than two months without any communication from the search committee. If the committee has no specific information to report, a general announcement that "the committee continues to meet on a regular basis and candidate applications are being given consideration" would be sufficient.

Don'ts

1. *Don't be in a hurry.* Some committee members will be tempted to hurry the process, especially if they have been at it for a year or more. Many people who are new to the process of finding a senior pastor enter the experience with an expectation that they can have it all wrapped up in a few short weeks, perhaps three months at the longest. That simply isn't realistic. Each of the various steps outlined in the next section is essential and requires time to complete. Any shortcut taken along the way brings with it the possibility of making a poor selection. Learn this important lesson now: It is far better to take a little longer and find the right person than to select the wrong person in a hurry and have to live with the consequences of that hasty decision for a long time.

2. *Don't fail to take advantage of this strategic period of transition.* This is an opportune time for your church to reassess its goals, make needed budgetary changes, and refocus its ministry direction.

3. *Don't remove other staff members unless circumstances warrant such action.* Except in the case of someone who is causing dissension, avoid dismissing pastoral staff during this time. To do so implies that there was something more going on behind the scenes than what the pastor communicated in his letter of resignation. This, in turn, may create an atmosphere of panic within the church membership. If a staff member's removal seems necessary, it usually is better to delay this decision until it can be discussed with the newly selected senior pastor.

3. *Don't publicize the previous pastor's shortcomings.* It may be tempting for a church to discredit its former pastor. Especially if members believe that the pastor left because he expected something more attractive elsewhere, they will feel hurt and rejected. Bad-mouthing him may help lessen the sting of disappointment, but such criticism is clearly not biblical, even if it seems justified.

The Step-by-Step Search Process

Once the search committee is formed, an orderly progression through the following steps will reassure the congregation that well-qualified candidates will be identified and that the final selection will be appropriate to the needs of the church. (Obviously, the church's constitution, denominational procedures, or board guidelines may require altering some of these steps.)

Step One. Prepare a church-and-community profile. Since you called your last pastor, your church and the surrounding community have undoubtedly changed. Therefore, it is essential for the pastoral search committee to examine the current demographic conditions. Consult the local chamber of commerce for updated statistics about the area's population. Also survey the demographics within the congregation (age distribution, marital status, ethnic composition). Prepare a report that summarizes all this information and then distribute copies to the church board(s) and staff members for their review and critique. Since this document will eventually be sent to prospective pastoral candidates as well, it should include a copy of the church's mission statement, history, constitution, bylaws, policies, procedures, and previous year's budget.

Step Two. Conduct a congregational survey. While the search committee is reviewing demographic trends within the church and community, a congregational survey should be conducted to gather input from members regarding their vision for the church. Extreme patience will be required of the committee during this time! Most people will have an opinion and try to have their ideas heard above the rest. An open forum might be used, but I have found that a written survey works better, since it allows each member equal representation.

The survey's primary purpose is to explore the membership's criteria for a new senior pastor. Issues such as level of education, gender, ethnic background, experience, and family life should be examined. Don't be afraid to ask hard questions. It is better to get any prejudices out in the open now than to begin dealing with them once a candidate is being seriously considered by the committee. Obviously, not everyone's wishes can be incorporated into a list of pastoral qualifications. However, just by conducting the survey, you let the members know that you care about their concerns. Later, you will be able to communicate to the candidates that you know precisely what you are looking for!

The most fatal mistake a search committee can make is to begin seeking candidates before both the community profile and the congregational survey have been completed. It may take several months to tabulate and analyze this material, but efforts spent on these activities will help narrow the search and shorten the overall time required.

Step Three. Review and update the job description for "senior pastor." Demographic and staffing changes over the past few years may suggest a reassessment of which qualifications and responsibilities will be required of this person. This revision should also reflect the information gathered from the congregational survey. (The church's board should be involved in this process, since they carry the responsibility of working with the pastor once one is hired.)

Step Four. Advertise the vacancy through existing channels. Because the most common way to publicize a pastoral opening is by word-of-mouth, the search committee will probably start receiving résumés from potential candidates long before the position is officially advertised. If so, no attempt should be made to screen the applications until the first two steps in the search process have been completed.

There are a number of other advertising sources available. For example, because most seminaries have placement offices to help a church find suitable candidates, they should be notified of the opening, especially if a younger pastor might be considered. Denominational representatives should also be informed about the vacancy. The church might want to consider broadening its search by placing ads in Christian magazines, journals and/or newsletters. Additional sources of publicity include other local pastors, denominational workers, conference leaders, and seminary professors who attend your church.

Step Five. Investigate all leads to possible candidates. Don't assume that the appropriate pastor for your church is already looking for a new job. In fact, the most eager applicant may be run-

ning from a problem of his own making! Many search committees make the mistake of concentrating on pastors who want to
change congregations, yet one can never predict how or when
God may prompt a pastor to make a move. The Spirit of God does
indeed work in mysterious ways.

Welcome pastoral referrals from every available source. Then
contact these people and determine if they might consider making a change. Ask any interested pastor to send the search committee a résumé for consideration. Many churches also request
an audio or video tape of a recent message, a list of references to
contact (in confidence), and a document stating the pastor's doctrinal position and philosophy of ministry.

At this time you should provide potential candidates with a
copy of the church-and-community study (Step One) as well as a
summary of the congregational survey (Step Two). Each candidate will thereby have the opportunity to get acquainted with the
church and can decide on that basis whether to proceed with the
process or back out *before* the time and energy of the search committee is invested.

Once a candidate has agreed to proceed and has given permission to contact his references, a written log of those communi-
cations should be maintained. Obviously, a candidate is going to
provide his most favorable references, so I prefer to dig a little
deeper and get secondary references as well.

Step Six. Evaluate all candidates' qualifications. Before long, the
search committee will have a file full of résumés. At this point its
members will need to compare their list of requirements with the
specifics mentioned in each application. Candidates eliminated
from consideration should immediately be sent a letter notifying
them of that decision. A candidate would much rather get a prompt
letter of rejection than have to wait for several months wonder-
ing where he stands.

The search process should continue until the committee members feel they have enough suitable applicants. The committee
will then narrow the field to a "short list" of three to four candidates, ranked according to preference.

Step Seven. Make informal contact with the most promising
applicants. First, speak with the top candidates to determine their

current level of interest. One or more of these pastors may no longer want to make a move. It is important to deal with only one candidate at a time, especially if working through denominational headquarters. Confidentiality will help prevent hard feelings among those who are later rejected.

After informal discussions with the most promising candidates and further review of their qualifications, it is likely that all but one of them will be eliminated from consideration. If at all possible, committee representatives should visit this candidate's church and evaluate his preaching style (if this has not already been done). The committee should now be ready to make a tentative selection, subject to final approval according to established church procedures.

Step Eight. Set up official interviews. The chairman of the search committee should now invite the candidate to the church for a formal interview with the entire committee and appropriate governing boards. The interviewing process should be moderated by a designated member of the search committee, although subsequent interviews may be requested by the elder and deacon boards. Some churches prefer to conduct several interviews with a candidate who has reached this stage: one by the search committee, a second by the church board(s), and another by the church staff. (Some of these meetings may include the candidate's spouse.) Generally speaking, the larger the church, the more interviews will be required.

An important consideration here is that the questions asked will be carefully planned and written down beforehand. Answers should be recorded and notes taken.

Note: In some churches the process stops here if the primary governing board has authority in this matter and votes to approve the candidate. The congregation is notified of their decision and is invited to attend a reception to meet the new pastor. (See Step Eleven.)

Step Nine. Schedule a formal visit for the candidate. In churches where a lay board does not have final authority to hire the senior pastor, the congregation should be informed (according to the church constitution) that the search committee and appropriate board(s) are recommending a specific candidate and will present him to the membership on a designated Sunday.

The candidate will probably want to arrive several days before the scheduled weekend so that he and his spouse (if he is married) can have time to observe the greater community. They will need to drive around the neighborhood, speak with realtors about housing costs (unless a parsonage will be provided), and visit local schools and shopping areas. There should be a chance to meet informally with the various groups with which the new pastor will be working if he is hired (e.g., deaconess board, choir, educational staff, etc.).

Although a prospective pastor should be given the opportunity to preach at both the morning and evening services, a potluck luncheon or supper might be arranged to introduce him to the congregation in a less structured setting as well. It would be inadvisable, however, to burden him with additional meetings or interviews between the two services. He and his family will need time to relax for a few hours on Sunday afternoon. They should be provided with a car and allowed to pursue their own agenda.

Step Ten. Vote according to established procedures. At some point, usually a week or two after the candidate's formal visit to the church, the congregation should vote on his acceptance at a general business meeting. (Most church constitutions state the percentage of congregational support required to issue a formal call.) A period of prayer to ask God's guidance in this important decision should precede the vote. Although the results should be announced as soon as possible, the congregation should be asked to keep them confidential until the candidate has been officially notified. (See Step Eleven.)

Step Eleven. Formalize the call. The candidate should be contacted immediately by phone and told the results of the vote. If the church has voted to accept him as its new pastor, he will need a couple of weeks to pray about his decision, notify his present church, and report back with his response. Follow up the telephone conversation with a written statement of the employment terms. Spell out specifics such as salary, vacation time, medical and other benefits, training opportunities, and car allowances, even though they have been discussed during the screening process.

If the congregation does *not* accept the candidate, the search committee should interview several parishioners to determine specifically what they did not like about him. This will suggest areas in which future candidates should be screened more closely. It will be natural for committee members to be discouraged and disappointed if their recommendation was not approved. The chairman should do whatever is possible to renew their spirits and encourage them as the process continues.

Implications

Few decisions affect the life of a local church as deeply as the selection of its shepherd. This process requires time, research, and a great deal of prayer. It is important for the governing board to keep the membership informed about the general movements of the search committee. This will help people understand that progress is being made, even though they may not be in a position to see it. Without this knowledge, some members may feel that the ministry is stalled indefinitely, and they will begin to look for another church family.

Despite the worthy intentions and diligent efforts of a search committee, very few senior pastors are called with a unanimous vote of affirmation. Lay leaders who are aware of this reality will avoid setting their expectations too high. This is a very opportune time for church members to take a hard look at who they currently are and where they would like to see themselves in the near future. With these issues resolved, the congregation is more likely to select a new pastor who can get them to their desired destination.

Questions for Discussion

1. If you have ever served on a pastoral search committee, how would you describe the experience?
2. If a pastoral vacancy occurred at your church, would you feel that you have enough grasp of the congregation's needs to serve on the search committee?

3. What would be your critical issues of concern if you had to serve on such a committee today?
4. Has your church prepared a church-and-community profile in the past five years? If not, would such a document be helpful for you now?

For Further Reading

Belt, Charles. "Preparing to Meet with a Search Committee." *Church Administration* 33, no. 6 (Mar. 1991): 7–8.

Buchanan, Doug. "Finding and Interviewing Prospective Staff." *Church Administration* 33, no. 7 (April 1991): 18–20.

Bullard, George, Jr. "A Historical Look at Forced Termination." *Search* 21, no. 1 (Fall 1990): 9–14.

Collins, Philip. "Make Me a Perfect Match: A Concerned Look at the Causes of Poor and Painful Pastoral Placements." *Crux* 23, no. 2 (June 1987): 18–25.

Green, Ken. "Tips for the Pastor-Search Committee." *Church Administration* 33, no. 6 (Mar. 1991): 23.

Hardin, Gary. "Being Intentional with a Search Committee." *Church Administration* 33, no. 6 (Mar. 1991): 3–6.

Harrison, Deanna. "Surviving Search Committee: Advice for Husbands and Wives." *Church Administration* 33, no. 6 (Mar. 1991): 18–20.

Kageler, Ken. "Surviving the Senior Pastor's Departure." *Youthworker,* Winter 1991, 63–65.

Keire, Anita. "Long-Term Interim Ministry." *The Christian Ministry* 21, no. 3 (May–June 1990): 9–11.

Miller, Greg. "Seeking a Staff Minister: Some Considerations." *Church Administration* 33, no. 3 (Dec. 1990): 29–30.

Morris, Lee. "Ethical Factors in Forced Termination." *Search* 21, no. 3 (Fall 1990): 50–58.

Quick, Kenneth. "Candid Candidating." *Leadership* 11, no. 4 (Fall 1990): 71–75.

16

Moral and Ethical Dilemmas

*W*ithout doubt, one of the hardest challenges a church leader may have to face is dealing with immorality and unethical conduct within the congregation, whether the wrongdoing involves a fellow parishioner, a staff member, or the senior pastor. Few issues have the potential for creating as much emotional pain, stress, and soul-searching as moral and ethical violations by members of the body of Christ.

No other vocation is expected to model morality as scrupulously as those who serve in church leadership. Ministers today, as well as their staff and church boards, walk an ethical tightrope. At one moment they serve as a prophet, priest, or administrator. At the next, they may be an educator, counselor, or leader of worship. Each of these roles raises moral and ethical dilemmas unlike those of most other professions.[1] Church board members need to be aware of these dilemmas, since they will find themselves cast into the center of them on numerous occasions.

Although this chapter will identify two critical areas of concern, an in-depth discussion of either of them would require far

208

more space. Indeed, entire books and long articles have been written about the subject. However, I will attempt to provide a concise introduction to each topic.

Moral Dilemmas in Church Ministry

The most obvious examples of immorality in the church relate to sexual misconduct. The church has traditionally tried to ignore such problems, especially when they involved members of the clergy. Says one Roman Catholic Bishop, "Our solution in the past was to keep such issues as quiet as possible. Where problems existed we damage controlled and transferred the priest. We can no longer get away with that posture."[2] Protestant churches have responded in similar fashion. The media and the legal system are forcing church officials to deal more openly and honestly with the issue. Sexual indiscretion now generates public outrage among members of all denominations. Victims of sexual abuse and exploitation by members of the clergy are suing in large numbers all throughout North America. In one Minneapolis case, an entire congregation was held partially responsible by a jury, and paying the judgment may cause this church to face financial bankruptcy.[3]

But what is a church to do when it discovers immoral or unethical behavior by one of its members? Scripture clearly teaches that religious leaders are to involve themselves in correcting misconduct within a congregation, and the Bible provides several examples of how this was done in both the Old and New Testament church. "Immoral behavior" includes (although is not limited to) adultery, sexual misconduct between consenting single adults, impure motives on the part of a church leader toward a parishioner while serving as counselor or care-giver, and sexual exploitation of a minor by an adult (which is both immoral and illegal).

Step One. There are a number of steps that a church can take when faced with immoral behavior among its membership. Prayerfully consider the best way to resolve the problem. As with most church conflicts, there may be a number of actions that could be taken. Much like walking through a minefield, issues involving immoral behavior can have devastating effects if they are not handled appropriately, ethically, and (in some cases) legally. Prayer is needed for guidance throughout the process.

Step Two. Once there is knowledge of an offense, those with a "need to know" should be informed. This must include the senior pastor, and in most cases it should also include the chairman of the primary governing board. Together they should seek a biblical response to the violation. This may call for going to the individual(s) involved and asking for clarification of the facts, trying to establish whether sincere repentance has occurred (if indeed an offense has been committed), and discussing future consequences, if any are deemed appropriate.

Step Three. Some attention should be given as to whether or not the information should be communicated to secular authorities. For example, if an adult has been involved in sexual misconduct with a minor, the laws of your state will specify whether the police or a child protective services agency must be notified. In most states, "ministerial rights," or penitent-priest privilege, do not apply when the health and safety of a minor are at risk.

Step Four. Safety measures should be established to ensure that similar violations cannot happen again. For example, if an adult leader has inappropriately fondled a child during a Sunday school class, it should be clearly stipulated that two adults must be present in a classroom at all times. A written list of such safeguards should be distributed among the members. It should also be required that all church workers sign a statement indicating their knowledge of these policies and their willingness to abide by them. (Chapter 17, "Legal Issues in Ministry," has more to say on this subject.)

Step Five. In cases of immorality involving a church leader, action should be taken to remove the offender from office. There should be no double standards within a church. If the misconduct is by a member of the church staff or a volunteer leader, allow that person the opportunity to resign before having to bring the matter to a church vote. A public excommunication of the offender usually involves a public display of the victim. The victim's rights to privacy should always be taken into consideration and held in high value. The innocent party may choose to remain in the church, but unnecessary publicity may force the victim and his or her family to leave.

Step Six. If, because the infraction was minor, it is deemed unnecessary to remove the person from a position of leadership, some system of accountability should be set up to ensure that the violation does not occur again.

Step Seven. As a board member, research all the facts and be careful not to overreact or become so emotionally involved that you are unable to make rational and objective decisions. Charges of immorality should be evaluated on an individual basis. A church that has had a history of such cases may be tempted to swing so heavily in a judgmental direction that a minor violation results in a major punishment. Be sure the corrective action fits the offense. Not every infraction warrants a public dismissal or written reprimand.

Step Eight. If the immoral behavior was by a member of the pastoral staff, it is usually advisable to include the chairman of the governing board in the resolution of the conflict. On the other hand, if the senior pastor is the offender, it may be appropriate to discuss the matter with denominational representatives (e.g., bishop, executive minister, state director). Otherwise, the pastor might simply move to another church and repeat the offense because he has not been disciplined and/or received the counseling help that is needed. (Highlighting the reality of pastoral misconduct, *Leadership* conducted a survey of their clergy readers and discovered that 24 percent of the respondents had had sexual experiences outside their marriages.)[4]

Step Nine. As much as possible, seek a redemptive outcome. Although legal action may also need to be taken, never neglect the unique position and role of the church as a redemptive community. Where there is confession of sin and repentance, love and forgiveness should be generously provided. This does not negate the behavior or eliminate its consequences, but it does provide the groundwork for future emotional and spiritual healing, which goes far beyond any decisions made by the congregation or by denominational or legal authorities.

In this light, the church should not overlook the obvious needs of the families of both the victim and the offender. Help will be needed for their emotional pain, spiritual suffering, and social isolation. The wrongdoer's children may be confused, and the spouse may feel anger, resentment, and even irrational guilt. The wife of a pastor who had been forced from his church over allegations of immoral misconduct once spoke to me of feeling terribly isolated from her friends and fellow church members afterward, even though she had spent twenty years in the congregation. In essence, she was made to share the punishment for her husband's alleged offense.

Obviously, there are a number of choices that occur throughout this entire process. Scripture provides some general principles to guide us in the correction and reconciliation of those involved in immorality. However, since it does not give us a clear procedure to use in every setting or scenario, tremendous wisdom is needed to apply biblical principles appropriately.

The "For Further Reading" section at the end of this chapter includes some excellent resources for additional guidance. I would also suggest that the board members of every church spend some time discussing which actions they would take in various hypothetical situations, so that a logical order of procedure can be established before emotions, personalities, or politics are involved. Such discussions should also set clear lines of authority for communication and decision making in the event that the senior pastor is out of town when a moral crisis occurs in the church.

It has been said with some degree of accuracy that the church is the only army that shoots its wounded. I am aware of recent actions on the part of several congregations that testify to the truth of this saying. The church, above all other institutions, must model the biblical paradoxes of mercy and justice, forgiveness and accountability, grace and restitution. Although we must hate the sin, we must not reject the sinner. In this, as in all things, love must abound.

Ethical Dilemmas in Church Ministry

The church board, pastoral staff, and general membership can be thrown into an ethical quandary over any number of ethical issues. Some of these include abuse of power and authority, dishonesty, exaggeration, failure to use church funds for their intended purpose, manipulation of others, mishandling of church resources, too loose an interpretation of the church's constitution, breaches of confidentiality, forced termination of a pastor, involvement in certain political causes, and simply not saying or doing what seems appropriate for a servant of God.

At the outset of this discussion, it should be mentioned that very few seminaries offer training in ministerial ethics. For those few that do, such a course is rarely required of all the students. In the words of one Southern Baptist pastor, "Neither biblical knowledge nor a 'divine call' to ministry gives the clergy automatic answers to ethical questions. Ministers must build strong moral character, understand the nature of the pastoral office and develop the ability to make good ethical decisions."[5] The same characteristics should be expected of church board members.

"Ethics deal with how people make decisions and act on them."[6] Ethical matters are often difficult to discuss rationally, since emotion and personal preference enter into the method by which an important decision is made. It is not easy to use ethics to invalidate another person's behavior without demeaning the value of the person. Choices often reflect an individual's basic beliefs and convictions—and to challenge a particular value is often to critique the person, even if unintentional. That is why so many discussions of an ethical nature become heated and fraught with misunderstandings.

Biblical References to Ethical Decision Making

The Bible speaks a great deal about ethics, and all responsible church board members will have to deal with this issue at some point during their term of service.

It is easy to take a verse of Scripture and make it seem to apply to any setting you want. Those who develop doctrine for the cults do this on a regular basis. However, biblical hermeneutics require a historical-grammatical approach to Scripture interpretation. This involves giving due consideration to the history and cultural background of a particular passage before deciding on its meaning. If a passage is taken out of context, with no reference to preceding or following material or the original text, people with opposing views can use the same verse to argue different views.

Although I may run the risk of violating those rules, I have identified some verses in Scripture that clearly teach the principles of ethical reasoning and behavior. Obviously, the Ten Commandments and the Sermon on the Mount are excellent examples. Others would include:

> He has told you, O man, what is good;
> And what does the LORD require of you
> But to do justice, to love kindness,
> And to walk humbly with your God? (Mic. 6:8 NASB).

> Do not move an ancient boundary stone or encroach on the fields of the fatherless, for their Defender is strong; he will take up their case against you (Prov. 23:10).
> The righteous care about justice for the poor, but the wicked have no such concern (Prov. 29:7).
> For if you forgive men when they sin against you, your heavenly Father will also forgive you. But if you do not forgive men their sins, your Father will not foregive your sins (Matt. 6:14–15).
> And just as you want people to treat you, treat them in the same way (Luke 6:31 NASB).

Decision making for Christians is "ethical" when it is firmly grounded in the Word of God, for it is only there that we find a basis for understanding the mind of God. As the apostle Paul wrote: "For the mind set on the flesh is death, but the mind set on the Spirit is life and peace, because the mind set on the flesh is hostile toward God: for it does not subject itself to the law of God, for it is not even able to do so; and those who are in the flesh cannot please God" (Rom. 8:6–8 NASB).

Church leaders must give close attention to Scripture and allow the Holy Spirit to guide them in the proper interpretation and application of God's moral and ethical principles. Since God's teachings are moral absolutes, they should be the basis for all decision making, especially when it affects the life of the church.

Resolving an Ethical Conflict: Forced Termination of a Pastor

It would not be possible in this section to present a step-by-step procedure for resolving each of the previously mentioned ethical dilemmas. Each issue must be approached on a case-by-case basis. For example, how board members would work through an abuse of power would be different from the way they would handle the misuse of designated funds. However, for illustrative purposes, I will deal briefly with one of the most difficult ethical issues a church board will ever have to face: the forced termination of a pastor.

Perhaps the most devastating experience for church leaders is arriving at the decision to remove their pastor from his position of spiritual leadership. Few actions by a church board have the potential to divide and split a congregation as quickly as a forced termination. Because it involves taking sides, airing deeply felt emotions, and unleashing verbal attacks, it is politics at its worst. Heart-wrenching as it is, this decision is made in some church every week.

Forced termination of a pastor can occur for a variety of reasons. The *Los Angeles Times* recently reported on a Baptist church that had "involuntarily terminated" its sixty-one-year-old pastor. Although he had been its spiritual shepherd for over ten years, and in that time the church had experienced consistent growth, the congregation simply wanted somebody new. A 1988 study by the Sunday School Board of the Southern Baptist Convention revealed that 116 congregations had fired their pastors during that year. This represented a 27 percent increase since 1984, the last time the figure was determined. Even in denominations that give bishops control over such matters, such as the Episcopalians and United Methodists, congregations can usually get their way by withholding financial contributions or signing petitions.

Once a congregation and/or its lay leaders face such a decision, it is imperative that they handle the matter according to the principles of Christian ethics. The following guidelines should apply:

1. *Since a pastor has been called by God into a position of spiritual leadership, he deserves a certain degree of respect and reverence.* He is still "the Lord's anointed" shepherd over God's flock, even if the

sheep no longer want to follow him. All pastors should be held in honor, and everything that is communicated to and about them should be done accordingly. This principle is drawn from David's words about Saul: "Don't destroy him! Who can lay a hand on the LORD's anointed and be guiltless?" (1 Sam. 26:9).

2. *The church should exercise self-control and restraint in its criticism of the pastor.* Once a fracture in the congregation has become evident, the appropriate board chairman should meet with the pastor to discuss the difficulties with honesty and frankness. This is not the time to beat around the bush. Communication should be direct and to the point, yet not sharply punctuated with accusations and blame. The chairman should present the complaints of the congregation in writing and also verbally spell out specific actions that were offensive, attitudes that have become disruptive, and/or job responsibilities in which the pastor has been derelict. It is possible that the pastor may not even be aware of his shortcomings. If he does not agree with the chairman that his behavior has been inappropriate, the chairman should return with several other members of the board. The case should be presented again with sufficient documentation and specificity.

3. *If the second attempt at board intervention does not convince the pastor of the need for change, the matter should be submitted to the church body in accordance with the bylaws in the constitution.* However, this should not happen until the pastor and all board members have had ample opportunity to meet and discuss their various views. Options might be presented at this time and "cards laid on the table." If this fails to resolve the conflict, the congregation should be brought into the picture. This will usually involve a public announcement by a board representative (preferably the chairman), followed by a written statement in the church bulletin, indicating the time and location of a general meeting when relevant dialogue can occur. Allow at least two weeks for parishioners to gather information, cool their emotional level somewhat, and collect their thoughts. This period should not be seen as a chance for members to form voting blocs, pool their collective political clout, or hold secret meetings.

4. *Board members should decide in advance what the agenda for the general meeting will be.* The primary board chairman must be will-

ing to exert his authority to insist that the meeting flows according to stated expectations. Because a meeting that gets out of control will serve no constructive purpose, its agenda should be posted and strictly followed.

5. *The moderator for the meeting should assume a neutral position and allow the various views to be aired without bias.* Everyone who has come prepared to speak should be allowed to do so. However, this should not be a time for personal attacks, demeaning statements, or malicious slander. Such dialogue is strictly forbidden, according to Ephesians 4:2–3, 15 and Colossians 3:8; 4:6. These verses should guide the conduct and communication at all church meetings.

6. *Love should characterize our actions toward one another, even in the midst of church conflict.* Paul demonstrated his love for the believers in the Corinthian church even though he vehemently disapproved of many of their actions. We should respond in like manner. Using a foundation of love as the ethical basis for our attitudes and behavior is what distinctively sets the church apart from secular institutions. If the body of Christ does not model love, how will we ever convince a lost world that we have a better way of dealing with conflict and pain?

7. *If it seems apparent that the outcome of the congregational meeting will be a vote of termination, the board should allow the pastor to resign before the actual vote is taken.* This may seem like a matter of semantics, but there is good reason to make the separation "voluntary." If the pastor resigns, acknowledging his inability to bring unity and reconciliation to the fellowship, it can diffuse some of the emotion and hostility within the congregation. Even if most members are resigned to the fact that the pastor will not be able to stay, letting *him* make that choice makes it much easier to accept than a forced termination. Furthermore, the pastor may prefer to resign before an official vote is taken, thus avoiding the embarrassment of having to admit to a future congregation that he was fired. It also allows him to offset further polarization of members and preserve his own dignity.[7]

8. *If a termination vote is taken and passes by the percentage stipulated in the church constitution, the pastor should be allowed ample time and resources to relocate.* He should be given about four to six

months of severance pay and a continuance of his health insurance benefits for a designated period. The church may even provide assistance toward his moving expenses, especially if he has been living in a church-owned parsonage.

Some churches have softened the impact of a forced termination by providing an unsatisfactory pastor with a one-year paid sabbatical leave that will allow him to return to seminary for further training and instruction.[8] Since the pastor is not expected to return after the year is up, the church can use that time period to seek his replacement. Departing the church for an extended leave is less emotionally traumatic than an immediate termination.

9. *If the forced termination is particularly destructive to the pastor, the church may want to consider making several months of professional counseling available to him at the church's expense.* This would be an honorable and loving gesture that clearly goes beyond the call of duty. It clearly communicates to the pastor that the parishioners care about his well-being, even in the midst of what is a hurtful decision.

10. *Every attempt should be made to avoid litigation over the termination.* The Bible is clear that any noncriminal disputes among believers should be settled within the fellowship, rather than by the civil courts. However, if a pastor feels that he has been grossly mistreated, he may not want to let the matter rest there. Three major passages of Scripture relevant to this issue are Matthew 5:25–26; 1 Corinthians 6:1–7; and Acts 25:1–12. Referring to these verses, Lee Morris summarizes five practical considerations that can be applied to serious minister-church conflicts of this nature.[9]

First, exhaust every resource within the church and denomination to settle the dispute. Not to do so admits grievous failure. If a hearing of the case by a body outside the congregation seems necessary, it should be conducted by mature representatives from affiliated churches in your diocese, district, or presbytery (see 1 Cor. 6:5).

Second, only when everything else fails—in cases in which a minister's employability has been seriously damaged or delayed (six to twelve months) and the church has not adequately provided for his/her needs on termination—a terminated pastor should consider making an "appeal to Caesar" (see Acts 25:11).

Third, the terminated minister should take care that vindictiveness and revenge are not his motivation for turning to the courts, although some degree of anger is bound to influence his decision. Litigation should be delayed until sufficient time has passed for cooling off and regaining perspective.

Fourth, a civil lawsuit may well exacerbate the accusations against the minister. (After all, Paul's appeal to the courts led him to Rome!) Taking legal action may mark the minister as a "problem pastor" for the rest of his career.

Finally, realize that the lawsuit will probably damage the credibility of the church (especially among nonbelievers) for years to come. Sometimes beating a fire to put it out only succeeds in spreading it.

Obviously, these same principles apply if the church, rather than its pastor, is considering taking this matter (or any other internal conflict) to the civil courts.

Implications

God has provided the church with scriptural guidance for what some church leaders refer to as "the dark days of ministry." Almost every church faces moral and ethical dilemmas at some point in its history. Certainly many of the churches described in the pages of the New Testament had their share of such problems.

In a world of imperfect human beings, no pastor or board member can ever guarantee that incidents of immorality or unethical behavior will not occur within the congregation. However, if church leaders are prepared to face these situations, they will be better able to handle misconduct before it has a chance to damage the fellowship. The best preparation consists of a good working knowledge of God's Word, open communication between the pastor and congregation, and a calm, well-controlled temperament in time of crisis.

Questions for Discussion

1. What other steps might church board members take to solve some of the moral dilemmas that they might face?

2. Share a past experience that illustrates how one or more of these steps were used to resolve a moral or ethical dilemma.

3. Does the church have any written guidelines regarding what is deemed inappropriate moral and/or ethical conduct for its staff and volunteer workers in the performance of their duties?

4. How can church leaders prepare to meet moral and ethical dilemmas before they occur?

5. What other resources are available to the church to help either prevent or resolve a moral or ethical conflict within the congregation?

For Further Reading

Brock, Raymond T., and Horace C. Lukens, Jr. "Affair Prevention in the Ministry." *Journal of Pastoral Psychology* 8, no. 4 (1989): 44–55.

Browning, Don S. *Religious Ethics and Pastoral Care*. Philadelphia: Fortress Press, 1983.

Crowell, Rodney. *Musical Pulpits: Clergy and Laypersons Face the Issue of Forced Exits*. Grand Rapids: Baker Book House, 1992.

Faulkner, Brooks. "Ethics and Staff Relations." *Review and Expositor* 86 (1989): 547–59.

Fortune, Marie. *Is Nothing Sacred? When Sex Invades Pastoral Leadership*. San Francisco: Harper & Row, 1987.

Hart, Archibald D. "Being Moral Isn't Always Enough." *Leadership* 9, no. 2 (Spring 1988): 24.

Hopkins, Nancy M. "Congregational Intervention When the Pastor Has Committed Sexual Misconduct." *Pastoral Psychology* 39, no. 4 (1991): 247–55.

Kantzer, K. S. "The Road to Restoration." *Christianity Today*, 15 May 1987, 19–22.

Muck, Terry C., (ed). "How Common Is Pastoral Indiscretion?" *Leadership* 9, no. 1 (Winter 1988): 12–13.

Muck, Terry C. "The Bakker Tragedy." *Christianity Today*, 15 May 1987, 14–15.

Simmons, Paul D., (ed). *Issues in Christian Ethics*. Nashville: Broadman Press, 1980.

Stafford, Tim. "Great Sex: Reclaiming a Christian Sexual Ethic." *Christianity Today*, 2 Oct. 1987, 24–44.

"When a Pastoral Colleague Falls." *Leadership* 12, no. 1 (Winter 1991): 102–11.

Legal Issues in Ministry

With the exception of defining what constitutes a nonprofit corporation for income tax purposes, the federal government has, for the most part, steered clear of legislating measures that would restrict the activity of church and para-church ministries. It has been the general opinion of the federal courts that each state has the freedom to enact what it feels are appropriate laws to govern these ministries, so long as those laws do not infringe on an individual's right to freely exercise his or her religion, which is guaranteed in the first amendment of our nation's constitution. For this reason, regulations that might affect a church or religious organization differ greatly from state to state.[1]

If you are a church board member, you have been entrusted with the responsibility of overseeing certain matters that could have a legal impact on your church if mishandled. For example, the laws governing contractual agreements, taxes (property, payroll, income, etc.), liability, and professional malpractice apply just as much to the church as they do to private individuals or secular organizations. Failure to provide adequate supervision in

222

those areas can have devastating effects on the ministry and the morale of the congregation.

The Proliferation of Litigation

There is no denying that we live in a society where people are quite willing, if not eager, to litigate an issue when they feel they have been wronged. Access to the courts is a basic right that has been honored in North America since colonial times. Although other means for settling disputes may fail, most people believe that the legal system has the capacity to remedy every wrong by punishing the offender and/or compensating the victim. For this reason, virtually every important issue has ultimately had its day in court. Contemporary America certainly has not seen any let-up in the number of litigation cases that appear on the court dockets each year.[2] Jethro Lieberman notes in *The Litigious Society* that the American tradition of seeking legal redress for every injury, whether it be real or imagined, has grown to epidemic proportions, which in turn has invaded previously immune areas and drastically raised the costs and frustrations of operating a profession or business.[3]

The National Center for State Courts estimates that more than 15.7 million new civil cases and 11 million new criminal cases were filed in state trial courts in 1986. Those figures represented a 5 percent increase in the number of civil filings since the previous year. The appellate courts have experienced a 10 percent jump over the same period of time.[4] No matter which statistical comparatives are used, the court calendars are getting more and more crowded.

In light of these findings, it is not surprising to see lawsuits being brought against professionals that would have been unimaginable twenty years ago. The church is no exception. In recent years there has been a major increase in the number of cases filed against churches in America (and their personnel) for a variety of reasons, including breach of contract, improper church discipline, and defamation of character. However, most lawsuits that affect a church revolve around either malpractice or negligence, each of which will be discussed in this chapter. In addition, I will present some guidelines to help the church avoid falling prey to lit-igation in these two critical areas.

Ministerial Malpractice

Malpractice can be loosely defined as professional misconduct or unreasonable lack of skill in carrying out one's job responsibil-ities. To "win" a malpractice suit (and recover damages), a plain-tiff must prove four things:

1. That the profession has a standard of conduct or care.
2. That the professional owed him/her a duty to conform to this standard of conduct or care.
3. That the professional breached his or her duty.
4. That the client suffered damages as a result of the alleged misconduct.

If one of these four elements is missing, malpractice suits are rarely successful.[5]

Charges of clergy malpractice usually involve either sexual mis-conduct or counseling incompetence.

Sexual Misconduct. There are no reliable figures regarding the number of sexually-related malpractice cases that have been brought against members of the clergy. Jeffery Anderson, a nationally known Minneapolis attorney who specializes in litigation involving the clergy, estimates that the Catholic Church alone has spent over $300 million since 1985 to settle charges of sexual abuse by its priests. Anderson has handled more than a hundred such cases in the past seven years and has so far settled thirty of them, earning more than $15 million for his clients.[6]

An example of this kind of lawsuit is the case involving one of my former students, who was a youthworker in his local church until he was accused of molesting several of the children in the junior-high group. The parents have joined together to confront the young man and are seeking legal action. A church has very lit-tle grounds for defense in a malpractice suit of this nature.

Counseling Incompetence. This particular area of church ministry has come under increasing scrutiny since *Nally v. Grace Commu-*

nity Church of the Valley, a case filed in 1980 by the parents (as heirs) of a seminary student who committed suicide while receiving counseling from a church pastor.[7] After several years of debate in the courts, the senior pastor was exonerated from blame, but the residual effects have been felt by clergy members across the nation.

One of the aftereffects of this case was a decision by the American Association of Pastoral Counselors (AAPC) to automatically include professional liability insurance as a membership benefit. Pastors who counsel members of their congregation (and most of them do) set themselves up for possible litigation that may be difficult to win.

Professional counselors (psychologists, psychiatrists, etc.) who are licensed by their state have to subscribe to a written code of ethics that becomes the standard by which their competence is measured. Because most pastors are not *licensed* to practice counseling, they are not technically accountable to the same set of standards. In essence, parishioners who are counseled by their pastor should not expect the same standards of competence required of licensed members of the profession. However, pastors who represent themselves as "counselors" invite being held accountable to the same set of professional standards as AAPC members and would do well to acquaint themselves with the association's code of ethics. This written code can be brought into court as evidence of assumed competence. In addition, other pastors who perform counseling may also be brought in as material witnesses to substantiate what is considered "normative conduct" in pastoral counseling.[8]

Malpractice insurance is becoming popular among members of the clergy. Some denominations automatically provide such liability coverage for their ordained ministers. Examples of this are the Presbyterian Church in the U.S.A., the Lutheran Church in America, and the United Methodist Church.

Negligence Litigation

The second common source of litigation against churches and those who serve in church leadership positions is negligence. It is surprisingly easy to be held negligent in a civil lawsuit.

A number of years ago, while serving on the staff of a para-church organization, I took a group of teenagers to the Montreal Olympics for witnessing and other forms of ministry. On the way back across Canada in the van, we took time off for a float down a beautiful river. Since I had never been down this particular river before I had no idea what lay around each turn. As we rounded a sharp bend, we were all suddenly sucked into an incredible hole that held us underwater for what seemed like an eternity. In fact, I nearly drowned and a high school student nearly drowned with me. If that student had died in the river that day, I probably would have been sued for negligence, and the organization might have lost all of its capital assets. I learned a valuable lesson that day about clergy negligence.

Negligence can occur in any number of church-related activities. The list seems endless: camp-outs with the youth department, recreational games during Vacation Bible School, improper maintenance of church vehicles, disrepair of buildings and grounds, construction code violations, even skits that get out of hand during a meeting.

Lowering the Risk of Litigation

It is unfortunate that so few churches know how to protect themselves against charges of malpractice or negligence. Some church boards overreact by canceling all youth activities that even remotely look dangerous, including missions trips. The apostle Paul would never have been sent out to spread the gospel message to the Gentiles under the guidelines that some church boards have felt necessary because of their fear of litigation. Clearly there must be some middle ground to help calm the leaders of our churches![9]

Nothing can prevent an angry parishioner from filing a lawsuit against the church and/or one of its workers. However, there are a number of things that a church board can do to lessen the risk that charges of negligence or malpractice could be brought to the litigation stage. In the event that a case is actually brought to court, the following suggestions may help the church win the case—or at least reduce the size of settlement awarded if the court finds in favor of the plaintiff.

Suggestion #1. The church's leadership needs to be honest about the amount of risk that may be involved in the activities it sponsors. Whether it be through announcements from the pulpit or notices in the bulletin, any potential dangers should be clearly communicated to the congregation. This is especially true for such activities as backpacking, rock climbing, water-skiing, car rallies, dances, physical-contact sports, skin diving, and so on. For example, if the church is sponsoring a jog-a-thon to raise money for the youth group, those who participate should be warned of the hazards of indulging in strenuous physical exertion without the consent of a physician. This way, if an accident or health crisis occurred during the activity, the church could submit evidence in court that everyone was made aware of the risks involved.

Suggestion #2. When minors are going to participate in a church outing, the adult sponsors should have a parent-signed medical release form in their possession for each child or youth involved. (A sample of this form appears at the end of this chapter.) Some states require that these release forms be notarized before they can be deemed valid for medical attention in the event it is needed. Members of the church board are ultimately responsible for the specifics of the laws as they relate to their state. Pastors who move frequently are rarely informed of the unique laws of each state they might live in.

I have often spent many hours trying to convince a hospital physician that I have verbal permission from a sick or injured student's parent to secure medical attention if needed. Take a lesson from me—if you don't have a current medical release form signed by the minor's parent or guardian, save your breath. Medical personnel won't take your word for it! Bring the forms with you on the outing, as they will do you little good sitting on your desk back at the church.

I have spoken with several attorneys regarding the use of medical release forms and liability waivers, and they all agree that there is no guarantee that you will not be sued just because you have obtained one or both of these signed statements. However, it will provide some proof that you gave adequate warning of the risks if the statements are printed on the same form that the parents signed to give permission for involvement.

Suggestion #3. Whenever possible, rent vehicles (cars, vans, busses, trucks) from a national car-rental company instead of using church-owned vehicles for outings. Most churches that I have been acquainted with are pretty lax regarding the care and maintenance of their vehicles. When the church budget gets tight, one of the first things to get postponed is vehicle maintenance. The consequences of this frugality have been disastrous for some churches.

Because national car-rental agencies cannot afford to take risks, they have an extremely high standard of vehicle maintenance. They have discovered it is much cheaper to maintain their vehicles than pay for the attorney fees, court costs, and legal settlements that are the result of negligence litigation. In addition, their insurance coverage will be much higher than what most churches can afford. In the event of an accident involving a vehicle rented by your church, the car company will be listed as the primary litigant in any lawsuit that might ensue.

I am aware of a church in Southern California that used its own bus to transport a high school group to camp. On the way, the bus was involved in a freeway accident in which several students were killed and many others were seriously injured. During the subsequent lawsuit, it was charged that the vehicle maintenance records indicated inadequate care. The church lost the litigation and was forced to mortgage its building and conduct a major fund-raising campaign to pay the settlement. This could have been avoided by simply renting a vehicle from a legitimate agency. This may cost a little more on paper, but in the long run a church can save lives, ministry effectiveness, money, and a great deal of emotional stress by doing so.

Suggestion #4. Be sure that your church has established high standards for the recruitment and training of all volunteer workers. Proof of thorough screening and training is essential in litigation. Church board members should want to screen all applicants to guarantee (as much as possible) their qualifications and good character. A good screening process involves three elements:

APPLICATION FORM. This form should include the volunteer's name, address, phone number, work record, date of availability, type of work preferred, marital status, physical or mental conditions that might prevent the applicant from providing adequate care of others, prior criminal convictions, and any court proceedings that involved child abuse or sexual molestation. A church board has the legal right to know as much as possible about everyone who assists in the church programs. Those who are unwilling to complete the application should not be allowed to serve in the ministry. It isn't worth the risk.

PERSONAL REFERENCES. I prefer to have written references on people I do not know, but I may just check out the names by phone if the applicant has been a member of the church for some time. If it is a telephone interview, I will take notes on the comments. Whether written forms or records from a telephone conversation, be sure to keep them on file. You will need to produce these in the event of a court case. I once avoided serious problems with a new volunteer worker by calling his previous church to ask about his background. I discovered that he had been asked to leave because of his "emotional instability" while working with children. A simple three-minute phone call can save you countless hours of clean-up.

ORAL INTERVIEW. This dialogue is for the purpose of following up on any questions that came up after reading the application form or while gathering personal references. The interview can be conducted by any number of people, but it is essential to include a member of the church pastoral staff on the screening committee. This may be the only time when you feel the freedom to ask direct questions of the applicant, so don't shy away from sensitive issues. Believe me, if problems develop later and lead to court action, the attorney who questions you will want to know exactly what you asked, and what you did not—and why.

Suggestion #5. Secure a reference waiver form. Because I request references from all church volunteers, I consider it important to ask for a "right to privacy" waiver to be signed by the applicant. This form simply states that the applicant waives his or her right to see the results of my reference checking. That way, I am more assured of the accuracy of the information I receive in the process.

If, however, the applicant does not sign the form, I am very cautious about what I write down about the candidate during a telephone interview, since I cannot guarantee confidentiality to the person giving the reference.

The last two suggestions can make a big difference in the selection and supervision of your volunteer workers. Church boards from rural communities may find these measures to be somewhat extreme, given the fact that they have probably known all the members of their church for many years. However, for most suburban or city churches, where there is far more turnover of members, it is more prudent to err on the side of caution than to avoid collecting this important information. In the long run, since this process communicates to the parishioners that you want to safeguard their families, you will gain their respect and confidence. Because a thorough screening process gives the church added protection against crime and potential litigation, it is well worth the effort.

Insurance Needs

Obviously, every church should have a standard insurance policy that covers items such as fire, theft, flooding, and basic liability. However, insurance coverage for clergy liability and medical claims can be a bit more complicated. Knowing whether or not to purchase such policies and how much coverage is needed can be a source of lengthy deliberations at the board level. The following information should prove helpful in those discussions.

Liability Insurance Riders

Basic liability coverage provides financial protection in the event that someone falls down in the parking lot, trips on a loose piece of carpet in the sanctuary, or has some other accident on church property. You may be surprised to learn that most church insurance policies have certain exclusionary clauses. This usually means that the church is not covered in its use of church-owned vehicles and during high-risk activities. These additional areas of coverage are available by adding "riders" to the policy. A separate rider will be needed for each area for which coverage is desired. For instance, if the church owns a vehicle, the board will want to purchase a separate rider for it. The age and condition of the vehicle and who will be authorized to drive it will determine the cost of this inclusionary rider.

Riders can be added to a policy for short periods of time as well. For example, if the youth pastor is taking a group of students on an overnight camp-out in the mountains, a separate two-day rider can be purchased to give the church liability protection for the duration of the trip. Any outing that has an element of risk involved should be covered by such a rider. This is simply a matter of calling the insurance agent on the phone and providing the details of the trip. The cost is usually quite minimal, but the coverage is well worth it.

Full Coverage vs. Co-Insurance

Another important decision that should be made is whether the church is going to provide full liability coverage or co-insurance coverage for participants in church activities. Full coverage means that the church's insurance company is the primary provider. So, in the event of an accident, the church's policy will cover the full amount of damage and related expenses.

With a co-insurance arrangement, the injured party's insurance company is the primary provider, up to the limits of his or her coverage. If anything additional is needed, the church's policy takes effect. If the person who is injured does not have any coverage of his or her own, the co-insurance policy of the church automatically becomes the primary provider.

For obvious reasons, the cost difference between the two types of policies is considerable. The popularity of the co-insurance policy has grown substantially among churches because of the significant increase in premiums for full-coverage protection. Small churches are almost forced to use the co-insurance approach if they are to have any coverage.

Liability Coverage for International Missions

While serving as the associate pastor of a local church, I wanted to take some young people to work at an orphanage in a foreign country. The church board had recently heard of an unfortunate incident involving a church that had taken a group of students to Mexico. While helping to build a house for a Mexican family, a young student was killed in an accident. My church board, fearing the possibility of such an accident and a subsequent lawsuit, required the purchase of a separate liability rider to cover the missions trip. Thus began my year-and-a-half search for a company that was willing to provide this coverage.

None of the church-oriented insurance companies that I consulted was able to provide such a policy. Some of the major insurance companies would sell me a rider if my church was willing to switch its entire coverage to them. The overall cost was unreasonable, so the trip was cancelled while I continued my investigation.

On hearing my monthly reports, the board concluded that acquiring insurance was not possible, so they decided to do the next best thing. They wanted to draft a liability waiver that would clearly state the risks of international travel. The form would have to boldly declare that the church had no insurance coverage for the students going abroad, and that they would be participating at their own risk. In the event of an accident (whether or not there was a lawsuit), the board members felt they could present a convincing argument for the unavailability of coverage and use the liability waivers to show they were up front with the participants about the risks involved.

I eventually contacted a well-known law firm in the Los Angeles area with significant experience in church litigation. We hired an attorney to draft an international liability-waiver form that the church could use for all student missions experiences. The attorney stated frankly that such a document had never been used in court, so its effectiveness had not yet been tested. "However," he said, "simply securing and using this document will convince a judge or jury of your forthright intention to be honest with those who will be going on the trip." The church board required the parents of all participants to sign the form before the trip. This was a lengthy and frustrating experience for me. However, I am convinced now that the church board was exercising responsible spiritual leadership by protecting the congregation from possible litigation. This international "liability release agreement" is supplied for your use at the conclusion of this chapter.

Implications

It is simply not possible to take all risk out of church ministry. Whether it is during a counseling session, in an act of church discipline, or during a church activity, there will always be the possibility that professional malpractice or negligence (or an accident for which no one is to blame) will subject the church to subsequent legal action. The issue is not to try to eliminate all risks but to minimize them as much as is reasonably possible. Ultimately, the sovereign hand of God must be relied on to protect the congregation from harm.

The church board should conduct thorough periodic reviews of the activities of the church to determine where risk can be eliminated without restricting the effectiveness of the ministry. These reviews should include insurance policies, which should be updated on a regular basis. The church's insurance agent should be invited to a board meeting to explain exactly what is covered (and what is not) in terms of clergy, medical, and other liability insurance needs. This will be a learning experience for the board, and it will inspire confidence within the congregation to know that each board member is informed about the specifics of the church's coverage.

Questions for Discussion

1. In what ways do you think your church is taking risks?
2. Do you believe these risks are making the church vulnerable to litigation?
3. What kinds of insurance does your church currently have? What limits of coverage exist in each area?
4. What exclusionary riders are attached to any of your church policies?
5. Has your church purchased any inclusionary riders? If so, which ones?

6. When was the last time your church board reviewed the specifics of the church's insurance policies?
7. Would it be beneficial for your church board to invite your insurance agent to a board meeting to explain the coverage that your church has and what else might be needed?

For Further Reading

Anders, M. Maureen. "Religious Counseling—Parents Allowed to Pursue Suit Against Church and Clergy for Son's Suicide." *Arizona State Law Journal,* 1985, 213.

Bergman, Ben Zion. "Is the Cloth Unraveling? A First Look at Clergy Malpractice." *9 San Fernando Law Review,* 1981, 47, 48.

Burek, Lawrence M. "Clergy Malpractice: Making Clergy Accountable to a Lower Power." *14 Pepperdine Law Review,* 1986, 13, 141.

Ericsson, Samuel E. "Clergyman Malpractice: Ramifications of a New Theory." *16 Valparaiso University Law Review,* 1981, 163, 164.

Gumper, L. L. *Legal Issues in the Practice of Ministry.* Franklin Village: Psychological Studies Consultation Program, 1981.

House, Wayne. *Christian Ministries and the Law: What Church and Parachurch Leaders Should Know.* Grand Rapids: Baker Book House, 1992.

Kasper, Dennis. Talbot School of Theology, 1986: "The Clergy and Legal Liability." (A seminar for pastors in ministry offered every couple of years and taught by a professional attorney who specializes in first-amendment protection.)

Klee, Kimberly A. "Clergy Malpractice: Bad News for the Good Samaritan or a Blessing in Disguise?" *17 Toledo Law Review,* 1985, 209, 248.

Maloney, H. N., and T. L. Needham. *Clergy Malpractice.* Philadelphia: Westminster Press, 1986.

Sample Medical Release Form

Central Baptist Church
Medical Permission Slip

Name _____Phone_____
Address _____

The person named above has an unusual medical need as stated below:

_____
_____
_____
_____

I/we the undersigned do hereby give permission to Central Baptist Church and its representatives to obtain any necessary medical treatment for the person named above during the conduct of any program, ministry, or activity sponsored by Central Baptist Church.

_____ I want the person named above to ride only with adult drivers approved for coverage on the church's liability insurance policy.

_____ I will allow the person named above to ride with adult or teenage drivers not officially approved for coverage on the church's liability insurance policy and I/we have our own insurance coverage for this person in the event of injury.

_____
    (signature of parent or legal guardian)   Date

Note to Parents: Central Baptist carries only liability co-insurance. This means that should your child become injured or ill on a church sponsored activity, your own family medical insurance will be billed first. If you have no insurance or if your insurance doesn't cover all necessary medical costs, our policy will make up the difference.

Source: Ken Garland, "Legal and Ethical Issues in Christian Education," in Michael J. Anthony *Foundations of Ministry: An Introduction to Christian Education for a New Generation* (Wheaton: Victor Books, 1992), p. 291.

Liability Release Agreement

The undersigned (herein the "Individual") wishes to participate in the following activity:

_____
_____
_____
_____
_____

(herein the "Activity") sponsored by_____
_____

a non-profit religious corporation (herein the "Church") _____
Church and the undersigned agree that the activity poses a risk including the following specific risks _____

_____
_____
_____
_____
_____
_____

as well as similar and dissimilar risks (herein the "Risks"). _____

For and in consideration of the Church allowing the Individual to participate in the Activity, and other good and valuable consideration the receipt and sufficiency of which are hereby acknowledged, the undersigned, for himself or herself, assigns, heirs, and next of kin (herein the "Releasors"), release, waive, discharge, and covenant not to sue the Church and its officers, employees, and agents (herein the "Releasees"), from all liability to the Releasors, on account of injury to the Individual or death to the Individual or injury to the property of the Individual, *whether caused by the negligence of Releasees or otherwise,* while the Individual is participating in the Activity.

The undersigned is fully aware of the Risks and other hazards inherently in the Activity and is voluntarily participating in the Activity, and voluntarily assumes the Risks and all other risks of loss, damage, or injury that may be sustained by the Individual while participating in the Activity.

The undersigned warrants that he or she has fully read and understands this Liability Release Agreement and voluntarily signs the same, and that no oral representations, statements, or inducements apart from the foregoing written agreement have been made to the undersigned.

Caution: Read Before Signing

Date: _____   _____
                                            (signed)

                        _____
                                        (please print name)

Source: Michael J. Anthony, "Reaching Beyond Our Singleness," cited in Carolyn Koons and Michael Anthony, *Single Adult Passages: Uncharted Territories* (Grand Rapids: Baker Book House, 1991).

Healing a Divided Church

ny pastor who comes to a church that has recently been split apart faces a frightening task. Though he may gallop onto the scene like a knight in shining armor, amidst back-slapping support and cheers from an enthusiastic crowd of spectators, once he sits down at his desk during the first week of ministry, reality will soon set in. He will quickly arrive at the stark discovery that this church has been a combat zone. Casualties litter the field. Snipers are still firing. Many combatants remain mortal enemies. Morale is low, and the church's reputation in the community is in rags. Soldiers are deserting their post and slinking off in the night. Welcome to the war-torn church![1]

Jesus said, "Every kingdom divided against itself will be ruined, and every city or household divided against itself will not stand" (Matt. 12:25). These words could easily be applied to the local church, for any church that is expending most of its energy fighting battles waged within its own walls will eventually be devastated by the experience. There are no winners or losers in this kind of warfare—only weary survivors with wounds that need healing. Meanwhile, the ministry will have been stripped of its spiritual vitality by the emotional trauma, caustic interpersonal strife, and tireless political maneuvering that always precedes a church split.

In my search for materials on healing a divided church, I discovered that there was very little in print on the subject. However, a little over 10 percent of the senior pastors in my survey had experienced a church split, and I knew that personal contact with these pastors would be my most accurate source of information. By visiting half of them in person and conducting phone interviews with many of the rest, I gained much valuable insight into the dynamics involved in the restoration of a strife-torn congregation. Their stories were punctuated with pain, both personal and corporate. This chapter is based almost exclusively on my interviews. For obvious reasons, I cannot cite the real names of the pastors and board members or the location of their churches, but I do want to credit them for their willingness to share their thoughts with me, and ultimately with those who would read this book.

I had originally wanted to title this chapter "Managing the Church Split." However, one battle-weary senior pastor told me that there was no such thing as "managing" a divided church. He said, "Once the church is on a collision course to split apart, there is no such thing as managing it. At best, all you can do is survive it. You'd be far better off helping pastors and church boards learn to heal their church after it happens than telling them how to avoid what may be inevitable." As you can see, I have taken his advice and directed my energies toward helping pastors and church boards deal with the important task of picking up the pieces and getting the church back on course again.

I have chosen to divide this chapter into three sections. The first section deals with identifying the warning signs that usually precede open warfare within a church. The second provides practical advice about how to bring healing to a church after a split, and the third deals with the personal consequences that a senior pastor or board member experiences during and after the fracturing.

Warning Signs of an Impending Split

Knowing some of the signs that warn of a church split can sometimes help the pastor and church board slow the process. With a large dose of help from God, they may even prevent it altogether. The key is catching it soon enough. Although in some cases a split may seem to be the lesser of two evils, the dissension that comes before the separation and the negative consequences of the painful split itself are seldom advantageous for the church in the immediate future. If positive results do occur, it is usually only after many months, perhaps even years into the future life of the church, assuming it is able to survive that long.

Obviously, a church split can be precipitated by any number of factors. I have listed four common causes, but by no means is this list meant to be comprehensive. Keep in mind that there may be both surface issues and hidden elements in the equation. The church may be up in arms about the senior pastor's mismanagement of the budget, but that may only be the most obvious complaint. Since disagreements over money are so easy to identify, the opposition party may choose to focus there, when the real issue may be disillusionment with the pastor's speaking style, abrasive personality, or inability to get along with his wife. Or there may be some other problem that is even more difficult to communicate.

Warning Sign #1: Ineffective Conflict Resolution

One of the first signals that a church is moving toward a separation is the inability of the senior pastor and/or church board to handle conflict within the congregation. Especially when the issue involves a church leader, the process of resolution can be long and tedious. Everyone involved in ministry is going to face some degree of opposition and turmoil. A cursory look at the Book of Acts reveals a significant number of disagreements in the early church. Whether caused by fraudulent misrepresentation (5:1–11), disgruntled church members (6:1–7), pressures exerted by a hostile community (8:1–3), inability to agree on doctrinal issues (15:1–21), or pastoral competition (15:37–40), the body of Christ has always had the potential for strife, tension, and interpersonal animosity.

Conflict within the church seems to be inevitable. That doesn't make it right, but we must understand that Satan—in opposing the work of God—often encourages dissension among believers to try to prevent us from accomplishing the purposes of our Commander-in-Chief. When these conflicts become so inflammatory that they cannot be controlled or resolved, they can build to the point of explosion, crippling the ministry and splitting the church apart. "Divide and conquer" has always been an effective military strategy.

Warning Sign #2: Increased Political Maneuvering

Politics in ministry may be a source of tremendous disillusionment for a board member who has never had a behind-the-scenes look at church administration. Although concern over who exerts more power and influence or maintains the highest level of prestige is certainly not biblical, it is a reality in most churches in America.

When warring factions within a church feel that their opinions are not receiving adequate attention from the responsible parties, they will usually try to gather support. Lobbying for a voice in church matters may take the form of unofficial meetings in a church member's home, circulating a petition, requesting a hearing by denominational representatives, trying to get a spokesperson elected to a church office, and/or even disrupting a business meeting or worship service. Whatever the method, the motive is generally the same: to win new supporters and discredit the views of "opposing" members. When these activities become noticeable, a church split may be on the horizon.

Warning Sign #3: Unusual Attrition in Membership

Every church has a certain percentage of its members in rotation. Because of job transfers, retirement, and changing community demographics, church membership is seldom stable. The hope, of course, is that there will be more people coming into a church than are leaving it. If a disproportionate number of members have departed without an apparent reason, a church split is probably impending.

This is particularly true when those who leave the church are upset and angry. Their hostility may be channeled into phone calls to friends who have remained behind, requesting that they join them in their search for a "better church" to attend. Eventually, once enough people join forces and leave, the pastor and church board will look around and realize that they have experienced a silent split. This form of church division is not as common as one that occurs after an explosive or prolonged battle, but it is every bit as effective in dismantling an existing ministry.

Warning Sign #4: Dictatorial Leadership

A split may be seen as the only possible alternative when church leaders become arrogant and overbearing. Opposition members may remain in the church as long as they feel there is still a chance that their voice will be heard and their desires met. However, once they lose that sense of hope, they may call for a separation. Any number of incidents can bring a congregation to the breaking point, but the critical, negative, or sarcastic spirit communicated by autocratic leadership will speed up the process.

Being on the receiving end of criticism or hurtful comments first produces a defensive attitude and resentment, but eventually there are counterattacks. Battle lines are drawn and people go scurrying for ammunition. War parties are commissioned to develop strategies for "getting back" at the leaders who have hurt or publicly humiliated them. Proverbs 15:1 says that "a gentle answer turns away wrath, but a harsh word stirs up anger." The end result of dictatorial church leadership may be the fracturing of the local body of Christ.

The Healing Process

Because there are as many ways to rebuild the spirit of a church as there are reasons for its division, there is no single formula that will heal the hurts that a split has inflicted. In many cases, only time can revive a sense of peace, unity, and love within a wounded congregation.

The following guidelines come mainly from senior pastors who have learned them the hard way—after a church split. Although every prescription reported here was successful for someone, none of them will be truly effective unless the congregation has utmost confidence in the healing power of the Great Physician.

Prescription #1. Healing a war-torn church must start at the board level. In almost every church split, the governing board is at the center of the storm. After the split has occurred, board members will feel abused, betrayed, and disillusioned. Because a congregation usually reflects the attitude demonstrated by its leaders, the board must be in agreement about its direction and its ability to get there. This is a critical component of church stability, since people will assume that if there is strife at the board level, there must be a justifiable reason for it. The congregation may not have all the information about the conflict, but if the board is not united, chances are pretty good that the congregation will not be united either.

If there are several boards, each must deal with the problems in its designated area of responsibility. Perhaps a joint board meeting is needed to clear the air and get everyone back on track again. This may require a purging of critical board members who do not truly want to reunify the church. Those who are so inclined should be given the opportunity to remove themselves from the board in a face-saving manner. At any rate, board members who remain must be committed to a single focus of ministry direction. They must demonstrate confidence in their spiritual leader by agreeing to follow his lead.

Prescription #2. Don't get caught up in fixing blame. To do so is to live in the past at the expense of the future. At some point everyone must be willing to forgive the hurtful remarks that were expressed in the heat of conflict. Verbal battering can leave deep wounds that may never heal properly if attention is fixed on condemning those who inflicted them. In the words of one California pastor, "You have to be willing to just let it go. It isn't worth the emotional turmoil of fixing blame, no matter how justified it may seem at the time. Just let it go."

One way for board members to implement peace negotiations is to dispel the "we against them" attitude that may exist within the congregation. For healing to occur in interpersonal conflicts, there should be less emphasis on blaming "the other side" and more attention paid to rebuilding a team spirit. Find and use words that communicate mutuality of interest and harmony. Phrases like "shared vision" and "team unity" can do much to turn the focus from past division to new beginnings that instill hope for the future.

Prescription #3. As painful as it may be, the pastor and church leadership must eventually draw a line and force people to decide where they stand on whatever issues caused the division. After a church split, there will always be those who remain in the congregation even though they are not enthusiastic about the current leadership. Anyone who is actively undermining the leadership of the church should receive a visit from the senior pastor for the dual purpose of confronting the issues and seeking reconciliation. If that attempt is unsuccessful, representatives from the church board should follow up with their own visit. If this, too, fails to reconcile the differences, the dissatisfied member should be encouraged to find fellowship elsewhere. Without fixing blame or pointing fingers, both parties must come to grips with the reality that they have agreed to disagree and will do it in different locations. Whether through individual meetings, group gatherings, or messages from the pulpit, members who continue to cause division and strife must be notified that their actions will not be tolerated (see Prov. 6:19; 1 Cor. 1:10; and Eph. 4:31–32).

Confrontation in love, with the intent of reconciliation, must be the chief ingredient in any prescription for healing. Confrontation is probably the least-preferred pastoral responsibility, but it comes with the biblical job description. Much like a medical professional, a pastor must sometimes be willing to use extreme measures to save the life of the body. A cancerous growth does not heal itself—it must be cut out if healing is to occur. Until it is, nothing but further harm can be expected. Removing disruptive church members from fellowship is drastic action indeed, and it should be done only if the people who are causing division indicate an unwillingness to change their behavior. As one senior pastor put it, "You've got to preach the bad ones out, so you can preach the good ones in."

Prescription #4. The church leadership will have to approach disenfranchised members and reach out to them in love. This is particularly difficult when dealing with people who have been perceived as active participants in the split. Members who are still unhappy but have chosen not to leave with the departing group should be sought out and spoken to concerning their need for personal healing.

If words were spoken in haste, the pastor and church board must take the lead in seeking reconciliation, although "peacemaker" may be one of the most difficult roles required of a spiritual leader. Give former adversaries the benefit of the doubt and be the first to extend a hand of friendship. Welcome them back into the fellowship if they are willing to return.

One pastor from Iowa said that for almost a year after his church experienced a split, he and other board members visited every disgruntled member of the church. He was convinced that removing any residual hard feelings was the first step in preventing further misunderstandings and initiating reconciliation. He explained, "They may have chosen to reject our hand of friendship, but that was going to be their decision to make. Ours was to go and seek their understanding and fellowship." Most of the pastors who spoke about this step in the healing process said that a one-on-one meeting was the most effective way to communicate with alienated members. Getting them alone allows them to express their own opinions as opposed to the opinions of their friends. It also communicates that you value them enough to meet individually with them, that they are important, and that you really care about them.

Prescription #5. Once putting the hurts and pains of the split behind you is no longer your primary concern, focusing on the driving values of the church will keep the congregation's confidence and motivation alive. People must have a vision of the future to feel secure. Otherwise, they gradually become disillusioned and begin to drop off in their commitment to the church.

One pastor compared the split at his church to a bitter divorce. This young pastor had come to the church in the wake of a controversy that caused the former pastor to leave, taking the majority of the congregation with him. He began another church just four miles away, literally in the shadow of the church he had left. "In essence," said the pastor who replaced him, "the handsome husband left the house and took everything of value with him, leaving the wife to feel ugly and unwanted." The new pastor had the difficult task of renewing the hope and vision of an embattled congregation. "One of the biggest obstacles I faced," he said, "was to help the remaining remnant of the congregation believe in themselves. They needed to learn to see their own beauty, to be renewed in their calling, and to regain a purpose for existing." Eight years later, this young pastor has one of the most dynamic churches in his city. Its people needed to dream new dreams that were not tied to the past. At first, the new pastor had to dream those dreams for them and then pass them down. As the members began to believe in themselves, they were able to share in the pastor's vision and ultimately rebuild their hope for the future on the ashes of their former disillusionment. One of the tasks set before a new pastor who arrives at a church shortly after a split is to protect the church members from early setbacks. When old dreams are shattered, people are often left with a poor self-image and are easily discouraged by failure, no matter how minor.

Prescription #6. Create an environment where people can be successful in ministry. This starts by generating a high level of enthusiasm and excitement. One pastor said every Sunday he told stories from the pulpit about what God had done in the lives of church members during the past week. These were stories of spiritual victories, answered prayers, and people who were being changed by the providence of God. It was his way of convincing the congregation that the Holy Spirit had not abandoned the church. As a result, these people began to believe that God still wanted to use them as his vessels for ministry in the community. As their pastor explained, "Once they caught the momentum of what God was doing in their lives, they took their eyes off their past and began to look ahead to a glorious future."

Beyond communicating the message of God's ever-present movement in their lives, this pastor also enveloped the congregation with opportunities to share in the ministry. Soon the people tasted for themselves the rewards of servanthood and began to ignite in spiritual passion. If the pastor anticipated that a particular programmed event was going to be very successful, he made sure that people who especially needed to experience success were part of the leadership for the event. Later he would recognize their leadership and affirm them on Sunday morning from the pulpit. This created an atmosphere that said, "Things are moving here at this church, and you're an important part of it." As this attitude became contagious, people began to reinvest their spiritual gifts and talents into their church with new enthusiasm. It shifted the focus from mere survival to healthy growth.

Prescription #7. Preach the truths of Scripture to the congregation and model those truths in your own attitudes and behavior. In the heat of battle, people can lose their sense of what is really important. Although emotionally charged encounters may make standards of conduct seem ambiguous, the Word of God always stands as our guide for what is right and wrong.

Scripture speaks very clearly about how we are to treat our fellow brothers and sisters in Christ and how we are to show our respect for those in authority. If the Word of God is taught on a consistent basis, God's standards become the guide for all our words, attitudes, and behavior. We must also trust in the Holy Spirit's ability to stimulate a sinner to repentance, to soften a hardened heart, and to change an inappropriate pattern of behavior. Some people may disagree with their pastor's message, but if that message is clearly tied to the authority of Scripture, it is ultimately God to whom they are accountable for their thoughts and actions.

One pastor chose a series of messages based on Paul's letter to the Ephesians, a book whose theme is unity in the body of Christ. Another pastor preached for several weeks on acceptance, encouragement, and hope. Each of those topics was directly tied to Scripture and was designed to bring people to God through a tender message of love. One pastor said, "You have to preach like mad, and love them like mad—but not always in that order."

Prescription #8. The need for tenacity and conviction was mentioned by most of the pastors with whom I spoke, both those who came into the church after a split and those who had remained behind to bring healing. One survivor said, "A pastor must be sure of his calling if he is going to remain at a church after a split has occurred. We must remember that we are not commissioned by the church but by God. Until he reassigns us, we can't let the circumstances get us down." Another pastor, after commenting on the emotional strains of his responsibilities during the storm's aftermath, said that he was encouraged to remain on as spiritual leader after talking with a military general at a conference where he had gone to speak. After the meeting, the two men went for a long walk, and the pastor began to share his deep hurts and pains. The general's advice was clear and direct: "Son, the military doesn't send a general into a battle to play games. It sends a general in to take command and clean up the mess. As the spiritual leader of your church, you must return to that position and *lead*. Get back there and clean up the mess. Take command and move ahead!" It was the turning point in this pastor's ministry.

These prescriptions for healing a fractured church must be seen only as helpful suggestions. The speed with which reconciliation is achieved will depend on the issues involved and the character qualities of those responsible for restoring harmony and trust.

Personal Consequences for the Peacemakers

Even if bringing healing to a divided congregation goes fairly smoothly, there are many consequences for the pastors and board members who have served as peacemakers. Anyone who lives in the center of interpersonal fires can expect to get burned, sometimes severely.

One of the side effects mentioned by virtually every church leader I interviewed was personal pain and suffering. All the pastors said that trying to bring healing to a church that had split was a high-risk and stressful assignment. If they had been present *during* the split, the experience was even more devastating.

The pastors expressed disappointment over lost trust, personal integrity that had been called into question, friends who had betrayed them, and the shattering of ministry dreams. Several of them spoke with trembling voices as they related their stories and relived painful moments that had been temporarily forgotten. A few began to weep.

A number of the pastors or board members said they regretted losing their Christian perspective. I was told that even a desire to correct a wayward brother in love could deteriorate in anger to a verbal attack, which later had to be confessed as sin. It was apparent that the polarization of church staff and board members had caused months, even years, of wasted ministry and was now viewed with remorse.

Most of the people I interviewed confessed to bringing their work-related stress home with them and allowing it to affect their families. When the tension of being a peacemaker was added, some homes became riddled with strife and discord. Pastors and their wives argued about the will of God for the church, and board members took phone calls from angry parishioners, resulting in a loss of valuable family time. Eventually, entire families paid a price for the peacemaking process.

One of the most disheartening consequences of being a peacemaker at church can be the loss of motivation for service. Several pastors confessed their desire to leave the ministry and do anything else that wouldn't cause so much personal pain and tension. One of the pastors I tracked down by phone had left the ministry because he had been so badly abused by the members of his church. Verbal assaults and threats of legal repercussions or even physical retaliation had taken their toll.

Implications

Healing a divided church is not something to be taken lightly. Although the rewards of seeing a church renewed and spiritually productive bring a deep satisfaction, peacemaking is not without its own set of risks and dangers. Therefore, the pastor and church board must enter into this phase of ministry with an extremely large measure of prayer, mutual respect, and trust. Reactivating a team spirit is the first step in the healing process. The pastor and lay leadership can then serve as a support group for each other's pain. Once its energies are consolidated, the leadership team can infuse mutual respect, tenacious leadership and purposeful vision, even in the midst of seemingly overwhelming odds. A church divided against itself cannot stand, but when the spiritual leaders of that church are united, not even the unleashed powers of hell will be able to shake their determination.

Questions for Discussion

1. What warning signs of an impending split would you add to the list presented in this chapter?

2. Would you say that there is a low, medium, or high level of politics operating at your church? Give some reasons for making that generalization.
3. If you have experienced a church split, share your feelings about living through it. Which prescriptions given in this chapter were beneficial?
4. Can you identify any other prescriptions that you would add to this list?
5. What personal consequences have you already experienced as a result of serving as a church leader? How might it be different in the context of a church split?

For Further Reading

Flynn, Leslie B. *When the Saints Come Storming In*. Wheaton: Victor Books, 1988.

Gunnink, Jerrien. *Preaching for Recovery in a Strife-Torn Church*. Grand Rapids: Zondervan, 1989.

Hicks, H. Beecher. *Preaching Through the Storm*. Grand Rapids: Zondervan, 1987.

Leas, Speed, and Paul Kitlos. *Church Fights: Managing Conflicts in the Local Church*. Philadelphia: Westminster Press, 1973.

Issues Involved in a Church Day-Care Center

*D*ue to the growing number of women who are actively involved in the work force throughout North America, there is an ever-increasing need for safe and affordable child-care centers. Especially in most large cities, the demand far exceeds the supply, forcing many families to search for acceptable alternatives. Although some parents are able to rely on grandparents, neighbors, or friends for child care, others must resort to leaving their children at home without supervision or face the stark reality of losing an income that may be needed for economic survival.

Recent news reports of day-care center workers who have been accused (and in some cases convicted) of child molestation have created fear and apprehension among parents who must leave their children in the custody of such a facility. Many churches have responded to the need for a safe environment for children of working parents by providing child care for its members (and others in the local area). This allows many anxious parents to feel

250

more secure about their children's well-being since the church is generally regarded as a place where high moral and ethical standards are upheld.

Many questions must be addressed when a church entertains the possibility of beginning its own day-care center. Will the facility be an extension of the ministry of the church and seek to bring each child to Christ? Or will it simply be a baby-sitting service for church members and parents in the community? Some pastors and board members see church-sponsored day care as a year-round Vacation Bible School, while others want to make it a broader experience that will prepare a child for entering the public or private educational system. Beyond purpose and curriculum, the church must also examine all the financial, legal, health, and staffing issues involved in providing day care for young children. If a church already has a day-care facility, new board members should receive some orientation regarding those issues during the early stages of their term in office. That way, they will be able to make informed decisions about church policies that might affect the program.

In four of the five churches where I have served on staff, there has been a care facility or school for young children, and I have seen both excellent and poorly operated programs. I have also served on the board of directors for a day-care center. Dr. David Beckwith, senior pastor at Woodbridge Community Church in Irvine, California, has also worked with both good and bad programs. In his over twenty years of pastoral experience, he has supervised and been involved in the management of numerous day-care facilities. He conducts a seminar for pastors entitled "Day Care: Dream or Disaster?" Much of the material in this chapter comes from his seminar notes, which he kindly allowed me to use in this book. In a very real sense, Dr. Beckwith should be seen as a co-author of this particular chapter.

Reasons for Operating a Church Day-Care Center

If many churches were honest, they would admit that they began or currently maintain a child-care facility primarily to make money! It is unfortunate that a financial motive enters into the scenario, since churches are seen as nonprofit organizations in the eyes of the government. However, there are many reasons why a church may want to establish a day-care center, including the following six possibilities.[1]

1. *To find new ways to minister to those in need.* Families with two working parents or a single parent desperately need secure care for their young children. One way a church can make inroads into the lives of people in its surrounding community is by providing good child care. This is why some churches limit the children who attend their day-care facility to those who live within a few miles of the church. It is a way of making sure that this ministry reaches people in the immediate neighborhood. It is hoped that when parents appreciate the outreach of the church in this area, they will feel a greater measure of shared ownership in other church programs as well. This bond with local families can eventually translate into opportunities for evangelism through special activities sponsored jointly by the care facility and the church. Evangelistic outreach is a legitimate reason for providing child care at a local church, since it affirms the mission and overall purpose of the body of Christ.

2. *To provide a safe and secure child-care environment.* Because of the shortage of quality day-care centers, some parents must leave their children with baby-sitters who may not have to meet the stringent licensing requirements of the state (because of the small number of children involved). This may result in understaffing and other unsafe conditions. Of course, baby-sitters are not necessarily unsatisfactory care-givers, but if their facilities are not subject to legal regulations, only their concern for the children's welfare will determine whether adequate safety provisions are made.

3. *To encourage children's overall development.* Scripture confirms that Jesus had a well-balanced childhood. Luke 2:52 tells us that he "grew in wisdom [mental discrimination] and stature [physical development], and in favor with God [spirituality] and men [social skills]." A church day-care facility is a healthy environment where a child's character can develop in a balanced manner. In particular, the church is better equipped to handle spiritual training than most other organizations are. A church can provide support personnel (pastoral staff and lay teachers), adequate physi-

cal space (chapel, playground, classrooms), and study materials from the children's ministry program. Publicly funded day-care centers and most private care-givers lack the resources (and usually the will) to stimulate the spiritual maturation of the children for whom they are responsible.

4. *To plant biblical truths during a child's formative early years.* Child specialists agree that preschool experiences (from one to four years of age) have a lasting influence on how a child's character and value system will develop. Children are able to learn and understand moral concepts well before entering kindergarten, and church day-care personnel can communicate biblical principles in a way that young children can understand and assimilate into their lives. The spiritual commitment of the staff members can be monitored to ensure that their teachings and lifestyle are in agreement with the church's statement of faith and standards of conduct.

5. *To help parents learn skills that are based on biblical teaching and sound principles of child development.* A church can provide parental guidance through magazines, books, and videos available in its lending library and by inviting parents to special seminars and support groups that deal with child-rearing issues. (These may already be part of the overall ministry.) Finally, in cases where individual counseling may be needed, this could be handled by the regular pastoral staff and/or through referral to appropriate community agencies.

6. *To make better use of church facilities, which in many cases would otherwise be empty during the week.* As faithful stewards, we should seek to find ways to maximize the availability of church resources for ministry purposes. On a practical level, the income from a child-care center can contribute to the amortization of church property. It is important to note here that a day-care center should not be charged rent by the church. Rent is considered taxable income, and a church that lists child-care revenue as rent on its monthly financial statement is in danger of having to pay taxes on that income, even though it is considered a nonprofit organization. If revenue from the program is listed as "day-care income," it is treated in the same way as church contributions. It is then

nontaxable and can be used toward the upkeep and maintenance of the overall church facilities.

Starting a Day-Care Center

The issues involved in starting a day-care center are so varied that it is beyond the scope of this chapter to deal with them in depth. In addition, each state has its own set of licensing criteria. When one church tried to claim that its child-care facility was exempt from state licensing regulations, the government promptly shut the operation down.[2] In a general sense, it is best for a church that wishes to begin a day-care ministry to proceed as follows:

Step One. Start by contacting the Department of Social Services and ask about procedures for beginning a child-care facility. A knowledgeable employee will explain in detail what is needed from a state perspective. It is highly advisable that one or more church board members attend an introductory meeting with a governmental spokesperson. This will be an opportunity to ask questions and get specific information about regulations that apply to insurance, staffing ratios, square footage per child, qualifications for administrators and teachers, and so on.

Step Two. Decide who at the church will serve as liaison between the day-care facility and the church. This might be the senior pastor in a small church, but in larger churches it will probably not be realistic to add this requirement to an already full job description. Some churches give the responsibility to either the director of Christian education or the director of children's ministry, while others create an entirely new position.

Step Three. Create a separate board of directors for the day-care center. Regular church board members (trustees, elders, deacons) should not have to supervise this program in addition to their other responsibilities. However, I recommend that one or two members of the existing church board(s) serve on the new board, so that church administrators have a voice in the way the day-care center is operated. The day-care center is first and foremost a ministry of the church and should not compromise or control the church's regular agenda.

Step Four. Have the day-care center's board of directors draw up a manual of personnel policies and procedures and submit it for approval to the governing board of the church. This assigns the ultimate overseeing of the day-care facility to the church administrators without requiring them to be involved in program or mundane decisions. Once these overarching policies are stipulated, the governing board of the church is freed from getting bogged down in minute details of the program. Most decision making will be delegated to the day-care board. Only major policy decisions should be referred to the church board for approval.

Personnel Management

The key to any effective ministry is the acquisition of quality staff. A church might have superb physical facilities and a fine program for young children, but without trained and highly motivated personnel, it might as well lock the doors of its day-care center. There is simply no substitute for excellent directors and teachers. How do you find them and—having done so—how do you ensure proper training and supervision? Although the answers depend on what resources are available, there are a few things that almost every church can do to get off on the right foot when it comes to staffing a child-care program.

Selecting the Day-Care Director. The most important person in terms of implementing the church's philosophy and purposes in the area of day care is the center's director. This individual will be responsible for selecting curricula, hiring and training staff, complying with licensing regulations, following board policies, and a host of other important details. The church should have clear-cut policies written down before any hiring is done, for it is on the basis of these policies that any screening of applicants (and review of personnel performance) will be conducted.

In terms of qualifications, first examine the state regulations regarding educational background, teaching experience, number of centers one director may manage, and continuing education. These requirements are probably clearly listed in a Department of Social Services manual for day-care centers. Since a church cannot obtain a license without complying with these standards, you should use them as the basis for determining the director's qualifications. The church's special requirements in the area of spiritual commitment should also be added to this list. A sample job description for a day-care director is included at the end of this chapter.

Staffing the Day-Care Center. Since this facility will be an extension of the church's ministry, the staff should meet the same standards of character and conduct as the pastoral staff and lay leaders. In addition, as in the matter of the director, there may be state requirements for the teaching staff with which you must comply. Many church boards want to know if they can legally restrict the staff of a day-care center to people who support the doctrinal views of their congregation. This form of "job discrimination" is allowed provided a staff member's religious beliefs are an integral part of job performance, much like any other member of the church staff. Under those circumstances, a church is not forced to hire a non-Christian or member of a different denomination. This legal precedent has been upheld by a number of state-level court rulings.

It is best to state all staffing requirements in both the church constitution and the day-care center's policy manual. For example, one church where I served on staff specified that *all* day-care employees must (1) have a personal knowledge of Christ as Lord and Savior; (2) have a belief in the Bible as the Word of God; and (3) be in agreement with the church's constitution and bylaws.

Hiring Procedure. Beyond completing an application form and supplying references, each applicant should be interviewed by the day-care center's director and perhaps also by the center's governing board. As a courtesy, I would suggest that each newly hired employee be introduced to the senior pastor. If a member of the pastoral staff is trained in psychological testing, it would be wise to administer a standard personality profile to every applicant (or at least every new employee). Some churches also require written testimony of an applicant's salvation experience.

Never neglect to check an applicant's references. In addition to those provided by the applicant, you might ask each of the references for an additional name to contact. These can serve as secondary sources of character reference. A few extra minutes of preventive inquiry during the hiring process can save the hours of painful clean-up required when a candidate who has been hired needs to be terminated later. Keep asking yourself whether you would want this person to be responsible for the health, safety, and spiritual guidance of your own child. Unless the answer is a definite "yes," do not proceed any farther with the hiring process.

Child Abuse and the Church

One of the evidences of our troubled times is the increasing incidence of abuse that is directed toward children. It has been estimated that child abuse—physical, emotional, or sexual—occurs in approximately 60 percent of homes in the United States. Some of those children will die from the abuse they experience.[3] Many others will be permanently traumatized in one way or another.

The church itself has not remained untouched by this disturbing sociological phenomenon. Whether in the day-care facility, the children's ministry, or in the youth group, child molestation and other forms of abuse have been found to occur in the church. Such abuse has resulted in increased litigation against the church. The subject is quite broad and deserves careful examination. I have included some excellent resources at the end of the chapter on this subject.

I am not aware of any state that does not require staff members to report suspected occurrences of child abuse in the home (or in church-sponsored day-care facilities) to the local authorities. Neither the separation of church and state nor pastor-penitent privileges extend to this area. It would be wise for each day-care board and church board to establish policies for reporting such suspected abuse. Clearly state: Who will make the call? Will the senior pastor be included in the decision? Will the police be notified in addition to the Department of Social Services? Important questions like these must be discussed and decided.

Implications

Establishing a day-care center as part of its overall ministry is an excellent way for a local church to make full use of its resources, answer the practical needs of some of its members, and reach other families in the community. If such a facility is truly to be a safe haven for children who might otherwise receive less adequate care, it must meet all state licensing requirements and be staffed with concerned personnel who are in accord with the purposes and moral values endorsed by the congregation.

Although church administrators should provide broad overseeing of the day-care program, they should feel free to assign specific responsibility for its operation to an auxiliary board of directors. Because the church's primary governing board is ultimately accountable for the management of any church-sponsored activity, its members must be knowledgeable about the broad issues involved in providing child care and be kept informed of any problems that develop. Forming a team approach to this type of ministry requires full cooperation between the pastoral staff, the lay leaders of the church, and the director of the day-care facility. If this can be achieved, the church will have found one more way to implement its desire for community outreach.

Questions for Discussion

1. If your church already has a day-care program, what were the reasons for establishing it?
2. If your church does not have a day-care program, what reasons have been given for not establishing one?
3. If you were to prioritize the reasons for having a day-care facility in your church (from the list of reasons given in this chapter), in what order would you place them?
4. If your church has a day-care facility, do you (as a pastor or church board member) have a copy of its policies manual? Do you have a copy of the director's job description? If so, have you taken the time to read this material?
5. Are there any policies for your church's day-care center that you do not understand or would like to see revised?
6. To whom does the director of your day-care center report? How often is he/she given a performance review? Are the standards for this review in writing?
7. Does your church have a written procedure for reporting suspected child abuse?

Sample Job Description: Director of Church Day-Care Center

Job Title: Director of Church Day-Care Center

Responsible to: Minister of Christian Education

Qualifications

1. Personal faith in Jesus Christ as Lord and Savior.
2. Belief in the Bible as the Word of God.
3. Adherence to the church constitution.
4. Member of an evangelical church.
5. Meets all state requirements regarding education and experience.
6. Ability to develop a positive relationship with children, parents, day-care board, pastoral staff, and church boards.
7. Certified in CPR and Advanced First Aid.
8. Exhibits a cooperative spirit and is a team player in regard to church goals and activities.
9. Strong commitment to help individuals and families know Jesus Christ as personal Lord and Savior.

Specific Responsibilities

1. Plan, organize, staff, direct, and evaluate the overall ministry of the day-care center according to state regulations and the church's policy manual.
2. Develop the annual budget for the center, setting tuition rates and overseeing the financial expenditures in conjunction with the center's board of directors.
3. Maintain current files on all personnel and students at the facility.
4. Purchase supplies, materials, and equipment.
5. Report to the day-care board on a monthly basis and serve as an *ex officio* member.
6. Maintain an emergency plan in the event of fire, earthquake, tornado, flood, etc.
7. Monitor the cleanliness of the facility and communicate with the maintenance/custodial staff about any needed improvements.
8. Plan and coordinate special events.
9. Plan and coordinate the curriculum.
10. Plan one special activity per month based on curriculum theme.
11. Develop and maintain a consistent discipline policy.
12. Recruit, interview, and train all personnel for the facility. Staff hiring and termination will be handled by the board of directors on the recommendation of the center's director.
13. Arrange staff work schedules, substitutes, and vacations.
14. Conduct staff performance evaluations on an annual basis.
15. Write and update staff job descriptions.
16. Supervise classroom use and time organization and the organization of classroom furniture and equipment.
17. Develop regular communication with parents through appropriate means.
18. Conduct parent-orientation seminars and education programs.
19. Maintain sensitivity to parents' needs and requests.
20. Develop promotional materials and advertising as needed.
21. Participate in related professional organizations.
22. Plan for and maintain a safe and attractive education environment.
23. Conduct a monthly fire drill and keep appropriate records.
24. Coordinate facility set-up and change-over for Sunday usage.
25. Assist in any other duties assigned by the minister of Christian education.

For Further Reading

Anthony, Michael, and Ruth MacLean. "A Child Abuse Awareness and Prevention Plan for the Local Church." *Christian Education Journal* vol. 12, no. 2, 9–15.

Hightower, James. "Ministering to the Abused and Their Families," in *Equipping Deacons in Caring Skills,* Robert L. Sheffield, ed. (vol. 2). Nashville: Convention Press, 1988.

Lester, Andrew. *Pastoral Care with Children in Crisis.* Philadelphia: Westminster Press, 1985.

Lund, Jan. "Ministering in an Abusive Crisis," in *Ministry with Youth in Crisis,* Richard Ross and Judi Hayes, ed. Nashville: Convention Press, 1988.

MacLean, Ruth, Director of Children's Ministries at First Baptist Church of Lakewood, California, has developed extensive materials and has served as a consultant to churches on this important topic. She may be contacted at: First Baptist Church, 5336 Arbor Road, Long Beach, CA 90808.

Martin, Grant. *Counseling for Family Violence and Abuse.* Waco: Word Books, 1987.

Monfalcone, Wesley. *Coping with Abuse in the Family.* Philadelphia: Westminster Press, 1980.

Gossip, Complaints, and Nitpickers

egardless of their position in the church, denominational affiliation, years of experience, gender, or level of education, the one common denominator among those who serve in ministry is that they all face rumors, complaints, and outright opposition from members of the congregation. The nature and frequency of such problems can, at times, be the determining factor as to whether a pastor or board member is satisfied in his or her present church or will move elsewhere.

Dealing with complaints from people you are trying to serve is emotionally draining, at the very least. Whether congregational dissatisfaction takes the form of rumors and gossip, sly innuendoes, or boisterous shouting, being on the receiving end of massed opposition can be an overwhelming experience. In fact, spiritual warfare can seem like wrestling with young children compared to the forces that church members can muster when they are unhappy with their leaders.

What follows in this chapter are some suggestions about what you can do when these forms of opposition come to the surface in your church, particularly how you can handle them in a way that does not destroy the valuable effects of your ministry.

Responding to Opposition

No matter how much you might be tempted to resort to physical violence or verbal abuse to defend your reputation or position, this method of solving problems is, of course, not biblical. Neither is it effective! Although I have known some church leaders who resorted to strong-arm tactics to settle their differences, the end result was always worse. They may have won a battle, but in the process of winning it they lost the war—because they were soon removed from office or "convinced" of the need to find another church in which to worship. There are far more constructive ways to respond to gossip, complaints, and nitpicking in the church.

1. *Realize that all church leaders at some time or another will face opposition.* Scripture confirms that those who pursue God's agenda will be vulnerable to attacks by either hostile outsiders or dissenters within the fellowship. Moses' leadership was challenged by Korah and his friends; Joseph faced the hostility of his own family members; Nehemiah's plans were criticized by Sanballat, Tobiah, and Geshem; and Daniel had his share of problems from the city's commissioners and satraps. The apostle Paul's ministry was questioned by many people, but the Ephesians Alexander and Demetrius are mentioned specifically by name. And, of course, Jesus' authority was disputed by the religious establishment and even by Judas, one of his own board members. Those whom God has used to accomplish ministry have always had to contend with rumormongers, complainers, and less subtle adversaries.

Too often the harmful effects of an internal conflict could have been avoided if a church leader had seen trouble coming and taken necessary action before extensive damage could occur. A survey taken by *Leadership* found that a stunning 85 percent of all pastors had at one point in their professional lives "felt betrayed by persons I thought I could trust," yet only a small percentage said that they had anticipated the conflict.[1]

2. *As soon as you hear a potentially dangerous rumor (or a complaint), try to determine what degree of truth is involved.* Most rumors and gossip contain an element of truth, but the facts have become distorted and twisted. The key to resolving the matter is to gather information about who started the rumor and why. The "why" may be a hidden complaint caused by miscommunication.

Boyce Bowden, in an article entitled "Slowing Down the Rumor Mill," says we should ask ourselves five questions if we want to analyze a rumor:

Is the rumor true?
Who started the rumor?
Why was it started?
How extensively has it spread?
What do our key publics think about it?[2]

3. *If you determine that the truth has been distorted, clearly communicate all the facts in an appropriate manner.* This may take the form of a public statement, a written letter to those involved, or a notice in the church bulletin or monthly newsletter. However, if the rumor is of little importance and the consequences minimal, printing a public notice may create more harm than good! In this case it is best to simply contact the people involved by phone or in person and personally clarify the issues.

If, in all honesty, you feel that you have somehow contributed to the misunderstanding, admit your error and apologize for it. An apology can snuff out the damaging effects of a rumor quicker than written notices that seek to direct accusations toward others.

4. *Once you have made every effort to resolve the issue, accept the fact that some people will not agree with the direction you are taking.* You must answer to a higher authority, and if you truly feel that what you are doing is right, you will have to weather the storm and continue pressing ahead in spite of opposition. (This is much easier to say than do, but unless it is done, nothing of lasting value will come from your ministry.)

This is also where having the security of board approval will enable you to sustain the strength that you need. When other church leaders also feel you are taking the right course, their support will provide you with encouragement. However, be aware that the board may later begin to fragment under the pressure of complaining church members.

5. *Anticipate gossip, complaints, and nitpicking before they occur.* Rumors and complaints generally come from the same group of individuals. Some personalities seem to enjoy controversy. Because such people are never satisfied, they tend to incite dissension in any organization to which they belong. If you could follow them around the community, you would find them stirring up trouble in other places besides your church—perhaps in the PTA or at a city council meeting. They will write articles to the local newspaper complaining about something that is (or isn't) happening to their satisfaction and will shout at their child's football coach for not calling the right plays. No matter where these malcontents go, they stir up trouble. Luther Thompson identifies several common complainers in the local church: "Generally there are limited numbers or types of difficult personalities. This has been noted repeatedly by students of human behavior. There are the hostile or angry; the self-centered; the snipers given to sarcasm and satire; the negators who love to say 'I told you so'; the super agreeable; the silent ones who refuse to respond; and the victims who indulge endlessly in self-pity."[3]

If you have people like this in your church (and most churches do), you can minimize the effects of their caustic negativism by doing some advance planning. Realize that each personality type requires a different approach, an individual manner of confrontation. Having a working knowledge of the proper techniques to be used with each one will soften the blows of their criticism and perhaps lessen the damage they cause.

6. *Remember that not all opposition has negative consequences.* It has been helpful to me to realize that even the attacks of people who desire to bring me harm can be used by God to increase the fruitfulness of my labors. I encourage all church leaders to keep a long-term perspective on their ministry-related problems.

I discovered that principle from my own pain and hurt in dealing with gossip, complaints, and nitpicking. As I mentioned in the chapter on conflict resolution, while serving as director of a camp (in eastern Canada), I had hired some staff members who apparently had their own agenda for the program. Within a couple of months, these individuals had created enough false rumors, complaints, and criticism that I was forced to leave my position. I was deeply hurt and confused about how God could allow such events to unfold when I knew in my heart that the decisions I had made were right.

Shortly after leaving this camp, I took another position at a camp in western Canada. After I had spent one summer there, the executive director resigned and the board asked me to become the new camp director. Still suffering from the wounds of the previous summer, I was extremely reluctant. But I accepted the job, and the result was four summers of the most fruitful ministry I have ever experienced.

Because staff members at the previous camp were motivated by greed and personal ambition, they masterminded my removal. Yet, looking back, I can honestly say that my pain and heartache were a small price to pay for the blessings I found in the new position. Sometimes it takes a few years before we gain a broader perspective on adversity, but keeping an open mind and a trusting spirit after a storm can make a big difference in how well we survive.

7. *Sometimes opposition is a signal that it's time to move on.* The consequences of remaining at the church may not be worth the painful compromises you must make. It isn't easy to leave a position of leadership in which you have invested time, energy, and your personal integrity. Although that decision may be viewed by the opposing forces as backing down or even admitting blame, it may ultimately be a more Christian response than prolonging the battle. Luther Thompson writes: "Love wants the best and attempts to bring out the best in every person, which is not to presume what that is. We are not called to reform people, but only to love them and trust God's grace can accomplish His purpose."[4]

Ministering to the Opposition

It may seem an outrageous command, but God calls us to love our enemies and minister to those who oppose us. We are expected to be a distinctive people who refrain from the retaliatory practices of the rest of the world because we model a higher code of ethics. As Christians we have a responsibility to serve even those who are trying to undermine our God-given objectives. Here are a few practical suggestions on how we can minister to those who start rumors, defame our character, or nitpick our every decision.

Suggestion #1. See your adversaries in the context of their environment. Sometimes they are not unhappy with the church, but with events in their personal lives—a dead-end job, financial worries, health problems, or a failing marriage—and are taking out their frustrations on you. By getting a behind-the-scenes look at a complainer's situation, you may learn that your leadership is not the real problem. That realization can raise your level of patience and forbearance.

Suggestion #2. Don't treat troublemakers as ambassadors of an evil empire, but as people for whom Christ died. See even their opposition as an opportunity to test your level of spiritual maturity. Sometimes we don't know how strong we are until we are put to the test. If we view these difficult individuals as stepping-stones to further growth and development, we can approach them with a more positive attitude. How we address them in conversation or behave toward them in public is a testimony of how Christ would deal with them. We must model respect, love, and compassion in all our words and deeds—as he did.

Suggestion #3. Spend some time with complaining individuals outside the context of the local church. If you usually see them only on your own territory, perhaps you can reduce some of the tension by visiting them where they work or live. Or you might invite them out for coffee at a local restaurant and discuss the matter privately without the obstruction of your desk and office. An informal setting can make a big difference in the tone of the conversation that takes place.

Suggestion #4. Attempt to resolve the dispute with a minimum amount of congregational involvement. If the problem is between a few people, keep the issue private. You will then lessen the risk of a public trial that may humiliate your opponents if they lose. Conflicts that are self-contained are easier to resolve than those that are allowed to spread through the church like wildfire. Once that happens, dousing the flames will require a major expenditure of spiritual energy that would be far better used in confronting the real enemy.

Keeping the conflict confidential is important, for as soon as the opposition hears that you are communicating your side of the story to others (and they will most certainly hear of it), they will feel the need to defend their views as well. The result will be a large-scale public-relations battle between two warring factions.

Suggestion #5. It may get to the point that the only way to deal with those who bring conflict into the church is to confront them with "tough love." You may then need to bring several members of the church board with you for support (see Matt. 18:15–17). The principles suggested in chapter 12 will be helpful at this point.

There are times when parents must be very firm with their children because they know it is the right thing to do. In the same way, there are situations in the life of a church leader that require administering loving discipline to a fellow believer. Otherwise, the whole assembly will suffer the negative consequences of one person's actions.

When parents have surrendered their authority to a child, the welfare of the entire family is in jeopardy. The same principle applies in the life of the church. Disciplinary action should never be entered into lightly, but too often it is not used, even when it is necessary. If we are going to live by the analogy of the church as a spiritual family, its leaders must not shun their responsibility to serve as wise and loving parents of the congregation.

Implications

Gossip, complaints, and nitpicking have inflicted extensive damage on the church since its earliest days. Learning to deal with difficult people is a skill that all pastors and church board members must come to grips with if they are going to be effective servant-leaders. Survivors of a number of years in ministry have developed a set of coping skills that probably resemble the suggestions listed in this chapter. They may even have developed a few more that have worked for them. It can be very helpful for a church board to discuss potentially thorny issues before they have a chance to cause trouble. That way, a strategy of dealing with difficult people and situations can be mapped out in advance. By removing personalities from the scenario, conflict resolution becomes easier to achieve.

There may be no way to stop mean-spirited rumors and gossip from occurring, but much can be done to lessen their damaging effects. Since every congregation will include difficult people at some time in its history, pastors and board members should see this dimension of their job as critical to the life and health of their church. If they do not accept this as a high-priority item, they will be looking for a new senior pastor every few years! Better to deal with the real source of the problem once and for all than to have a revolving door on the pastoral office. Confronting difficult people in the church is never easy, but it goes with the territory. You can't avoid the inevitable, but you can reduce the pain.

Questions for Discussion

1. What kinds of rumors and gossip have you experienced as a church leader?
2. How did you feel when the rumor placed you in a bad light?
3. How would you measure the success of your church in stopping rumors and gossip from spreading?
4. What could your church do better to reduce the damaging effects of rumors and gossip?
5. How are complaints dealt with in your church?
6. Does your church board get involved in resolving complaints brought against the pastor by a church member? Why or why not?
7. How does your church board handle disputes between members of the board? Has this method been effective?
8. What can be done at your church to improve the manner in which nitpicking is dealt with?

For Further Reading

Bell, A. Donald. *How to Get Along with People in the Church.* Grand Rapids: Zondervan, 1960.

Biehl, Bob. *Increasing Your Leadership Confidence.* Sisters, Oreg.: Questar, 1989.

Jones, G. Brian, and Linda Phillips-Jones. *A Fight to the Better End.* Wheaton: Victor Books, 1989.

Rush, Myron. *Hope for Hurting Relationships.* Wheaton: Victor Books, 1989.

Shelley, Marshall. *Helping Those Who Don't Want Help.* Waco: Word Books and *Christianity Today,* 1986.

_____. *Well-Intentioned Dragons.* Waco: Word Books and *Christianity Today,* 1985.

Wilson, Marlene. *Survival Skills for Managers.* Boulder: Johnson Publishing, 1981.

Bringing Renewal to a Declining Church

Searching for the secrets to church growth would seem to resemble the quest for the Lost City of the Incas. Both hold the promise of rich rewards, but they also involve a little bit of luck, a map free of dead-ends or ambiguous markings, and a huge dose of sweat, frustration, and hard work. Furthermore, just as the directions to one cache of hidden gold will not lead to treasure buried elsewhere, a formula that spurs growth in one church will not necessarily work as well in another. So many issues are involved: leadership style of the pastor, changing demographics in the community, history of the church, climate of staff-board relationships, and so on.

It is important to note here that the field of church growth is expanding at an incredible rate. Therefore, this chapter is designed to serve simply as a brief overview of the topic, with no attempt made to be exhaustive in reporting on the current research. Church leaders who desire more detailed information in this area are encouraged to consult the resources listed at the end of this chapter.

The Elusive Goal of Church Growth

There is no doubt that the growth rate of a church is a measure of its vitality. The Bible speaks of the church as the body of Christ. As such, it should reflect all the characteristics of a living organism, including steady growth and development. We would worry about the health of a child who never grew. Likewise, we expect churches to increase in both size and maturity. Yet, if church growth is our reasonable expectation, why does the process seem so mysterious—and why is success in this area so elusive?

I once served in a church as "associate pastor of church growth." While in that position I read countless books, listened to taped seminars, and spoke with national consultants on the subject. However, none of the research material I surveyed at the time (and since) highlighted the two principles that I consider foundational to our understanding of the dynamics of church growth. They may seem obvious—but if they were obvious to others, I would have seen them in print, and frankly I haven't.

The first principle is this: *Ultimately, it is God's empowerment that produces growth in his church.* Like the ebb and flow of a tide, a church may experience periods of significant growth for no apparent reason. Simply put, when the Spirit of God is working in the life of a church, there is sudden and miraculous growth. On the other hand, there are times when all the right ingredients are present (at least according to the "experts"), but growth does not come. In fact, the church may actually experience a decline. Consultants swarm in and study every conceivable factor, only to conclude that the church *should* be growing—but it isn't. I believe it is normal for a church to experience such ebbs and flows. We can exhaust a lot of energy trying to "pump up" the body of Christ, but when all is said and done, it is God who brings the increase.

The second foundational principle flows from the first: *Total responsibility for bringing growth to a church cannot be laid at the door of the senior pastor.* Although clergy members form one of the most critical links in the growth process, far too many congregations have hired a pastor for the express purpose of building a megachurch, only to find out shortly after the pastor arrives on the scene that he did not bring a magic formula with him.

I recently spoke with a senior pastor about this issue, and he shared with me an insightful illustration from his own life. Shortly after graduating from seminary, this young man and his wife went to a quiet community outside of Phoenix and began a church in their home with just thirteen neighbors. For several years he labored to feed the flock and help them grow, but eventually he hit a spiritual wall and felt discouraged. No matter what the pastor did, he could not get his congregation to grow beyond about two hundred people. Wrestling with God over what seemed to be a failing effort, he begged, fasted, and nearly worked himself into the hospital with an ulcer. One day, while picking up a little girl for Sunday school, this man heard her ask from the back seat, "Are you the Lord of your church?" Out of the mouth of this innocent child had come a message from God. The pastor pulled the car over and began to weep as he realized that he had been trying to be *Lord* of the church, not merely its spiritual advisor. He gave up his fixation on increasing the membership rolls and began concentrating more earnestly on faithful service. Eventually, growth did come, and this church now has one of the largest congregations in the state. This man learned a valuable lesson about church growth that is seldom seen in any book but the Bible—Jesus said, "I *[not the senior pastor]* will build my church . . ." (Matt. 16:18).

What these two foundational principles tell us is that whenever the sovereignty and purposes of God intersect with the best that we humans have to offer, *he* will provide the blessings. Sometimes church growth (or decline) can be explained, but it often remains a mystery beyond our understanding. Having said that, I will describe the symptoms of decline that may deem it appropriate to close a local church's doors permanently. Then, on a more positive note, I will summarize what might be done to implement a renewal process that can sometimes bring new vitality to a stagnant or declining church.

To Close or Not to Close?

When—if ever—should a declining church be closed? Although making that difficult decision may seem on the surface the same as admitting defeat to the enemy, there are times when closing down a ministry may actually be in the best interest of the congregation. According to Gary McIntosh, church-growth consultant and editor of the Church Growth Network Newsletter, between three and four thousand churches close every year in the United States. He identifies several key factors to be carefully considered before deciding that a church is, indeed, dying, and therefore should be closed.[1]

1. *Public Worship Attendance.* A church needs at least fifty adults for a worship service that is celebrative and attractive to new people (having 20 to 40 adults puts the church in an unhealthy situation; less than 20 is a strong indication that the church should be closed).

2. *Total Giving Units.* It usually takes a minimum of 10 to 12 giving units to provide for a full-time pastor. It takes another 10 to 12 units to provide for the ministry of the church in terms of supplies, advertising, etc. A church reaches a danger point when it has less than 25 giving units.

3. *Lay Leadership Pool.* As a rule of thumb, a church needs one leader for every 10 members (junior high and up), 1 leader for every 6 elementary-school children, and 1 leader for every 2 children below school age. Less leadership than this will make it difficult to provide for the needs of a growing ministry.

4. *An Effective Ministry.* A church needs at least one ministry for which it is known in the community. For example, some churches may be known for their adult Sunday school, others for their children's program or ministry to senior citizens.

5. *Past Growth Rate.* A growth rate that has been declining for 5 to 10 years should serve as a warning signal. If a church is only about one-fourth (or less) of its original size, it is likely to be facing hard times that may force its eventual closure.

6. *Congregation's Spiritual Health.* A church's spiritual climate is another factor to be considered. Is a church characterized by peace, happiness, and love? Or by anger, bitterness, and discouragement?

7. *Average Membership Tenure.* How long have most of the members been attending? If the average tenure is more than 20 years, it is a sign that a church is having difficulty reaching and assimilating new people.

8. *Focus on Church Goals.* Is the main focus of a church on its own needs? Or does it reach out to new people? Do leaders talk about ministry, mission, and purpose? Or about paying bills, hanging on, the past, membership concerns, and real estate?

9. *Budget Expenditures.* Where is the money spent? On outreach and advertising the ministry's mission and purpose? Or are these areas the first to be cut when the budget needs tightening?

10. *Church Rumors.* Is there positive talk about God and his plans for the church? Are there people who believe that God can renew the church in the days ahead? Or do most people talk about the past, respond pessimistically to visionary statements, and fail to recognize God at work among them?

Obviously, no one indicator should be used as justification for making such a major decision in the life of a church. Many churches that are strong today were once on the verge of closing. Bear Valley Baptist Church in Denver (Frank Tillapaugh, former pastor) and The Church on the Way in Van Nuys (Jack Hayford, pastor) are but two examples of how God turned around a church that was in serious decline.

The Process of Church Decline

Mary Guy's insightful book, *From Organizational Decline to Organizational Renewal: The Phoenix Syndrome,* is an excellent resource for our examination of church decline. The subtitle refers to the legendary bird described by the ancient Egyptians as living for five or six centuries. Then, having been consumed in fire by its own volition, the bird rises again in youthful freshness out of the ashes. How wonderful it would be if that sort of rebirth could be duplicated in the life of a dying church! Guy depicts organizational decline as a downward spiral that is marked by eight phases.[2] I find them quite accurate when describing the process of decline in a local church.

Phase One: *Recognition.* A church that is in decline probably knows it but is refusing to admit the obvious. Although its members may look for any shred of evidence to the contrary, deep inside they know in their heart that their church is slowly dying. They have come to recognize it by the many funerals they have had lately and by how few weddings have taken place. They see it in the number of gray heads in the worship services and the vacant spaces in the parking lot. They may not verbalize their thoughts, but they do recognize the decline.

Phase Two: *Stress.* At this stage of decline, the church leaders begin to feel the pressure. As they verbalize their worries about surviving, they create a high level of anxiety within the congregation. Fear for the future begins to surface and is never far from anyone's thoughts.

Phase Three: *Circle the Wagons.* Now the church is concerned with keeping its assets and income safe from the practical demands of the outside world. Its leaders become frugal. They conserve on fuel, electricity, and office supplies. Sunday school material is recycled. There is a growing mentality of "preserve and protect at all costs."

Phase Four: *Restricted Information Flow.* At this point, those in leadership guard the records to avoid advertising the truth that the church is dying. Quarterly reports are late (on purpose, but nobody will admit it); evaluations of personnel or programs are not circulated; and reports to the denomination are incomplete and slow to arrive.

Phase Five: *Finger Pointing.* This is the stage where emotions have become so volatile that they are expressed in a negative and, therefore, counterproductive manner. Certain people are accused of poor decision making, and the past is relived with an eye to pointing out all the mistakes that have ever been made. Gossip creates a common enemy, and rumors suggest quick answers to long-standing problems.

Phase Six: *Collective Rationalization.* This is a protective belief in the correctness of whatever is being done. There are illusions of unanimity, but it is seldom truly experienced.

Phase Seven: *Defective Decision Making.* Since information has been restricted, it is difficult to formulate, much less implement, constructive plans. Decisions are piecemeal, alternatives unclear. This stage is essentially a desperate grab for solutions.

Phase Eight: *Continued Decline.* In this last phase, the few remaining faithful, described by themselves as "the remnant," feel invulnerable. Although this illusion peaks with feelings of inherent rightness and fiery optimism, the downward trend is probably unstoppable.

Eventually, even the most hopeful church leaders may come to the realization that it is futile to continue their efforts to keep the church open. They will then either look for a church with which to merge, change denominational affiliation, or sell the physical facilities to another congregation. (If the building is privately owned, the membership will disband, and the buildings may remain empty for some time.) But it doesn't always end that way! Some churches in serious decline have reversed the downward plunge and begin an upswing in membership and attendance. That they were able to do so is clear evidence of God's miraculous grace and provision for those who labor in his fields.

Moving Off the Plateau

Although approximately 1 to 2 percent of all churches in America permanently close their doors each year, many more are locked in a continual state of immobility. This is referred to in church-growth terminology as "being on the plateau." It describes a church that is no longer growing, but is not really dying either. Moving off the plateau has been the topic of numerous books, seminars, and seminary courses. A summary of their content is presented below.

Most church-growth consultants with whom I have become acquainted over the years agree that a church has ceased to grow when it maintains the same attendance figure—plus or minus 10 percent—for the past five years. Such a church is said to be on a plateau. Nearly 40 percent of the churches that I surveyed for this book were currently in that situation. It is estimated that 95 percent of our churches could grow if their leaders *and* their members really set their minds to it and are willing to make some sacrifices.

Peter Wagner, respected internationally as an expert on church growth, has written a great deal about what he feels makes some churches grow while others remain stagnated. According to Wagner, there are two indispensable preconditions for achieving sustained church growth: (1) a pastor who truly wants the church to grow, and (2) a congregation that also wants growth. And both must be willing to pay a substantial price if growth is to occur.[3]

The Costs of Growth for a Pastor

Many studies have been conducted in fast-growing churches to determine what is required of a pastor who wants to initiate (and sustain) a growth cycle in his church. In very few churches does growth occur spontaneously. It is almost always the result of concerted effort and careful planning. Because the costs can be high for a pastor, he must know about them in advance and decide if he is willing to pay them. Once he starts down this path, his church will never be the same! This may explain why some pastors do not want growth to happen in their church—they prefer the status quo and the stability of known activities.

Cost #1. The first cost of growth for a pastor is usually an initial drop in popularity. Every congregation has some members who resist change. They may not specifically say that they don't want growth, but their actions and remarks will clearly communicate their desire to see the church remain just as it is. The pastor will have to risk being misunderstood when he tries to convince these traditionalists that growth will be good for everyone in the church. Any congregation will instinctively recognize that growth will inevitably bring many changes to the church, and some members will be enthusiastic about the idea. Others will have doubts, but it is up to the pastor to confront the naysayers on the matter until he is able to create an atmosphere more accepting of his vision of the future.

Cost #2. A growth-oriented pastor must be willing to share his leadership and authority with others in the congregation. Some pastors find it very threatening not to be seen as the resident expert in every area of ministry, whether it be theology, counseling, education, or preaching. Being willing to share the reins of leadership is especially hard for those who feel insecure about their own abilities. However, giving up a degree of control over the planning and implementation of church programs is one price a pastor will pay in exchange for a more far-reaching ministry.

Cost #3. Pastors who want growth to occur must be willing to change their role from shepherd to general overseer. In the latter capacity, the pastor is no longer personally acquainted with each member of the congregation. Once a church reaches between 150 and 200 members, (about 85 percent of all Protestant churches in America are in this range), it becomes increasingly difficult for the pastor to shepherd all his parishioners on an individual basis. Some of his ministry must be through other servant-leaders to whom he has entrusted this responsibility.

The shift in approach to ministry is a particularly difficult hurdle for a pastor to overcome, because love for people was most likely his primary motivation for entering God's service. Many pastors prefer being at the center of *all* the church's activities. They want to lead people to Christ, counsel those in need of spiritual and emotional guidance, visit every sick member, monitor everyone's spiritual life, say grace at church suppers, prepare the bulletin and newsletter, pay the bills, visit the home of each parishioner at least once a year, write personal letters to all visitors, keep in touch with college students away at school and military personnel stationed overseas, distribute food to the needy, and preach forty-eight sermons a year.[4] A pastor who insists on doing all those things himself will not experience significant church growth. There will come a point when he will either realize that it is physically impossible or burn himself out trying.

Cost #4. To achieve the growth that he believes God wants to happen in his church, a pastor must courageously move off the comfort of the plateau and lead his congregation to higher ground. It is his vision for what is possible that will propel the church into the future, so his leadership must be strong and confident. A church has greater potential for growth if the pastor is more chieftain than top administrator, for he must create policy rather than implement someone else's. A church that is growing has a pastor who establishes objectives and measures progress toward them. This requires him to be at the forefront in all goal-setting discussions and actively engaged in each element of the planning process.[5]

The Costs of Growth for the Congregation

To move off a membership plateau, the congregation, too, must be willing to make sacrifices. The costs will vary according to the church's age, style, denomination, and neighborhood demographics, but some costs are common to most fellowships that have been able to achieve an upward growth cycle.

Cost #1. The first thing required of a congregation during the growth process is a willingness to accept change, even though it means discarding old ways of thinking, traditional worship patterns, and established church procedures. As attention is focused on the surrounding community, the ministry will have less to do with serving the needs of long-term members and place far more emphasis on reaching out to people beyond the walls of the church. This is what Frank Tillapaugh describes as breaking out of the fortress mentality.

If members are prepared for what their church will look like in the future, they will be more accepting of the changes that growth will bring. Are they willing to give up their favorite seat in the sanctuary to newcomers? Can they tolerate not having a parking space close to the church buildings? Can they adjust to having "strangers" around them on Sunday morning? Will they accept multiple services and an enlarged pastoral staff? The atmosphere will not be conducive to growth if there are too many negative responses to those important questions.

Cost #2. In a growing church, the congregation must be willing to get involved in the ministry. There must be general agreement that the professional staff cannot perform the work of the church without the help of volunteers. Present members must be recruited on the basis of their spiritual gifts and mobilized into an army that impacts the surrounding community. Since most church growth represents conversions rather than transfers, members must direct their attention to identifying the physical and spiritual needs of their neighbors and attracting them to the fellowship of believers through programs designed to meet those needs.

Cost #3. Leadership development must be a focal thrust of a growing church. Speaking of the weakness of churches to train and equip their member-ministers, Peter Wagner states, "Very few growing churches are 'adding daily to their number such as should be saved.' One of the problems is that they are led by ecclesiastical amateurs. Good-hearted people, yes; saints of God, yes; intelligent and generous and trustworthy, yes; but professional church leaders, no."[6]

Development of lay leadership takes place on three levels. First there must be basic orientation, which involves making sure that the member is genuinely saved and is modeling a Christian lifestyle. Next is basic job training that includes an overview of the essential elements of Christian faith (Bible doctrines, the need for a personal quiet time, the nature of the Holy Spirit, general teaching and counseling skills, etc.). The third requirement is advanced training in a specialized area of ministry (evangelism, small-group leadership, directing a support group, etc.).

I visited New Hope Church outside of Portland, Oregon, a few months ago to meet with their membership training director. This is one of the fastest-growing churches in America, and I was curious about how its growth has been sustained. The staff believes that the key to growth is a well-planned training program. All parishioners are automatically enrolled in the program when they join the church. This training raises the confidence level of the members and gets them actively involved in leading, teaching, serving, and/or counseling others in their community.

Cost #4. In an expanding ministry, church members must change their way of thinking about themselves. Instead of coming to church to hear an uplifting sermon and enjoy the company of people they know and like, members of growing churches must see their role as one of searching out visitors and making them feel welcome. For example, one of the biggest complaints among members of churches that initiate double services is that they may no longer get to fellowship with their friends as often. Multiple services usually attract new people, and it takes a concerted effort to incorporate these visitors into the body of Christ without making other changes in church programming. During the critical period of transition, the congregation must be willing to look outward and reach for new growth, rather than worry (unnecessarily) about maintaining existing relationships.

Implications

Attending and serving in a church that is declining or stagnated is a formidable challenge. Morale among the members begins to deteriorate, and ministry becomes tedious. On the other hand, there is something truly exciting about serving in a vibrant and growing church. Its leadership and congregation are alive with anticipation and excitement. Petty disagreements fade in importance because eyes are focused on the future instead of on past accomplishments. Testimonies of God's saving grace are heard on a weekly basis from new believers whose fresh ideas and enthusiasm are contagious.

Growth has a price tag, and the costs may seem unreasonable to congregations or pastors who are unwilling to break with tradition. However, there are countless examples of churches that were once on a plateau but have been able to renew themselves and begin a fresh new growth spurt within the body of Christ.

Questions for Discussion

1. How has the attendance at your church changed over the past five years? (Your church is "on a plateau" if the figures have not varied more than 10 percent.)
2. Do you feel that the members of your church would be receptive to the changes that would stimulate growth?
3. If not, what would it take to create an atmosphere conducive to change in your congregation?
4. What improvement in the training of lay leaders is needed to facilitate growth in your church? Who could direct such a program?
5. Do you feel that both the pastor and the congregation are willing to pay the costs of growth that are identified in this chapter?
6. Which of these costs will be the most difficult to pay?

For Further Reading

Brown, Truman. "Getting In and Getting Aboard a Plateaued Church." *Church Administration* 33, no. 2 (Nov. 1990): 9–11.

Charlton, Ed. "Renewal: A Mandate for the Church." *Christian Standard* 4 (25 Nov. 1990): 13–14.

Hadaway, Kirk. "What Helps Churches Move Off the Plateau?" *Church Administration* 33, no. 2 (Nov. 1990): 18–20.

Mattox, Guy. "Strategic Planning for the Plateaued Church." *Church Administration* 33, no. 2 (Nov. 1990): 15–17.

Mercer, Jack. "Building Morale in the Plateaued Church." *Church Administration* 33, no. 2 (Nov. 1990): 12–14.

Ogden, Greg. "The Pastor as Change Agent." *Theology News and Notes,* June 1990, 8–12.

Rein, Charles E. "Closing a Congregation." *The Christian Ministry* 21, no. 2 (Mar.–April 1990): 22–23.

Schaller, Lyle E. *Growing Pains.* Nashville: Abingdon Press, 1983.

_____. "Overcoming Resistance to Change." *Church Management* 32, no. 12 (Sept. 1990): 46–48.

Summer, David V. "Strategizing Innovative Ministry." *The Christian Ministry* 21, no. 3 (May–June 1990): 23–25.

Words of Wisdom from the Trenches

While working on my Ph.D. in human development, I spent several years listening to lectures, reading books, and writing reports on childhood, adolescent, and adult development. By the time I graduated, I thought I had a good working knowledge of the subject. However, once my daughter was born, I realized that knowing childhood theory wasn't going to help me become a better parent. None of my books told me how to convince a crying baby to go to sleep at 3:00 A.M. For that kind of practical information, I had to talk with experienced parents. And did I ever talk with a lot of parents!

I have also discovered over the years that—although research on leadership can provide us with some helpful insights—theory seems of limited value when you are in the midst of leading a church out of a crisis. What you really need then is some advice from those who have already come through the battles.

In gathering materials for this book, I wanted to provide church leaders with content that would be relevant to their ministries and helpful in managing God's resources. So I asked each of the board members and senior pastors in my survey this question: "If you could offer some advice to a young pastor about pastor/board-member relations, based on your years of experience, what advice would you give?"

This section contains a selection of the board members' responses. Because these comments offer insights from a unique perspective, I believe they will be of help to you in your ministry, especially if they serve as a basis for productive dialogue between your senior pastor and the church's lay leaders. After each statement I have listed the responder's board position and geographical location.

"Get to know your board members real well. Go out of your way to socialize with them and know each of them. Set goals for your relationship with each board member and work at it."

Elder, PSW

"One of the biggest areas of advice would be a warning against the abuse of privilege. The church seeks to witness for Christ. It selects a disciplined and trained person who exemplifies the message of the church and gives him maximum exposure, opportunities and influence, oftentimes at great risk that these powers might be abused. I would warn him of the dangers of abusing these privileges."

Deacon, CN

"Listen to everything your board members have to say. Make them feel that everything they have to offer is appreciated and very important—even if it is terrible."

Elder, NE

"Don't be afraid to address pastor/board-member relations. It is very important. Unity of purpose and your method of direction are critical to accomplishing the most for the Lord."

Elder, PSW

"Seek to develop and articulate your vision of ministry, based on the Word of God. Ask the Lord to send you men from within the church who will share and support your vision. These men are your disciples, your team. Build them in their faith. Let them know you and love you. Accomplish your vision through them."

Elder, CN

"Your primary task is to equip the saints. This involves a continuum of leadership styles depending on the maturity of yourself and your board members. Follow your vision and allow your board members to develop and follow theirs. Walk carefully the tightrope between your strong leadership and empowering your board members to lead."

Elder, CN

"Go slow with changes in the church that has been in existence for some time, especially a church that has enjoyed success. Do not attempt to change it from a traditional style to a contemporary. They won't mix. Go to a separate service if you want a contemporary approach."

Elder, CN

"Concentrate on providing spiritual leadership to your board, but don't hesitate to cooperate with them as co-laborers with Christ. Encourage your board to trust God in difficult situations, and not to resort to clever manipulation to achieve results."

Deacon, PNW

"The nominating committee is probably the most important committee that you can ever serve on as pastor."

Church Council, PSW

"The board is not in existence to approve a program that has already been decided on by the pastor. Nor should it hold the reins so tight as to strangle his ministry (and the joy of doing it). It is there to assist in ministry, listen, pray, decide, discuss, and counsel."

Elder, PSW

"Learn to love people for what they are. As board members, we must already remember that Christ gave his life for all of them."

Elder, PSW

"Remember that board members have families and job responsibilities, too. Their time is at a premium, so try to be concise in your dealings with them and thereby optimize their time and effort."

Elder, CN

"Keep an open mind about the issues that you bring to the board for approval. Never forget that the Holy Spirit is also a member of the board and that many boards forget to consult with him for counsel. Let the board serve the church rather than allow the church to serve the board."

Deacon, CN

"When my pastor asks for my opinion, I try to be of help. If we don't agree, I love him and trust that he loves me. I pray that God will bless him and guide his leadership."

Trustee, CN

"Be teachable but take the initiative. Be willing to try new things that will touch the needs of the community. Do the work of the evangelist."

Elder, PSW

"Be up front about what you expect from your board members and what you will be doing. Then let them go and do the tasks that they feel God wants them to do. Set aside some time with them for mutual accountability."

Elder, CN

"Begin by establishing goals and a purpose. Pastors and board members should not hesitate to openly compliment each other when conditions warrant this. Really get to know your board members. Don't forget that we are both on the same side—or at least we should be!"

Deacon, CN

"When looking for board or vestry members, be sure they know the time commitment that is involved. Many people want to serve but really don't have the time. Also look at the women who are involved in serving. They have many of the skills required of members of a board. Make use of them."

Vestry, CN

"Trust ultimately in the Lord. Be open to new ideas and understanding in all situations."

Deacon, SO

"Be patient! God isn't finished with board members yet. Also, learn to lighten up."

Trustee, CN

"Be a good listener. Base your decisions on God's Word and not on man's. But you will still need to allow others to speak."

Trustee, PNW

"When programs or plans are designed at the board level, you will need to stay on top of them. Don't expect things to happen without *making* them happen."

Deacon, PNW

"Do not let your vision outpace your board members but grow with them."

Deacon, PNW

"Remember you are one leader among many. Listen and learn from older Christians. Don't change anything in the church until you have been there for one year."

Elder, PNW

"Expect that each board member will be Spirit-filled. If you pray that he/she will be, it will happen."

Deaconess, NE

"I believe the most rewarding time I ever spent with church staff was when, as a member of the board, I took them out for breakfast each Tuesday morning. We planned our programs, goals, budgets, etc. We also discussed problems in the church. You cannot reach goals or complete plans without this sense of community."

Trustee, PNW

"Church leadership is a teamwork job. The various members of the board all have a part to play, and the pastor should seek to use all the parts. Also, learn how something works before you change it."

Elder, PSW

Appendix **B**

Case Studies for Group Discussion

Case Study #1: The Mission Statement

Pastor Ken Nettleton was making his final preparations for the church's annual business meeting, which was to take place that evening. He had made sure that enough copies of the various reports had been duplicated and neatly assembled. As he glanced at the pages, a comment from the chairman of the Christian Education Committee's report caught his eye. The chairman was calling for the church to make a major emphasis on family life in the coming year. The report pointed out the changing demographics of the community and the obvious lack of attention to family-related issues at the church so far. Though a bit frustrated with the contents of the report, Ken made a note to speak with the chairman after the meeting. Ken was a bit anxious about all the last-minute details, but he felt confident about his vision for the church and his ability to lead the congregation toward making it a reality.

Pastor Nettleton was particularly excited because his opening message was going to be a summary of his philosophy of ministry. He had been at the church as senior pastor for two years now and felt it was time to make a few changes that would get the whole membership moving in the same direction. Tonight he would unveil his dream of a church that discipled people. He envisioned the congregation participating in a major discipleship campaign that would involve leadership training and development for everyone over the age of fifteen. Never before had such a major program been implemented at the church, but Ken was sure it would be well-accepted. He saw this new emphasis as the key to revitalizing the life of the church.

That evening, after the potluck dinner, the members assembled and were led in a few hymns by the minister of music. An atmosphere of excitement and enthusiasm was evident throughout the congregation. All that was needed was for the chairman of the board to introduce Ken, who was scheduled to open the meeting.

Instead, the chairman took the stage and made a speech of his own. First he pointed out the lack of motivation that he felt was characteristic of the congregation. He chided the members for their failure to get involved in several of the programs that had been offered the previous year. Next he requested a higher level of giving from them. Then came the bomb! The chairman proposed that evangelism be the primary mission of the church in the coming year. After outlining plans for a series of special seminars and other programs that would place an emphasis on outreach, he announced that the board was united in taking this new direction and expected everyone to "get on board."

Ken was amazed at what he was hearing, mainly because the chairman had not previously mentioned the evangelism project to him. This was something completely new to Ken, and he had mixed feelings of disappointment and rage. How dare the chairman communicate a vision for the church to the members before it was discussed with the pastor! How were the staff members going to respond to this idea? Shouldn't they have heard it first from their senior pastor? Wouldn't they wonder who was really in charge of the church? A hundred questions raced through Pastor Nettleton's mind in the minutes before he was due to speak.

Questions for Discussion

1. How would you feel if you were Pastor Nettleton? What would you say when you got up to speak?
2. What legitimate concerns did the pastor have? How should he express those concerns to the chairman of the board?
3. Whose responsibility is it to announce a church vision? How should that vision be established?
4. What could Ken have done to prevent such a situation from developing?
5. If you were the chairman of the board, what would you do after listening to the pastor's presentation?

Review chapter 7 for additional material on how to resolve the issues presented in this case study.

Case Study #2: Pastoral Overload

Keith King had been the senior pastor of First Church for nine years. When he first came to the church, it had averaged a hundred members for over a decade. Since Keith's arrival, the Spirit of God had done a marvelous work and was warming many hearts. When people responded to the movement of God in their lives, the congregation experienced a spiritual renewal they wished to share with others. And so, the church began to grow, as its members invited their friends to become part of the congregation. The broader community noticed what was happening at First Church, too, especially after the local newspaper carried an article about the transformation that had taken place. There was no doubt that this church had entered a phase of dynamic growth and was expanding its ministry and outreach daily.

Although Pastor King was joyous about "moving off the plateau," he was concerned about his ability to keep up with the increased workload the recent growth had created. Now there were more members who needed counseling, more people in the hospital to visit, concerns about supervising a larger church staff, and increased emphasis on the quality of the Sunday morning service. The phone seemed to ring off the hook with inquiries about upcoming events, requests for a visitation by the pastor, information about neighborhood needs, and invitations for Keith to speak at several community functions each month.

Several staff members had been hired to assist Pastor King in the ministry. The youth pastor was right out of seminary, so Keith insisted on meeting with him weekly in a supervisory capacity. The director of Christian education had been in the ministry for ten years, but Keith didn't feel at ease about giving him a lot of responsibility because the young man's wife was expecting their first child any week now. The church secretary was capable but not in the best of health. Although she had managed the office details of a small church with no difficulty, now the church was exploding with activity. Keith didn't have the heart to replace her, so he volunteered to answer the phones in the afternoon to help her out.

Pastor King soon began to realize that his enthusiasm for the activities of the church was dwindling. He had always wanted to see the kind of growth that God was providing, but now he wasn't sure he liked the way things turned out. He felt guilty for feeling this way. Hadn't God allowed First Church to grow because he trusted Keith to provide personal care for each of the members? Keith was growing so discouraged that he even thought of resigning. His health was showing the effects of stress, and his family life was suffering as well. Keith figured it was only a matter of time before he either gave up this ministry and sought a smaller church or had a nervous breakdown.

Questions for Discussion

1. What is Pastor King's real problem at First Church?
2. How could the church board step in and help Keith learn how to delegate ministry responsibilities?
3. What sermon topics would encourage the congregation to get involved in sharing the ministry of this church?
4. What passages of Scripture would you share with Pastor King if you were a board member at First Church?
5. Have you ever been involved in a church where the pastor went through physical and emotional burnout?
6. What steps could be taken to prevent such a situation from developing at your church?

Review chapters 3 and 6 for additional material on how to resolve the issues presented in this case study.

Case Study #3: Discord in the Board Room

One fall evening, Troy Hickerson, chairman of the board of trustees at Ninth Avenue Church, received an irate phone call from Dr. Stuart Bestrom, who had been a respected and influential member of the congregation for over thirty years. Stuart was not a man whom Troy could ignore! Although Dr. Bestrom had always claimed that his busy medical practice prevented him from accepting an official position on the governing board of the church, it was no secret that he was the largest contributor toward its budgetary needs. In fact, at the end of every fiscal year, Stuart phoned the church treasurer to ask how much money was needed to finish the year in the black. He invariably covered the deficit in full, though he never suggested how the funds should be allocated.

But now Stuart was very angry at John Black, the senior pastor, and was demanding to be heard. For the past few months, the pastor had been preaching a series of messages aimed at raising everyone's consciousness about meeting the needs of the surrounding neighborhood. Many of the parishioners agreed that they should all be doing something for their neighbors and had become quite vocal about directing more of the church's resources toward outreach and community service.

However, some of the older (and most influential) members of the congregation—including Stuart Bestrom—resented being told that they were neglecting their responsibility to people they viewed as outsiders. Because they had been accused of being second-class Christians for not endorsing Pastor Black's proposals, they had begun circulating a position demanding that he stop preaching "an extremist position on social issues."

Chairman Hickerson had been well aware of the growing tension within the church, but he had chosen to take no action until Stuart's phone call convinced him that the controversy could no longer be dismissed as a minor disagreement. He decided to call a special meeting of the board of trustees to discuss the matter. Hoping to protect the feelings of Pastor Black, the board chairman had not notified him of the meeting, but representatives of the warring factions were invited to come and express their views.

As the meeting progressed, those who disapproved of Pastor Black's ideas began to make allegations of misconduct on his part. Rumors that had been circulating about him behind closed doors were now being openly verbalized. In this emotionally charged atmosphere, the debate was soon out of control. Finally, the opposition group summarized its position by demanding Pastor Black's resignation. Otherwise, they said, they were prepared to leave the church and form another congregation.

The end result of the meeting was that both parties had spoken their minds, but neither was persuaded to change its position. Therefore, the board decided to take a vote of confidence within the entire congregation to determine whether the pastor's focus on social action should be continued.

Just then, Pastor Black walked in. He sat down quietly at the front of the room and asked why the board had assembled without his knowledge—and what was the topic of discussion.

Questions for Discussion

1. What should Troy Hickerson have done after receiving the phone call from Stuart Bestrom?
2. Should Stuart's high record of giving have been a factor in determining how important it was to resolve the issues involved?
3. How could the board and pastor have worked together to resolve the problem *before* it threatened to split the congregation?
4. What are the next steps that should be taken to diffuse the tensions and bring harmony back to the church?

Review chapter 18 for additional material on how to resolve the issues presented in this case study.

Case Study #4: Fiscal Confusion

After only three weeks as senior pastor at Christ Church, Brendon Michaels was sure that his decision to come to this small suburban community had been a good one. The parishioners were warm and friendly, and he already knew most of them by name. Brendon's previous church, back in the state capital, was so large and difficult to direct that administrative responsibilities had taken up most of his time.

As he began to acquaint himself with church policies and procedures, Brendon discovered that the financial records were being handled by John Babcock, a retired C.P.A. who had been a member of the church for many years. This elderly gentleman, a former board member, wanted a way to continue serving his church, even though poor health now kept him housebound most of the time. Each Sunday after worship services, John's wife, who was the church treasurer, brought home all the financial files so John could record the weekly receipts and expenditures. Until recently, John had been able to complete the work in a few days and send the records back to the church before the next Sunday. Lately, however, the bookkeeping had fallen so far behind that serious inaccuracies had been discovered in the monthly financial statements presented to the board of trustees.

Soon Pastor Michaels began to receive phone calls from several businesses in the area about church checks that had been returned for lack of funds. The bank had also called to ask why the financial condition of the church was in such a state of disrepair. Apparently several mortgage payments had been late, and the church's bank deposits were not keeping pace with its expenditures. As far as Brendon could determine, the problem was traceable to poor recordkeeping, so he called for a meeting of the church board to discuss the problem.

Questions for Discussion

1. If you were Pastor Michaels, what would you say to the board to convince them of the need to change their financial procedures?

294

2. What are the issues involved besides just the need to change these procedures?
3. If you were assigned to serve on a committee to plan new financial procedures for the church, what specific recommendations would you make?

Review chapter 14 for additional material on how to resolve the issues presented in this case study.

notes

Chapter 2: The Mythical Church Board Member

1. Larry Osborne, "The Most Important Meeting," *Sundoulos* (Alumni Newsletter for Talbot School of Theology), Fall 1990, 4.

2. Wayne Jacobsen, "Five Reasons *Not* to Equip Lay People," *Leadership* 9, no. 3 (Summer 1988): 49.

Chapter 3: The Biblical Basis for Pastors, Elders, Deacons, and Trustees

1. James H. Pragman, *Traditions of Ministry* (St. Louis: Concordia, 1983), 126.

2. David Leuke, *New Designs for Church Leadership* (St. Louis: Concordia, 1990), 16.

3. D. Edmond Hiebert, "Behind the Word 'Deacon': A New Testament Study," *Bibliotheca Sacra* 140, no. 558 (April–June 1983): 155.

Chapter 4: The Ministry of the Deaconess

1. Marvin R. Vincent, *Word Studies in the New Testament* (Peabody, Mass.: Hendrickson Publishers, 1988), 176–77.

2. J. D. Douglas, *The New Bible Dictionary* (Grand Rapids: Wm. B. Eerdmans, 1968), 287.

3. Ibid., 286.

Chapter 5: A Historical Overview of Deacon Ministry

1. Bob Sheffield, "An Historical Look at Deacon Ministry," *Search* 20, no. 4 (Summer 1990), 7.

2. Charles W. Deweese, *"The Emerging Role of Deacons,"* (Nashville: Broadman Press, 1979), 12.

3. Cyprian, "Epistles, X.1" in *The Ante-Nicene Fathers* 5:291; "Constitutions of the Holy Apostles II, *3,* 16," in *The Ante-Nicene Fathers* 7:402; and Joseph Bingham, *Antiquities of the Christian Church,* 3 (London: William Straker, 1834).

4. *The Emerging Role of Deacons,* (Nashville: Broadman Press, 1970), 14–15.

5. Shefield, 8.

6. Ibid., 9.

Chapter 6: Job Descriptions for Church Officers

1. Richard Hansen, "The Sound of Clashing Expectations," *Leadership* 5, no. 3 (Summer 1984): 79.

2. Marshall Shelley, "The Problem of Battered Pastors," *Christianity Today,* 17 May 1985, 35–37.

3. "Jobs Where Stress Is Most Severe," *U.S. News and World Report,* 5 Sept. 1983, 45.

4. Chris W. Tornquist, "Reading Between the Lines: The Problem of Unwritten Expectation," *Christian Education Journal* 10, no. 2 (Autumn 1990): 21.

Chapter 8: Organizational Structures in the Church

1. "Session Manual," Faith Presbyterian Church, Indianapolis, 3.

2. Bruce W. Jones, *Ministerial Leadership in a Managerial World* (Wheaton: Tyndale Press, 1988): 120.

3. "Session Manual": 8.

4. Jones, 23.

5. Wayman D. Miller, *The Role of Elders in the New Testament Church* (Tulsa: Plaza, 1980), 79.

6. This model is described by Dr. David Beckwith, senior pastor at Woodbridge Community Church, Irvine, Calif. Figures 3–6 also come from Dr. Beckwith.

7. Jones, 130.

8. Ken Gangel, *Leadership for Church Education* (Chicago: Moody Press, 1970), 56–57.

Chapter 9: Team Ministry: The Biblical Ideal

1. David Beckwith, "Keys for Team Ministry," a position paper for staff development, Woodbridge Community Church, Irvine, Calif. (Jan. 1988).

2. Kent R. Hunter, "A Model for Multiple Staff Management," *Leadership* 2, no. 3 (Summer 1981): 103.

3. Rod Wilson, "Team Players," *Interest* 56, no. 3 (March 1990): 16–17.

4. R. Dale Wicker, "Shared Ministry: Biblical Approach to Church Unity," *Search* 19, no. 1 (Fall 1988): 50.

5. Calvin Miller, "Fiddlin' with the Staff," *Leadership* 7, no. 1 (Winter 1986): 105.

6. Wayne Jacobsen, "Caught in the Middle," *Leadership* 8, no. 2 (Spring 1987): 87.

7. Miller, 105.

8. Henry Waller, "Building a Team," *Interest* 56, no. 1 (Jan. 1990): 8.

9. Ibid., 9.

Chapter 10: Effective Leadership in Ministry

1. Michael J. Anthony, "The Relationship Between Leadership Styles and Growth Rate of the Sunday School," *Journal of Christian Education* 10, no. 1 (Autumn 1989): 91–104.
2. Myron Rush, *Management: A Biblical Approach* (Wheaton: Victor Books, 1983), 226.
3. Ibid.
4. James N. Krouzes and Barry Z. Pozner, *The Leadership Challenge* (San Francisco: Jossey-Bass, 1987), xv.
5. Robert Sheffield, "New Trends in Leadership Practices," *Church Administration* 31, no. 4 (Jan. 1989): 18.

Chapter 11: Planning and Goal Setting

1. Robert E. Bingham, *Traps to Avoid in Good Administration* (Nashville: Broadman Press, 1979), 57.
2. David S. Luecke, *New Designs for Church Leadership* (St. Louis: Concordia, 1990), 131.
3. Bingham, 48.

Chapter 12: Resolving Interpersonal Conflict in the Church

1. Macklyn Hubbell, "Managing Conflict in the Church," *Church Administration* 30, no. 7 (April 1988): 26.
2. Homer G. Benton, "Coping with Church Conflict," *Christian Standard,* 14 Oct. 1990, 7.
3. Marshall Shelley, *Well-Intentioned Dragons* (Waco: Word Books and *Christianity Today,* 1985), 11.
4. Ibid., 12.
5. Norman Shawchuck, "Who Works for Whom?" in *When It's Time to Move,* ed. Paul D. Robbins (Waco: Word Books and *Christianity Today,* 1985), 70.
6. Calvin Ratz, "The Subtle Sin of Egocentricity," *Leadership* 7, no. 4 (Fall 1986): 29.
7. Robert W. Kirkland, "Conflict Management in the Church," *Search* 20, no. 4 (Summer 1990): 14.
8. Paul A. Mickey and Robert L. Wilson, *Conflict and Resolution* (Nashville: Abingdon Press, 1973), 27.

Chapter 13: Modeling a Biblical Lifestyle

1. Merrill O. Tenney, *Zondervan Pictorial Encyclopedia of the Bible* (Grand Rapids: Zondervan, 1970), 747.
2. Ibid.

Chapter 14: Financial Storms in the Church

1. Edward J. Hales, "The Role of Stewardship in the Local Church," in *Money for Ministries,* ed. Wesley K. Wilmer (Wheaton: Victor Books, 1989), 89.
2. George R. Grange, "Fund-Raising Constraints: Law and Ethics," in *Money for Ministries,* ed. Wesley K. Wilmer (Wheaton: Victor Books, 1989), 169.
3. Roger Hall, "How Important Is a Church Audit?" *Church Management* 66, no. 5 (March 1990): 48.
4. Ibid.
5. Luther Powell, *Money and the Church* (New York: Association Press, 1989), 182.
6. Carl F. Henry, "Heresies in Evangelical Fund-Raising: A Theologian's Perspective," in *Money for Ministries,* ed. Wesley K. Wilmer (Wheaton: Victor Books, 1989), 276.
7. Mel Rees, "Should We Use Professional Fund-Raisers?" *Ministry* 62, no. 3 (March 1989): 14.

Chapter 16: Moral and Ethical Dilemmas

1. Joe E. Trull, "Ministerial Ethics: A Matter of Character, Conduct or Code?" *The Theological Educator* 43 (Spring 1991): 5.
2. Mark R. Laaser, "Sexual Addiction and Clergy," *Pastoral Psychology* 39, no. 4 (April 1991): 214.
3. Ibid.
4. Terry C. Muck, ed., "How Common Is Pastoral Indiscretion?" *Leadership* 9, no. 1 (Winter 1988): 12–13.
5. Trull, 6.
6. Paul D. Simmons, ed., *Issues in Christian Ethics* (Nashville: Broadman Press, 1980), 17.
7. Brooks R. Faulkner, *Forced Termination* (Nashville: Broadman Press, 1989), 49–50.
8. Ibid.
9. Lee Morris, "Ethical Factors in Forced Termination," *Search* 20, no. 3 (Fall 1990): 55.

Chapter 17: Legal Issues in Ministry

1. Ken Garland, "Legal and Ethical Issues in Christian Education," in *Foundations of Ministry: An Introduction to Christian Education for a New Generation,* ed. Michael J. Anthony (Wheaton: Victor Books, 1992), 280.
2. John Collis, *Educational Malpractice* (Charlottesville: The Michie Company, 1990), 5.
3. Jethro K. Lieberman, *The Litigious Society* (New York: Basic Books, 1981).
4. National Center for State Courts, *State Court Caseload Statistics: Annual Report 1986* (Williamsburg, Va., 1988), 5.
5. Thomas E. Denham and Melinda L. Denham, "Avoiding Clergy Malpractice Suits in Pastoral Counseling," *Pastoral Psychology* 35, no. 2 (Winter 1983): 84.
6. Michael J. Anthony, "Living with the L Word: Can You Run an Active Youth Ministry without Risking Litigation?" *Journal of Youthworker,* Winter 1992, 65.
7. 157 Cal. App. 3d 912, 204 Cal. Rptr. 303 (Cal. Ct. App. 1984).

8. Denham and Denham, 85.
9. Anthony, 65.

Chapter 18: Healing a Divided Church

1. Michael E. Phillips, "Healing the War-torn Church," *Leadership* 12, no. 3 (Summer 1991): 118.

Chapter 19: Issues Involved in a Church Day-Care Center

1. Karen Collins and Margery Freeman, "Starting a Child-Care Program in Your Church," *The Christian Ministry,* July-Aug. 1989, 25.
2. "Pastors Charged with Operating an Unlicensed Church Day-Care Center," *Christianity Today* 30, no. 5 (21 Mar. 1986): 54–55.
3. Joe E. Richardson, "Child Abuse and the Church," *Search* 21, no. 2 (Winter 1990): 40.

Chapter 20: Gossip, Complaints, and Nitpickers

1. Kevin A. Miller, *Secrets of Staying Power: Overcoming the Discouragements of Ministry,* vol. 14 in The Leadership Library Series (Waco: Word Books and *Christianity Today,* 1960), 85.
2. Boyce Bowden, "Slowing Down the Rumor Mill," *The Clergy Journal* 66, no. 4 (Feb. 1990): 48.
3. Luther J. Thompson, "How to Cope with a Difficult Church Member," *Church Administration* 32, no. 9 (June 1990): 23.
4. Ibid.

Chapter 21: Bringing Renewal to a Declining Church

1. Gary McIntosh, "When to Close a Church," *Church Growth Network Newsletter* (Dec. 1990), 1.
2. Mary E. Guy, *From Organizational Decline to Organizational Development: The Phoenix Syndrome* (New York: Quorum, 1989), 62.
3. Peter Wagner, "Good Pastors Don't Make Churches Grow," *Leadership* 2, no. 1 (Winter 1981): 66, 72.
4. Ibid., 72.
5. Ibid., 69.
6. Ibid., 71.